# Camino de Santiago

SERGI RAMIS

# How to use this guide

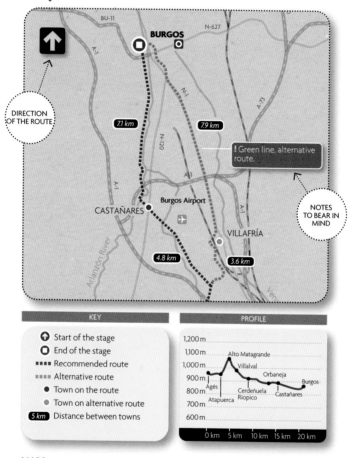

DIRECTION OF THE ROUTE

BURGOS

BU-11

N-627

7.1 km

7.9 km

Green line, alternative route.

CASTAÑARES

Burgos Airport

VILLAFRÍA

4.8 km

3.6 km

NOTES TO BEAR IN MIND

Arlanzón River

### KEY

- 🔼 Start of the stage
- ◯ End of the stage
- ■■■■ Recommended route
- ▪▪▪▪ Alternative route
- ● Town on the route
- ● Town on alternative route
- 5 km Distance between towns

### PROFILE

1,200 m
1,100 m — Alto Matagrande
1,000 m — Villalval
900 m — Orbaneja
800 m — Agés / Cerdeñuela / Castañares / Burgos
700 m — Atapuerca / Riopico
600 m

0 km   5 km   10 km   15 km   20 km

## MAPS

→ The route proposed in this book is shown in red. For some stages there are alternatives, shown in green. Reasons for choosing one route or the other are explained in the main body of the text. Symbols alongside the names of the towns at the start and end of each stage identify the services or facilities available. For intermediate points, symbols also show the availability of hostels and bars/restaurants. In addition, a profile next to each map shows the changes in elevation to expect each day.

# Contents

---

## SYMBOLS USED IN THE LIST OF HOSTELS

◉ All services

✛ Health centre
✚ A&E
✚ Pharmacy

▢ Bar/restaurant
▢ Bakery
▣ Patisserie
▢ Shop
▢ Supermarket
▣ Bike workshop
▢ Massages/
   physiotherapy

Ⓐ Accommodation
Ⓗ Hostel

▤ Taxis
▭ Buses
▣ Train
✈ Airport

▭ ATM
✉ Post office
☎ Telephone booth
⛨ Police

≋ Swimming pool
⦦ River beach
▯ Library
@ Internet
✺ Information for
   pilgrims

**Note:** The use of symbols has been simplified for greater clarity. In rural areas, shops can sometimes offer unconventional services.

## The Way as it is today

**F**rom the standpoint of the number of pilgrims who follow it, *el Camino de Santiago* (the Way of Saint James) is currently reliving the golden age of over a thousand years ago, when, with the support of the authorities, this route was opened up to everyone.

These days, pilgrims choose to walk the Way for many reasons: sport, tourism or the thirst for new experiences run side by side with religious motivation. Pilgrims who set out for Santiago de Compostela do not always do so for devotional reasons, but they soon discover that they are on a journey not only across the north of the Iberian peninsula but also into the depths of their own minds. In the course of that journey they will have the opportunity to visit some of the most impressive cathedrals in Spain, together with small villages they had never even heard of, and will come into contact with people from all over the world. However, their physical and mental endurance will also be tested. The Way of Saint James is many journeys in one.

Every year more than 300,000 people, starting out from different points, undertake the pilgrimage to Santiago de Compostela. The summer months remain by far the most popular, with more than 60% of the travellers doing it then. There are still improvements to be made: the signs, for example, could be a little more uniform and if

Walking through the leafy forests of Galicia

more amenities remained open in the low season, there might be a better spread of pilgrims through-out the year. It would also be great if something could be done about the conmen who try to take advantage of pilgrims. However, since they too have been around for a thousand years, that might prove impossible.

**The pilgrimage need not be devotional, but it rapidly becomes an introspective journey**

Such improvement is not the responsibility of the authorities alone. Pilgrims should also undertake certain improvements: some of their behaviour in the hostels or towns, especially at the height of summer, can come as a shock to the locals and other pilgrims who are not simply seeking a holiday but a meaningful experience.

Despite the need for changes, the Way is still an amazing journey, on which pilgrims discover as much about themselves as they do about the country they are walking through. Benefiting from the different perspective provided by a journey on foot, they more fully appreciate the architecture and landscape, while coming into contact with different people, cultures and languages. There is, furthermore, the sensation of spiritual purity, of being free from sin, if only for a day.

Though beautiful, the aridity can make the walk challenging

# Preparing for the journey

Deciding on the route to follow is essential. According to the records kept by the ecclesiastical authorities of Santiago de Compostela, every year over 300,000 pilgrims claim, upon their arrival in the city, the *compostela*, a certificate to show that they have travelled at least 100 km of the Way on foot, by bicycle or on horseback. August, July, June and September, in that order, are the months in which most of them arrive. During the rest of the year the Way is considerably quieter. However, comparatively few of those pilgrims make the whole of the journey from the classic starting points of Saint-Jean-Pied-de-Port (in Basque: Donibane Garazi) or Roncesvalles (in Basque: Orreaga). Most walkers choose to start out from some intermediate point, such as Burgos or León, while a vast number cover the Galician section alone, beginning either at O Cebreiro, a point of entry into the autonomous community of Galicia, or at Sarria, which is just far enough from Santiago de Compostela to provide the 100-kilometre distance required for the *compostela*.

This guide focuses on the Camino Francés (the French Way) right from its starting point on the French side of the Pyrenees. However, you could start from any point on the Way — the information provided is organized such that no useful data is missing from each relevant stage.

Given that the journey on foot will take over four weeks, covering almost 800 km, there are several critical organizational aspects to bear in mind.

## Dates and stages

According to statistics, close to half of the pilgrims are Spanish. This helps to explain why the greatest number of travellers come in the summer months, as it is then that the Spanish traditionally take their holidays. While June and September are very good months for undertaking the journey along the Way of Saint James, the midsummer months are most definitely not. Despite the traveller having the advantage of many hours of daylight at that time of year, there are also serious disadvantages to choosing that time: temperatures are extremely high, even from early morning, the sun is very strong and the amenities are crowded. As a result, in recent years pilgrims have been practically forced to engage in a race to see who starts the day earliest, completes the stage first and so manages to get a place at the next hostel (although a reserva-tion system has now made things a little easier). This is contrary to the very nature of the pilgrimage, which calls for calm, a measured pace and time in which to visit the places of interest along the way. If the journey becomes little more than a continuation of everyday stress, you are going to achieve very little.

The best seasons in which to undertake the pilgrimage are without doubt spring and autumn. Most of the hostels are open and temperatures are usually pleasant, while the days are long enough not to worry about it getting dark early. Only rain and the occasional flurry of snow test the resistance of the traveller.

Winter is only for the hardiest. Although ideal for those who are mentally and physically strong, a winter's journey entails crossing the Pyrenees at the toughest time, enduring the biting winds and low temperatures of Castilla y León as well the rains of

### PHYSICAL PREPARATION

→ The Way of Saint James is perfectly doable for people of any age, as long as they are physically fit. Except for the first stage and for a few later stretches (reached when the body has become accustomed to the effort), most of the route is gentle or with climbs of little difficulty. The aim is to walk for four to six hours a day on average, something that is within anyone's capacity. However, it is the overall duration of the journey that may give rise to problems. While it is true that everyone should be able to walk for several hours a day, even without preparation, it does not follow that everyone can maintain that rhythm for a month. The muscles will suffer and send out signals in the form of stiffness or pain. Worse still, a case of tendinitis might send us straight home. For these reasons it is particularly important to train a little during the weeks preceding the journey in order to tone up the body.

El Bierzo and Galicia. Further-more, many hostels, restaurants and bars are closed at this time of year. Careful planning is there-fore required if travellers are not to find themselves without accommodation at the end of a hard day's walk.

After deciding on the starting date, the next step is to carefully work out how long the various stages should be. Hardly any of the stages included in this guide cover more than 30 km in a day. Although you may hear other pilgrims boast of having walked 35, 40 or 45 km in that time, this is not something that we would recommend. The journey should be pleasant, allowing time to vis-it villages, churches and bridges, to take refreshment in a bar, to have a picnic in a meadow. The potentially adverse effects of long, sustained effort should also be considered.

Among hikers and mountain-eers it is customary to measure distances in terms of hours rather than kilometres. In this guide we have followed suit, as it seems a more logical way of estimating what can be done in a day. However, as the 'tradition' of the Way requires that distances also be indicated in kilometres, we have provided this form of measurement as well. These have been measured using a GPS, so they are fairly accurate. Even so, it is better to be guided by the hours and minutes mentioned in each case, as these indications are much more reliable and pro-vide walkers with references that

## MENTAL PREPARATION

Only a few of the pilgrims are experienced hikers or fell-walkers accustomed to making long journeys on foot. The others may be well advised to undertake a little mental preparation for the weeks ahead.

→ Your feet will be the means of transport, so walk at your own speed, neither faster nor slower than your body dictates.

→ Local people are generally friendly and even affectionate towards pilgrims. However, you will also come across those prepared to take advantage of the vulnerability of the traveller on foot looking for a place to sleep and a meal.

→ The hostels are not hotels but lodging places. The facilities may often be very basic or poorly maintained.

→ Many *hospitaleros* (those who receive the pilgrims and help out at the hostels) are unpaid volunteers. Try to make their work easier rather than more difficult by being polite and grateful.

→ There will be days when the wind, heat, cold, rain or snow will put a strain on your nervous system. Try to be positive and assertive in the face of these difficulties, aiming to find a solution rather than letting the problem get on top of you. Travelling without a sense of humour is of course possible, but not recommended.

are easier to follow, in the usual hiking tradition.

## Looking after yourself on the Way

On a long journey like this it is important that you are aware at all times that your body is your means of transport. You should therefore be sure to provide it with every possible care so that it may withstand the effort.

It is best to get up in time to start out at about eight o'clock, although in the summer an hour earlier, when the day will already have broken, is an even better time. This way you can walk for three or four hours before the heat sets in.

It is advisable to eat a full breakfast and, once on the path, to rest and have a drink of water every hour or so. Some prefer isotonic drinks to replace salts, but be warned, especially if you need to watch your sugar levels, that they are very sugary.

Lunch is best kept light but should naturally provide energy. A sandwich, dried fruits and nuts, fresh fruit or energy bars will suffice — and reduce the weight you have to carry — to enable you to conclude the day's walking in the early afternoon. You can then have a snack and, later, a hearty hot dinner, although even then you should avoid excessively heavy or greasy food as it could prevent you from sleeping well.

Alcohol not only impairs your awareness but also seriously dehydrates the body. Pilgrims should therefore keep their

**SIGNS**

→Signs bearing the characteristic yellow arrows have been erected all along the Way by the owners of hostels, town councils, the autonomous communities or the associations of friends of the Way of Saint James. The route is therefore marked from start to finish. There are, however, still some stretches where the marking is not entirely clear. If you encounter this problem it is always better to ask a local for assistance rather than walking on in the direction you think is right. In any event, this guide provides all the necessary help for negotiating places where the lack of signs or, at times, the abundance of them could give rise to confusion.

alcohol intake to a minimum. Although at the hottest time of the day or at the end of a stage you may feel that you have 'earned' a beer, it is wise to exercise moderation.

It is important to get a good night's sleep. On the Way you will meet many other people and it will clearly be tempting to stay up talking until late. However, the body needs at least eight hours' rest in order to recover from the efforts of the day and be ready to meet the next challenge. This is, after all, a test of your resistance.

You should take particular care over your feet, as they are your 'engine'. Comfortable, worn-in trekking or hiking boots with a good sole, are the appropriate footwear. Socks should never wrinkle or bunch and socks for hikers with reinforced toes, soles and heels are designed specifically to guard against that risk. While there are also traditional remedies for the much-feared chafes or blisters, sticking on a strip of artificial skin, available at all pharmacies, is the best solution. The pain disappears almost instantly and the dressing remains adhered until the wound heals.

It is vital to protect yourself against the sun — make sure you use sun cream on your face, arms and legs and wear a hat.

## Life at the hostels

As we have already said, the hostels are not hotels. They are modestly priced for a reason: you will be sharing rooms and facilities. It is therefore important to make an orderly use of the allotted space, to help ensure that the bathrooms and common areas do not get too dirty, to

### GEAR

Although the Way runs through parts of the Iberian Peninsula which have not developed any real tourist industry, all the services you will require are available. Pilgrims need therefore prepare only the lightest possible backpacks. If yours weighs more than 10 kilos, you have already made your first mistake: carrying it will be sheer torture. The well-prepared backpack should have a capacity of no more than 35 litres and contain:

➜ A sleeping bag
➜ A minimum amount of clothing (most hostels have a washing machine and drier if you need to do a quick wash)
➜ Flip-flops for the shower and for resting your feet
➜ A towel
➜ A small toilet bag
➜ A small first aid kit
➜ Basic rain and wind gear
➜ A water bottle
➜ Sunglasses and sun cream
➜ A hat or cap
➜ A guidebook, necessary documents, money and a camera

Subsequent needs that might arise can be dealt with in the course of the journey. There should be no difficulty in obtaining, for example, a particular medicine, additional warm clothing, lip balm or wipes, especially since the Way passes through small cities such as Pamplona, Logroño, Burgos and León.

Snow in the Pyrenees

leave the kitchen clean after use and to take the maximum care not to disturb the sleep of others. Unfortunately, snorers can prove a nightmare, although the number of hostels providing separate dormitories to group them apart is constantly increasing. It is therefore by no means a bad idea to carry earplugs, as they are the most effective solution.

Some hostels offer supper. Haute cuisine it is not, but the dishes are energy-giving and filling. Where that service is not available, there are bars and restaurants in the vicinity which will generally provide set meals at special prices for pilgrims.

To have the right to use the state-run hostels and also some of the private ones (although at others no questions are asked), pilgrims must be in possession of a pilgrim's pass obtainable at the offices of the Association of Friends of the Way of Saint James in Galicia and at some churches. It is also important to

**MOMENTS OF WEAKNESS**
→Doing the Way of Saint James is not difficult. However, on most days you will come across walkers who are limping, or suffering from horrible blisters or extreme fatigue. You should be cautious in your planning and have a few days' leeway. It would be ideal, for instance, to stop every ten days to have a day's rest. This gives the body some respite and lets you replenish mineral salts, hydrate and recover some of the weight you will have lost. In the event that things go wrong for you, you should have the courage to admit that you have had enough. If you have to abandon the Way, it will still be there for a future attempt.

remember that this document must be stamped on completion of each stage if you want to obtain the *compostela* at the end of your journey.

A traditional sign to help the walkers

## Precautions

The French Way is very well kept and pilgrims rarely have to walk unprotected on the hard shoulder of a road. However, there are some such stretches and you will need to concentrate on these. It is best to walk on the left, facing the oncoming traffic. In the dark wear brightly coloured clothes and carry a torch so that drivers can see you are there. It is, of course, important to take great care when crossing roads or railway lines. In some stretches of the last few stages you will often have to walk on the road, so be extremely careful. You will doubtless be reminded of this advice by the various memorials you will come across along the Way which commemorate pilgrims who died as a result of their own or someone else's carelessness.

The Way is, in general, safe from a personal safety standpoint, although some women have reported being attacked or harassed at particular places and times. In the hostels it is advisable to keep an eye on personal belongings, money and valuables, such as cameras, mobile phones and jewellery.

### AVOID GIVING OFFENCE ON THE WAY

→Many of the places the pilgrims pass through are not set up for tourists. Try to respect local traditions: remove headgear when entering a church, dress with reasonable decorum and refrain from bathing nude in lakes or rivers if local people might take umbrage. Your aim should be to relate to others without causing offence either visually or to their way of thinking, irrespective of your personal opinions or beliefs.

# Additional services on the Way

There are numerous services that allow pilgrims not to have to worry about carrying their backpacks or about what to do with their bikes, which many will find appealing.

## Camino Cómodo

This company offers a backpack transport service all along the Way, between Roncesvalles and Galicia. It also hires and transports bicycles and will take pilgrims who are short of time or injured and need to skip some of the stages.

→ www.caminocomodo.com
• They have different telephone numbers and email addresses for each stretch of the Way.

## Jacotrans

They will take your backpack and/or bike from Saint-Jean-Pied-de-Port to Finisterre. They also hire or sell some articles such as backpacks and have a system of backpack storage for unlimited time. They will transport your bike from your home to the starting point and check the bike for you.

→ www.jacotrans.es
• They have different telephone numbers for each town.

## Correos (post office)

Backpack and bike carriage, whether to the starting point or back home at the end of the journey in Santiago or Finisterre. This service is generally more expensive than those offered by local carriers in each town, but allows you to book it all online.

→ www.elcaminoconcorreos.com
• paqmochila@correos.com
• Tel. 683 440 022.

**ASK AT THE HOSTEL**
→ Most hostels advertise any additional services that they offer. But if you don't see any advertised, ask if they can take your backpack to the next destination or know of anyone who will. The answer is usually 'yes'.

**SPECIFICALLY FOR PILGRIM CYCLISTS**
A company focusing on services for pilgrims travelling by bike. It will take your bike to the start of the first stage and transport it back home from Santiago and is very competitively priced. It also hires bikes and additional items, and even has a list of second-hand bikes in case you want to buy one after the journey. They have bike workshops all along the Way.

→ **Bicigrino** • Tel. 972 908 727 and 627 928 213
• caminosantiagobike@gmail.com • https://bicigrino.com

Crêtes d'Iparla    Artzamendi 926m    Jara 812m    Baigura 897m    Garralda Mendi 470m    Arr...

St-Jean-Pied-de-Port

(XIIe siècle), attribué à Aimery Picaud, cite les treize étapes
jusqu'à Saint-Jacques de Compostelle. Il en situe le départ
...rt de Cize. Par la suite, l'extension de la ville de Saint-Jean
...val attirera le pèlerinage faisant ainsi évoluer le tracé.
...Guide évoque le passage des Pyrénées:

...Jacques franchit un mont remarquable appelé Port de Cize...
...nter et autant à descendre. En effet ce mont est si haut
...oit pouvoir de sa propre main toucher le ciel. "

Sur les chemins de
...Jacques de Compostelle
...ur le Pays de Cize

# STAGES

# From Saint-Jean-Pied-de-Port to Roncesvalles

**25.4 km • 7 h 10 min • Elevation difference ▲ 1,342 m ▼ 568 m**

### Saint-Jean-Pied-de-Port – Honto

**1 h 15 min ➜** You leave the charming town of Saint-Jean-Pied-de-Port (Donibane Garazi) by way of the central Rue d'Espagne, pass below the clock tower, cross the bridge over the Errobi River and go through the Porte d'Espagne. Right away you will see large signs showing the way. Take the uphill Rue Marechal Harispe.

The gradient is very steep; there are signs and yellow flashing lights to help you follow the correct path. Scattered houses give us a glimpse of the elegant suburbs of the capital of Lower Navarre. There will be practically no rest until you reach Ferme Ithurburia.

### Honto – Refuge Orisson

**2 h ➜** The village of Honto lies in the bend below you as you pass by Ferme Ithurburia, a rural guest house. The route is still tarmac, but barely 350 metres further on you come to a well-signposted detour to the left taking you onto a grassy path. This gives you a respite from the road and, although it is a stiff climb, it allows you to advance in a virtually

■ Izandorre, a precarious but useful refuge if needed

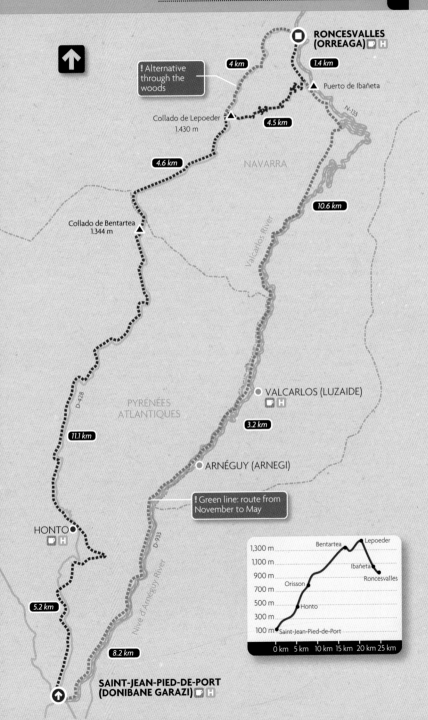

**RONCESVALLES (ORREAGA)**

4 km

1.4 km

! Alternative through the woods

Puerto de Ibañeta

N-135

Collado de Lepoeder 1.430 m

4.5 km

NAVARRA

4.6 km

10.6 km

Collado de Bentartea 1.344 m

Valcarlos River

VALCARLOS (LUZAIDE)

D-428

PYRÉNÉES ATLANTIQUES

3.2 km

11.1 km

ARNÉGUY (ARNEGI)

! Green line: route from November to May

HONTO

D-933

5.2 km

Nive d'Arnéguy River

8.2 km

**SAINT-JEAN-PIED-DE-PORT (DONIBANE GARAZI)**

1,300 m
1,100 m
900 m
700 m
500 m
300 m
100 m

Bentartea       Lepoeder

Ibañeta

Roncesvalles

Orisson

Honto

Saint-Jean-Pied-de-Port

0 km   5 km   10 km  15 km  20 km  25 km

straight line and avoid the much longer way around the hillock.

Coming out once again onto the road, you will see a fountain with a tap and, 30 metres further up, an orientation table. On this you can locate the peaks of Iparla to the north.

Having paused to enjoy these views, you only have to walk up the road for another 15 minutes to reach the Refuge Orisson. You will have covered almost a third of the day's stage and the best parts are yet to come.

### Refuge Orisson – Arnéguy turn-off

**3 h 15 min** →Once again follow the solitary road upwards, now far more unprotected as you walk through grassy hillocks. Small short-cuts straight across allow you to tread softer terrain and offer a shorter route than the road. Some of these are marked, while others are so obvious that they need no sign at all. All you have to do is continue to climb while keeping an eye on the ribbon of tarmac. After three and a quarter hours, on the right, you will see the turn-off to Arnéguy (for an alternative route in winter, see box on this page). Don't take it; instead, follow the sign indicating 'liaison Urkulu'.

### Arnéguy turn-off – Fontaine de Roland

**4 h 30 min** →The time has come to part company with the road. While this leads on towards mount Urkulu, you need to follow the signs pointing in the direction of Roncesvalles. Barely 20 metres further on you will see Thibault's cross and a monolith dedicated to some victims of Nazism. The path continues straight on, through soft fields of upland grass, towards the Col de Bentartea.

You will soon come to a narrow stretch between rocks, where there is a metal plaque fixed to the stone bearing a long legend in French.

You will begin to see large beech trees, while a wire fence protects you on the right from the danger of the slope falling away to the Arnéguy River below.

It is at this point that the gradient which has demanded some four hours' intense effort

---

**THE STAGE IN WINTER**

→Pilgrims undertaking this first stage in the low season may encounter a lot of snow between November and May. It is therefore always important to ask at the hostels in Saint-Jean-Pied-de-Port whether the mountain route is passable. If it is not, the winter route, which is perfectly well marked, should be used. This leaves the town via the Porte de France and then partly follows the road to Valcarlos (Luzaide). Whenever possible it runs through the woodland and it has some very pleasant stretches through Ganekoleta and Gorozgarai. It is longer but safer, and joins the main route at Ibañeta.

becomes less severe; there will be no more such steep climbs. A large sign warns people not to pass through here between November and March; it should be much lower down the path. There is little more climbing to do up to the Col de Lepoeder. The path, now flatter, is of compact clay.

The Fontaine de Roland, with its stone bench, is a pleasant spot to have lunch, refill water bottles and take a rest before undertaking the least difficult part of the stage.

### Fontaine de Roland – Col de Lepoeder

**5 h 15 min** ➔ Continue along the same mountain track among the beech trees and very soon you come to marker stone 199, which stands on the border between France and Spain. There is also a large sign with a map showing your precise position, together with another marker stone indicating the point of entry into the *Comunidad Foral de Navarra* (Chartered Community of Navarre). Following a few short, fairly undemanding climbs, you reach the 'roof' of the stage, the Col de Lepoeder at a height of 1,430 m. To get there, follow the numbered signposts which, in thick fog – quite common in this area – help you to avoid getting lost. In the most difficult areas there is a shorter distance between them, leading up to the hill and next to a HELPoint, a facility for calling for help in emergencies.

### Col de Lepoeder – Puerto de Ibañeta

**6 h 40 min** ➔ The signs are quite explicit: either a steep downhill path to the left, or a gentler one to the right. Choose the second path, so as not to miss the historic point where the earlier pilgrims rejoiced in having overcome the formidable Pyrenees and, according to legend, the death of Roland, which gave rise to the epic poem *Chanson de Roland*, took place.

The descent follows the well-signposted GR-11 and cuts out the bends of the road. In little more than half an hour you reach Ibañeta, where you can take a certain pride in having now overcome the north face of the mountain range. The day's walk will soon be over.

### Puerto de Ibañeta – Roncesvalles (Orreaga)

**7 h 10 min** ➔ A straightforward descent by the side of the road leads in less than half an hour to the back of the collegiate church of Roncesvalles. Go around the buildings and find the tunnel and patio leading to the hostel.

You can visit the church, the chapter house and the museum. Less than 50 metres further down the road, there is a chapel and the crypt where Roland is said to have died. In the evening there is a mass at which pilgrims receive a blessing. The toughest stage of the journey (due to the steep gradients) is now over.

# From Roncesvalles to Larrasoaña

**26.9 km • 7 h • Elevation difference ▲ 395 m ▼ 850 m**

### Roncesvalles – Burguete (Auritz)

**45 min →**On taking the road downwards out of Roncesvalles (Orreaga) you immediately come upon a large sign reading 'to Santiago, 790 km'. This might be a little discouraging, although you may find some consolation in the knowledge that 790 km is the distance by road, whereas the pathways provide numerous short cuts. And look on the bright side: a great journey full of wonders lies ahead.

A few dozen metres further on, another sign invites you to follow the path through a leafy beech wood on a carpet of leaves. It is wise to tread carefully. The path is in shadow and there may still be puddles on the ground, even weeks after the last rains. Small holly trees adorn the slightly downward path. Thirty minutes after starting out you reach the white cross of Roland.

At this point you leave the wood and take the road. You are now on the outskirts of Burguete (Auritz), a typical town of the Navarre side of the Pyrenees where big houses, their fronts white with the stone partially showing, line the road on either side. As you walk down the main street you will see the family crests which many of them display.

### Burguete (Auritz) – Espinal (Aurizberri)

**1 h 45 min →**The Banco Santander office marks the point where you should turn, go downhill and cross the wooden bridge over the Urrobi River. Then walk for a good while on a level, broad, unsurfaced track, observed by the many birds perched on the fences to the side. You will pass a cattle farm and cross several stone bridges; some streams are forded simply by means of stepping stones. The path is clearly indicated with markers and the traditional scallop shell symbols. You join the road a quarter of an hour before reaching Espinal

### ABANDONED BOOTS

→The two Pyrenean stages are not the easiest way of starting your journey. It is therefore necessary to be mentally and physically prepared, and above all to review the equipment you are going to use before you start off. It is by no means unusual to see worn-out boots abandoned in the woods of Navarre.

Make sure you take worn-in, comfortable boots with a good pattern on the soles.

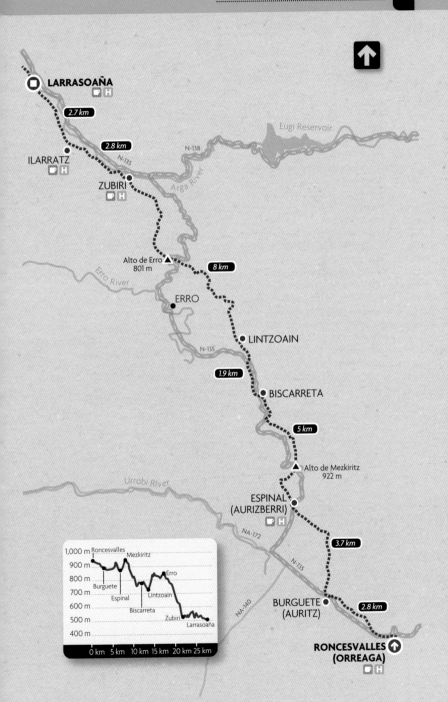

**LARRASOAÑA**

2.7 km

ILARRATZ

2.8 km

N-135

ZUBIRI

Arga River

N-138

Eugi Reservoir

Alto de Erro
801 m

Erro River

8 km

ERRO

N-135

LINTZOAIN

1.9 km

BISCARRETA

5 km

Urrobi River

Alto de Mezkiritz
922 m

ESPINAL
(AURIZBERRI)

NA-172

3.7 km

N-135

NA-140

BURGUETE
(AURITZ)

2.8 km

**RONCESVALLES
(ORREAGA)**

1,000 m   Roncesvalles
900 m              Mezkiritz
800 m                          Erro
700 m   Burguete
600 m      Espinal    Lintzoain
500 m           Biscarreta   Zubiri
400 m                              Larrasoaña

0 km   5 km   10 km   15 km   20 km   25 km

(Aurizberri), where the street leading into the town takes you past an enormous *pelota* court.

### Espinal (Aurizberri) – Alto de Mezkiritz

**2 h 15 min** ➜ Moving on towards Alto de Mezkiritz, take a muddy pathway which becomes progressively narrower. It leads upwards between wire fences intended to keep in the livestock. Provided you follow the markers, there is no chance of getting lost. You will come to a road, cross it and you will see a stele which, in Basque, Spanish and French, invites the traveller to say a Hail Mary. Five metres to the left of the image are the signs showing where the Way continues. The path now leads downwards but the going remains heavy. After about a kilometre, however, the mud gives way to a cement surface patterned to imitate paving stones. The going is easier but take care not to slip, particularly at the time of year when there may be ice very early in the morning. This "welcoming carpet" continues right up to the cattle-farming village of Biscarreta.

### Alto de Mezkiritz – Biscarreta

**3 h** ➜ Cross this village by way of the main street. Towards the end you pass a shop where you can buy food and directly opposite there is a drinking fountain. Upon leaving the village you once again encounter the imitation paving stone path which ends at a clearly marked fork. But stay sharp, because it is easy enough to take the wrong turn as you exit Biscarreta's Tiendica shop, for instance.

### Biscarreta – Lintzoain

**3 h 15 min** ➜ It takes just a quarter of an hour to reach Lintzoain. The village is small but the houses are imposing. A number of their owners now combine their traditional farming activities with the rural tourism trade. It is now time to take a short rest and prepare yourself to climb the Alto de Erro.

The second stage of the Way crosses a region where villagers produce the most sublime junket – you can even find it smoked. Not to be missed.

### Lintzoain – Alto de Erro

**4 h 30 min** ➜ From Lintzoain you take a broad, very good track. Stony at first, it subsequently becomes soft. Scented pines and decorative box trees line the way and provide shade. The path leads steadily upwards and is steep at times, twisting and turning. But at no time are there no visible signs. You come out onto the road and cross it.

## Alto de Erro – Zubiri

**5 h 25 min** →Descend through a leafy wood, a geographical feature that you will see very little of again for three weeks. Pass by the old Venta de Agorreta, formerly a pilgrims' hostel. Efficient signposting ensures you do not end up going the wrong way.

Carry on downwards along an undemanding path until you reach the valley floor. You soon come to the outskirts of Zubiri, which many pilgrims make the end of the stage, given that it is worth visiting and has good facilities. However, as it has not been a long day, it is better to keep going. This makes the next stage, the third, shorter and you'll have time to look around Pamplona.

## Zubiri – Ilarratz

**6 h** →To take a look at Zubiri, you must cross its medieval bridge, known as the *puente de la Rabia* (the Rabies bridge) and enter the town centre. It is said that the inhabitants of this Gothic town used to make their domestic animals walk around the pillar of its central arch to keep them safe from that feared disease. It is here that Martin Sheen dramatically loses his backpack in the film *The Way*.

The town is pretty and worth a visit, but the noise from its magnesite processing factory is rather more than background and detracts from the rural charm.

Barely a kilometre further along the Way, which is well marked in this stretch, you come to Ilarraz, a village with a fountain where you might have a last break before taking on the final section of the day's walk. From here you travel through wooded country. The path is not very wide, but is perfect for a peaceful walk, leaving the factory noise behind. The stretch that runs through land belonging to the extraction industry is helpfully signposted so that you avoid areas where lorries and machinery are concentrated.

You pass by another group of houses at the hamlet of Ezkirotz. The path runs right next to the Arga River and from time to time offers splendid views.

## Ilarratz – Larrasoaña

**7 h** →According to historical records, Larrasoaña has been giving shelter to pilgrims for almost a thousand years, although these days most travellers choose to spend the night at Zubiri, the previous town.

In the town centre you will find the municipal hostel and other privately-run hostels, as well as the thirteenth-century church of San Nicolás de Bari (Saint Nicholas). The town is no longer a pilgrims' paradise, but by extending the day's stage you will have the advantage of reaching Pamplona, the capital of Navarre, early tomorrow, allowing more time for some tourism. You also avoid the unpleasant noise of the factory at Zubiri.

# From Larrasoaña to Pamplona (Iruña)

**15.4 km • 3 h 55 min • Elevation difference ▲ 258 m ▼ 337 m**

### Larrasoaña – Akerreta

**20 min →** You may well wish to begin by looking back at the Pyrenean mountain ranges you crossed in the first two stages of the Way. Not until you reach the Montes de Oca, in about a week, will you see mountains of any size again, although they are by no means comparable in height or area.

You leave Larrasoaña via a cement track which leads slightly upwards, thus avoiding the main road, where vehicles pass close by at dangerous speeds. There is barely time to warm up before you reach the village of Akerreta, which has a guest house, a church and little else. This is farming country and you will have to pass through occasional wooden gates bearing signs in Basque reminding you to close them behind you. From time to time some curious *pottoka* (Basque ponies) may come up to sniff at the traveller's backpack.

### Akerreta – Zuriain

**1 h 10 min →** The path follows a level course though a wood. On your right, the Arga River guides you as reliably as Ariadne's

■ Medieval bridge over the Arga River

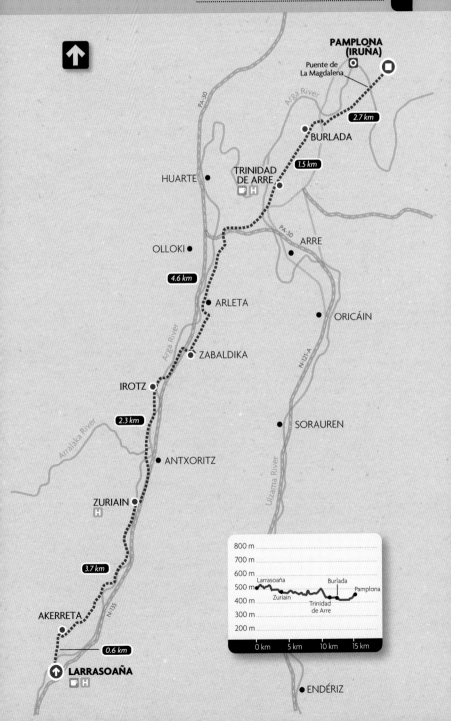

PAMPLONA
(IRUÑA)

Puente de
La Magdalena

2.7 km

BURLADA

1.5 km

HUARTE

TRINIDAD
DE ARRE

ARRE

OLLOKI

PA-30

4.6 km

ARLETA

ORICÁIN

Arga River

ZABALDIKA

IROTZ

N-121-A

2.3 km

Arralaika River

SORAUREN

ANTXORITZ

Ultzama River

ZURIAIN

3.7 km

N-135

AKERRETA

0.6 km

LARRASOAÑA

ENDÉRIZ

800 m
700 m
600 m
500 m    Larrasoaña          Burlada
400 m          Zuriain      Trinidad   Pamplona
300 m                       de Arre
200 m
      0 km    5 km    10 km    15 km

thread. Just before you reach Zuriain there is a fountain down by the water's edge, reached by means of steps with a wooden handrail. In Zuriain you will encounter something which will soon become ubiquitous: the drinks vending machine. This phenomenon has become fairly commonplace all along the Way of Saint James, but in this part of Navarre it is omnipresent.

### Zuriain – Irotz

**1 h 40 min →**A short, easy walk takes you to Irotz. From Zuriain there is the alternative of taking a riverside path, likewise leading to Pamplona, frequented by cyclists and people from that city out for a stroll. Our route, however, follows the official Way of Saint James, which is three kilometres shorter, although the final stretch runs through a series of urban avenues distinguishable only in that from time to time you see signs indicating that you are leaving one municipality and entering another.

### Irotz – Arleta

**2 h 15 min →**Leaving Irotz, you have to walk along the well-sign-posted path that runs halfway between a cement track and the tarmac road. To the right you will see the centre of Zabaldika until you reach a picnic area. This is a good place for a short rest, given that although the day's walk will not be a long one and you have already covered almost two thirds, you face a climb up a stony path. There are public

**DATES TO BE AVOIDED**
→Of the four cities that the French Way crosses, Pamplona is the nosiest. Although it is tempting to stay in the old quarter, consider it carefully, since you could find it hard to sleep, especially at weekends. Travellers should take note that the week of San Fermín and carnival are to be avoided at all costs: the city is full, prices rise and sleep is impossible.

toilets, picnic tables and stone barbecues here.

Rejoin the path, following the plainly visible yellow arrows, in the direction of Arleta, an enormous country house whose very stones speak of its splendid past. It even has a private chapel attached. When passing by the house, the path levels off for a moment. From here you have the best views of the valley of the Arga. The river has accompanied you nearly all day, but you will now lose sight of it until you reach the city.

### Arleta – Trinidad de Arre

**2 h 40 min →**Descend somewhat abruptly by a stony path, take an underpass to cross the dual carriageway and, just 45 minutes after leaving Zabaldika, you find yourself on the medieval bridge of Trinidad de Arre with its six arches. It is worth pausing in the middle to view the gentle waters of the Ultzama River. The medieval hostel used to stand just at the other end of the bridge.

You enter the town by way of the Calle Mayor (high street), a pedestrian precinct with bars on either side offering an enticing array of tapas. Soon, however, you come out onto a long straight avenue leading directly to Burlada.

### Trinidad de Arre – Burlada

**3 h 10 min →** While this is only a short stretch, it feels strange, after the leafy forests, the vast pastures of the Pyrenees and the idyllic rural villages of Navarre, to be walking along a pavement (which is wide, smooth and well marked with the customary yellow arrows). Certain striking buildings, such as the school, are worthy of attention, but the natural habitat of the pilgrim is rural rather than urban. This is a feeling that you may experience again when entering other towns and cities along the Way. It is likely to be particularly strong in Pamplona (Iruña), a very dynamic city whose old quarter is always teeming with life.

### Burlada – Pamplona (Iruña)

**3 h 55 min →** The more urban stretch continues until you come once again to the Arga River. Before you is the Magdalena bridge, an important milestone in the pilgrimage, marked with a cross and commemorative plaques.

On crossing the bridge you at once come to the walls of the city of Pamplona. From this point you must pay closer attention to the signs marking the Way, because they are at times positioned so unobtrusively that they can be missed. Turn to the right, follow the artificial city wall for a couple of minutes and you will find yourself between two high walls which lead up to the archway marking the entrance to Calle del Carmen. Just to its right stands the inn known in the city as the 'albergue de los alemanes' (the German hostel).

The urban part of the route ends, symbolically, at the door of the cathedral. Just as the Way always passes by the main church in the smaller towns, so in the cities it runs to the cathedral.

Today's stage was made shorter in order to allow time to look around the city, capital of Navarre. An interesting visit lies in store.

# Pamplona (Iruña)
**Distance behind you: 67.8 km**

→ **Cathedral** ◼ Gothic cathedral built between the fourteenth and fifteenth centuries. It is only from the inside that the beauty of this style may be appreciated, as the main façade, with its twin towers, is in a more sober, neoclassical vein. Noteworthy are the tombs of Charles III and Leonor of Navarre, the exquisite Gothic cloister and the choir stalls. Monarchs used to be crowned here and it was even, at one time, the seat of government, where the parliament of Navarre convened. The cathedral stands on a promontory which archaeologists have identified as the site of the ancient Roman city.

→ **Citadel** ◼ This fort was erected on orders given by King Philip II in 1571. It has the classic star shape, which, in theory, made it unassailable. It fulfilled its role as stronghold of the city more or less effectively well into the twentieth century, when it was converted into a park for use and enjoyment by the citizens. Today it is one of the city's green areas where, in addition, you may see works of art and shows are regularly organized. The pilgrims' path crosses this park via the Vuelta del Castillo (the citadel's glacis) and passes the San Nicolás gateway as it leaves the city.

→ **Portal de Francia** ◼ On arriving at the city of Pamplona (Iruña), pilgrims must cross the Arga River and then head for the maze of streets which make up the old quarter. Go up the steps that lead to the impressive gateway in the walls known as the Portal de Francia, a great arch bearing an imposing coat of arms. Its official name is Portal de Zumalacárregui, but nobody uses it.

→ **The bull-running route** ◼ During the second week of July hundreds of people take their lives in their hands by running ahead of a herd of bulls until they reach the bullring. Many will have heard of the streets involved – the legendary Calle Estafeta or the Cuesta de Santo Domingo – from media coverage of the event. Throughout the rest of the year tourists may find visitor information relating to the event on the panels placed along the route.

→ **Monument to Hemingway** ◼ The American writer Ernest Hemingway was a regular visitor to Pamplona. As he was attracted by the bullfights and the running of the bulls, the location of this hyperrealist bust, just at the point where the animals enter the ring, seems only appropriate. Hemingway also has his special "corner" in the popular Café Iruña.

→ **University of Navarre Museum** ◼ The museum, designed by the architect Rafael Moneo, lies in the grounds of the university campus and is home to a collection of

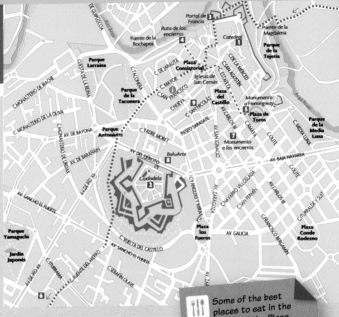

Some of the best places to eat in the city are around the Plaza del Castillo. The streets of San Nicolás, San Gregorio, Estafeta and Navarrería are the places to go for *pintxos*.

modern art that includes works by Picasso, Kandinsky, Tàpies, Chillida and Oteiza, as well as an interesting photography exhibition.

**→Monument to the running of the bulls 7** This vividly captures one of the tense moments where the runners are dangerously close to the horns. It is very realistic, lacking only the shouting and the smell of sweat.

**→BaluArte 8** Patxi Mangado is the architect who designed this spectacular conference centre which also hosts the city's main artistic events. A visit is well worthwhile not only to admire the building but also to check out the programme, as there are always theatre and dance performances, exhibitions and other cultural events going on.

**→Calle San Nicolás 9** When walking around the old quarter of Pamplona, visitors will repeatedly find themselves in Calle San Nicolás, which is at the centre of the *poteo*, the social custom of doing the round of tapas bars. There is a profusion of bars and restaurants and the citizens traditionally come out in their best clothes to take a walk there in the evening. Not to be missed is the fortress church of San Nicolás (Saint Nicholas). It stands in a wider section of the street and its tall tower dominates the old part of the city.

# From Pamplona to Puente la Reina

**24 km • 5 h 35 min • Elevation difference ▲ 534 m ▼ 660 m**

### Pamplona – Cizur Menor

**1 h 5 min →**The route out of Pamplona (Iruña) is pleasant, crossing the city from northwest to southeast and almost entirely avoiding the industrial suburbs or areas where pilgrims feel out of place.

The route is marked, but while still inside the city you may miss the signs if you are not careful. However, it is quite straightforward: set off from the cathedral though the streets Carmen, Mayor and Bosquecillo, following the markings on the ground; go past the gateway of San Nicolás and next to the citadel, and cross the park following a surfaced path known as the Vuelta del Castillo. On leaving the park, cross Avenida de Sancho el Fuerte and take Calle Fuente del Hierro in the direction of the university. After the roundabout, go through the pleasant landscaped grounds of the university until you reach the medieval bridge over the Sadar River. You should reach it some 40 minutes after having started out.

Once on the other side of the river you are in the outskirts of Pamplona. A *bidegorri* ('red path' in Basque; these are tracks which have been surfaced for use by cyclists and are coloured red) with a somewhat damaged surface takes you slightly uphill to a bridge over the A-15 or Ronda de Pamplona. After crossing the bridge, you at once come to the town of Cizur Menor.

### Cizur Menor – Zariquiegui

**2 h 30 min →**Cizur Menor is on the way to becoming the favoured end for the previous stage, as many pilgrims prefer the great hospitality and untroubled rest provided by its hostels (open only in the high season) to the noise and discomfort sometimes encountered in Pamplona. But it is too far for any urban tourism. You must decide which you prefer.

Leaving Cizur Menor behind, take a broad, level, unsurfaced track running between grain fields. After half an hour the track begins to narrow and is soon no more than a path. It is, however, very well marked. For a time it ascends, almost imperceptibly but constantly, until you draw near to Zariquiegui, at which point it becomes a slope. This is the preamble to the difficult part of this stage, the Alto del Perdón. Zariquiegui has two hostels and the odd basic shop. If the church of San Miguel (Saint Michael) is open, don't miss the opportunity to enter and admire the altar with its reredos and the

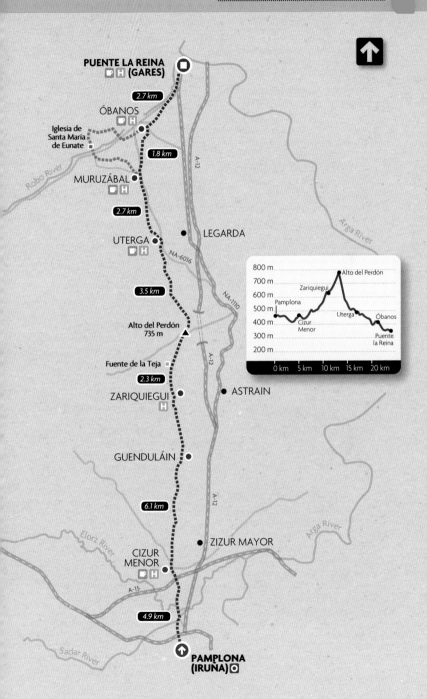

**PUENTE LA REINA (GARES)**

2.7 km

**ÓBANOS**

Iglesia de Santa María de Eunate

1.8 km

A-12

**MURUZÁBAL**

2.7 km

**LEGARDA**

**UTERGA**

NA-6016

NA-1110

3.5 km

**Alto del Perdón** 735 m

**Fuente de la Teja**

2.3 km

**ZARIQUIEGUI**

**ASTRAIN**

A-12

**GUENDULÁIN**

6.1 km

Elorz River

Arga River

**ZIZUR MAYOR**

**CIZUR MENOR**

A-15

4.9 km

Robo River

Sadar River

**PAMPLONA (IRUÑA)**

800 m
700 m
600 m
500 m
400 m
300 m
200 m

Alto del Perdón
Zariquiegui
Pamplona
Cizur Menor
Uterga
Óbanos
Puente la Reina

0 km    5 km    10 km    15 km    20 km

Gothic style that characterizes the church as a whole.

### Zariquiegui – Alto del Perdón

**3 h 5 min** ➔ At the previous hostel, you may have heard others talk about the fearsome Alto del Perdón. That is, however, nothing more than talk. The climb is undemanding, although the path is stony, and takes little more than half an hour. Furthermore, you are sheltered from the wind by the side of the mountain to your left. A few minutes after leaving Zariquiegui you will come to the fountain called 'fuente de la Teja', where, according to legend, the traveller could obtain water at the price of selling his soul to the devil. Perhaps too many agreed to the deal, as nowadays the fountain is dry for most of the year.

### Alto del Perdón – Uterga

**3 h 55 min** ➔ When you get your first view of the Alto del Perdón from the path you can immediately appreciate why it was chosen as the site for a wind farm. A strong wind blows constantly, leaving the landscape clean and allowing you a view of both plains to the north and south of the crest. At the highest point there is a stone cross, together with some silhouettes cut from sheet metal, erected by the electricity company and bearing an inscription reading 'where the way of the wind crosses that of the stars'. A memorial at the start of the descent pays tribute to those murdered here during the Civil War. Cross the road and follow the arrows, which at this point mingle with those of a GR footpath, and commence a rather steep descent made slippery in places by the pebbles lying on the clay soil. Luckily the tall box trees and a little holm oak wood will shelter you from the strong wind.

All the way down there are steps consisting simply of wooden sleepers that make the descent easier. There are also some benches where you can sit and take a rest. At the end of the steep slope, the way down to Uterga is much gentler.

### DETOUR TO EUNATE

➔ From Muruzábal you can visit the chapel of Santa María de Eunate (Saint Mary of Eunate). If you are feeling strong enough, the detour is well worth it. The return walk (5 km – you can also simply continue on to Óbanos along a signposted path) takes a little over an hour, but you are rewarded with a view of this unusual church surrounded by the ring of arches from which its name is derived (*ehun ate* means 'hundred gates' in Basque). It stands a little way off the road in a tranquil rustic setting. The church is octagonal and the ring of arches around it likewise has eight faces. Some say that it is a copy of the Dome of the Rock in Jerusalem. The vault also has eight ribs, but no central boss.

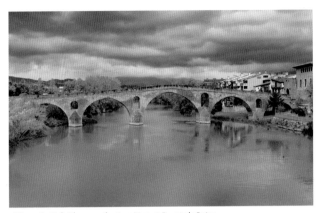

■ The majestic bridge over the Arga River at Puente la Reina

### Uterga – Muruzábal
**4 h 40 min** ➜ A path, initially stony and uncomfortable but subsequently sandy and pleasant, leads out of Uterga between fields and fruit trees. In spring the cherry trees decorate the landscape with their bright red fruit. It takes little more than half an hour to reach Muruzábal, a village from which you can make the detour to Eunate (see box). Normally you can expect to arrive in Muruzábal a little after midday. You might choose to have lunch at a bar in the village and then ask them to look after your backpack while you visit Eunate. In Eunate the French Way links up with the Aragonese Way, so another possibility is to carry on to Óbanos along a signposted path to the end of the stage at Puente la Reina (Gares), as planned, without having to walk the 2.5 km back from the chapel to Muruzábal.

### Muruzábal – Óbanos
**4 h 50 min** ➜ An easy walk along a broad, well-marked dirt track brings you in less than 20 minutes to Óbanos. The gateway to the town, the monumental church and cross and some ancestral houses with their coats of arms are the most striking features. Both the entrance to and the exit from the town are marked by scallop-shell symbols of the Way set in the ground.

### Óbanos – Puente la Reina (Gares)
**5 h 35 min** ➜ A country road leads from Óbanos to Puente la Reina, which you reach in barely half an hour. Puente la Reina is one of the most emblematic points of the Way on its passage through Navarre. It is here that it also converges, 'officially', with the route that comes from the Somport pass in Huesca.

# From Puente la Reina to Ayegui
**23.4 km • 5 h 45 min • Elevation difference ▲ 605 m ▼ 498 m**

### Puente la Reina – Mañeru
**1 h 20 min** →It is well worth taking a walk around Puente la Reina (Gares) before leaving it. The town developed thanks to the passage of pilgrims during the Middle Ages, when the Way was at its height. The most noteworthy buildings are in and around Calle Mayor, where most of the facilities are centred. After passing by the Padres Reparadores monastery, you come to the church of Santiago (Saint James), with its two Romanesque doors and Gothic nave, then to the church of the Crucifijo (Crucifix) with its two Gothic naves – a rare feature in Navarre – and next to the church of San Pedro (Saint Peter), which houses the figure

### DISQUIETING MEMORIALS
→From the very outset the traveller encounters, from time to time, simple monuments or plaques dedicated to pilgrims who died of different causes on the Way: pedestrian fatalities, falling off bikes, heat stroke, hypothermia, heart attack... This serves to remind us that, although the Way may not be difficult, it is necessary to be in good physical shape and to be alert to dangers.

of the revered Virgin of the Txori. The word '*txori*' means 'bird' in Basque and the Virgin is so called because, according to legend, a little bird used to come regularly to clean her face.

The town's best-known monument is the beautiful Romanesque bridge, with its six arches, over the Arga. It is via this bridge, one of the most impressive you will see along the Way, that you leave the town and every pilgrim feels something special when surmounting its paved hump.

After crossing the bridge, turn left, cross the N-111 road and follow a path running parallel to this road; take the broad track that crosses the valley. You will make easy progress on level ground for about an hour, but before reaching Mañeru you come to a long, steep slope with reddish soil and rather a lot of large pebbles which make the going awkward.

### Mañeru – Cirauqui
**1 h 50 min** →The pilgrim follows the winding streets of Mañeru, admiring its great, well-restored houses proudly displaying their coats of arms. The route takes you along Calle Forzosa, Calle Esperanza and Plaza de los Fueros, then passes close by the cemetery. From here you can see

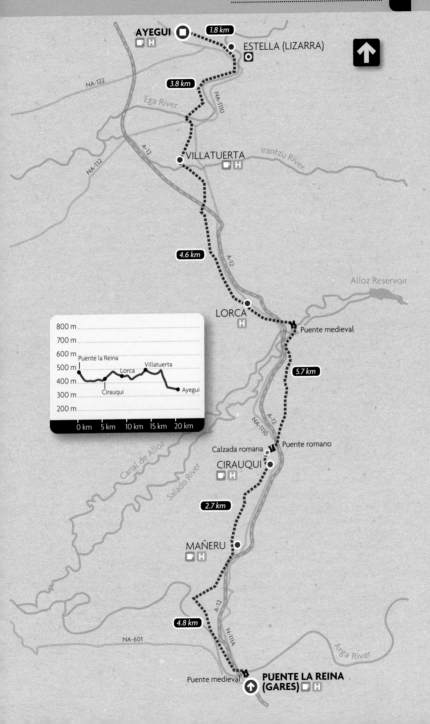

AYEGUI
1.8 km
ESTELLA (LIZARRA)
NA-122
Ega River
3.8 km
NA-1110
VILLATUERTA
Irantzu River
A-12
NA-132
4.6 km
A-12
Alloz Reservoir
LORCA
Puente medieval
800 m
700 m
600 m
Puente la Reina
500 m
Lorca
Villatuerta
400 m
Cirauqui
Ayegui
300 m
200 m
0 km    5 km    10 km    15 km    20 km
5.7 km
Canal de Alloz
Salado River
Calzada romana
Puente romano
CIRAUQUI
NA-1110
A-12
2.7 km
MAÑERU
A-12
4.8 km
NA-601
N-111A
Arga River
Puente medieval
PUENTE LA REINA
(GARES)

the outline of the next village. The two villages are linked by vineyards and a dusty trail. This is a view that epitomises the character of this part of the Way of Saint James.

### Cirauqui – Lorca

**3 h 15 min ➔** Cirauqui is another town with architectural delights which, to the majority of visitors, come as a surprise, as the town's name is not normally to be found on any list of major tourist attractions. The houses are imposing, with massive main walls and façades. You go under arches and along narrow streets towards the upper part of the town. Curiously, the path leads under the portico of the Town Hall at a point that looks more like a blind alley. There are two medieval churches in Cirauqui, that of San Román (Saint Raymond) and that of Santa Catalina (Saint Catherine), both with magnificent doorways.

As the town stands on a promontory, you leave it by way of a sharp descent and immediately come to the Roman road that linked Bordeaux and Astorga. It is pleasant to look at and is well preserved, however, what you see are the foundations, which were originally covered with a finer layer of gravel. As a result it is not comfortable for walking and can be dangerous for cyclists. Cross the bridge over the A-12, go down the steep slope and, paying attention to the signs, follow the path that leaves and rejoins the track, leading to a bridge, also

Roman, which crosses the Iguste River and helps to avoid the traffic on the dual carriageway. Cross this bridge to begin the ascent to Lorca.

### Lorca – Villatuerta

**4 h 10 min ➔** Lorca's Calle Mayor is the virtual backbone of the town. Halfway along it there is a small garden where you might want to take a rest, having now covered more than half the day's journey. The terrain gives the pilgrim no comfort. There is no shade and the wind blows dust from the vineyards. The stage is therefore more tiring than some, although it entails no particular difficulty in terms of length or topography.

On leaving Lorca, note the landscape beginning to change, as the vineyards give way to grain fields, but this will not last long. More days filled with vineyards lie ahead in La Rioja. Although you will be going downhill practically all the way to Villatuerta, the descents are no longer so steep as those you previously encountered.

### Villatuerta – Estella

**5 h 25 min ➔** The Way crosses the town, passing in front of the town hall and climbing up to the church. On your way through you will find grocery stores and other shops, together with various bars. A flight of steps leads downwards out of Villatuerta. Go down to the river, crossing it by means of a wooden bridge with an unusually pronounced

■ The Santo Sepulcro (Holy Sepulchre) church in Estella

arch, as though in Japanese style. The rest of the stage, up to Estella (Lizarra), is easy, although a few uphill stretches still lie ahead to test your stamina.

### Estella – Ayegui

**5 h 45 min →** The route into Estella could hardly be more spectacular. Just before reaching the built-up area you pass by the Santo Sepulcro (Holy Sepulchre) church, where you should pause to admire the doorway and the blend of Romanesque and Gothic styles. Go along the Rúa de los Curtidores, which dates back to the most prosperous era of the Way of Saint James. Once inside the city as such, you come to the church of San Pedro (Saint Peter), which is Romanesque, has arches revealing an oriental influence and a magnificent cloister. Then you find the church of San Miguel (Saint Michael), the monastery of Santo Domingo (Saint Dominic) and the palace of the monarchs of Navarre in the Plaza de San Martín, just opposite the tourist office and the church

of San Pedro. The large coats of arms hanging from buildings' façades point to the historic importance of the place. Leave Estella by crossing the Castilla gateway and continue along the Camino de Logroño road until you reach the N-1110. Follow this to the second roundabout, where you leave it to tackle the last uphill climb to the 'satellite' village of Ayegui, along the Calle de Carlos VII which leaves the roundabout towards the right, diagonally to the main road. There is little of note in Ayegui, but it is sufficiently far from the struggle to find accommodation when the flow of pilgrims is at its highest.

The advantage of Ayegui is that it is close enough to Estella to be used as a base so you can go down to the city for dinner. Between the two towns is a sign indicating the distance to Santiago de Compostela: 666 km, the number of the devil. Another figure you will see on signs is that Ayegui is located at precisely 100 km from Roncesvalles.

# From Ayegui to Torres del Río

**27.3 km • 6 h 50 min • Elevation difference ▲ 555 m ▼ 594 m**

### Ayegui – Irache

**20 min →** On leaving the Ayegui town centre you continue along the N-1110 which runs through the town. Soon, however, the yellow arrows point towards a broad, stony dirt track that veers away to the left and away from the road. In little more than a quarter of an hour, you come to something quite unique: the fountain of Irache. This was installed by a local winery and has two taps, one delivering water and the other wine. Bearing in mind that you will normally pass by this point early in the day and, furthermore, that a web cam is watching, it is advisable not to over-indulge. Better just to have a sober taste of the wine and then move on.

At the bottom of the hill you come to the impressive monastery of Irache. These days it is closed and unoccupied, but the size of the building and the church it incorporates on the left side bear witness to its magnificent past. Apparently it is to become a *parador* (a state-run luxury hotel), although no opening date has as yet been set. Entry to the monastery is free of charge (closed on Mondays; for further information, call 948 554 464 or 848 420 485).

### Irache – Ázqueta

**1 h 25 min →** Leaving the fountain and the monastery behind, walk for about half an hour along a tarmac road next to a housing development. Go past a campsite and then take the path, with ascents and descents, through a cool and pretty oak wood. To the right there are splendid views of the rocky face of the Sierra de Urbasa. You then come to Ázqueta, where a character by the name of Pablito de las Varas has made himself famous by making gifts of sticks to pilgrims. He is not always waiting by the side of the Way, but those eager to obtain the support of a stick will be able to find his house without difficulty, as everyone in the town knows him.

### Ázqueta – Villamayor de Monjardín

**1 h 55 min →** You leave Ázqueta via the valley floor and then begin to climb up a broad, dusty

¶¶¶ If you follow the Way during the cider season (January to May), make sure you attend a *txotx*, the act of opening the *kupela* or barrel containing a fresh batch of cider, during which anyone fancying a drink need only hold out their glass.

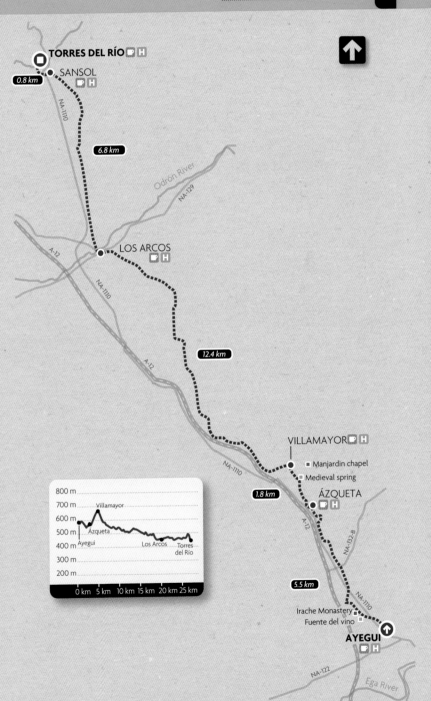

**TORRES DEL RÍO**

SANSOL

0.8 km

NA-1110

6.8 km

Odrón River

NA-129

A-12

**LOS ARCOS**

NA-1110

12.4 km

A-12

NA-1110

**VILLAMAYOR**

■ Manjardin chapel

■ Medieval spring

1.8 km

**ÁZQUETA**

A-12

NA-132-B

5.5 km

NA-1110

Irache Monastery
Fuente del vino □

**AYEGUI**

NA-122

Ega River

800 m
700 m — Villamayor
600 m
500 m — Ázqueta
400 m — Ayegui          Los Arcos    Torres
300 m                                del Río
200 m

0 km  5 km  10 km  15 km  20 km  25 km

farm-track running between vineyards. This is without doubt the most beautiful section of the stage and typifies the landscape of this part of the Way. The church tower of the next town, Villamayor, can be seen from the moment you leave Ázqueta. At the end of the town, a cement path descends to a cattle shed and then continues upwards through the scrubland along an easy winding track.

Before your reach Villamayor you come across a building fronted by two large arches giving passage to the inside, where there is a large well. This is the Fuente de los Moros (the Fountain of the Moors). It was restored a few years ago but dates back to the Middle Ages. Its origins are unclear, but documents show that it may have been used for ritual bathing or simply for the performance of ablutions, which pilgrims would no doubt have welcomed when travelling these dusty tracks.

From here again you will see, at a lower level, the church tower of Villamayor de Monjardín. On the rest of this stretch the going is easy, although just before reaching the town you come to a fairly steep descent: be careful not to slip on the sandy ground.

### Villamayor de Monjardín – Los Arcos

**4 h 35 min** → It is worth pausing to take a look around Villamayor de Monjardín. Up on the hill stand the ruins of the old castle of San Esteban (Saint Steven) de

**A NOT SO INNOCENT GAME**
→ In many hostels pilgrims will find a *juego de la oca* (literally, 'the game of the goose', a traditional board game along the lines of Snakes and Ladders) and may hear talk about its 'hidden messages'. Some believe this game actually embodies a secret code of the Knights Templar symbolizing the Way of Saint James, where the goal is Santiago de Compostela, square number 6 is Puente la Reina, the gaol represents Burgos, and the geese are the guards, as were the Templars themselves.

Deyo (the old Basque name of this region). The Romanesque church of San Andrés (Saint Andrew), which dates from the twelfth century, is very interesting, although the Baroque style of its bell tower is a little disconcerting. But, above all, be aware that for the time being you will be walking through bare, open country without any villages or towns between here and Los Arcos. This is therefore a good time to rest and have something to eat or to buy provisions, if necessary.

On leaving Villamayor you soon appreciate that this section is going to be rather monotonous. Although the trail leads slightly downward, the descent is barely perceptible most of the time and you may feel like you are walking on the flat. Twenty-five minutes out from

Villamayor you reach the last fountain before Los Arcos. Make sure that your water bottle is full. Here you will also see a sign with brief information on a place known as the Cueva de los Hombres Verdes (the Cave of the Green Men), in the nearby village of Urbiola. This is a burial place which has been dated to around 2000 BC. As it had been a copper mine, the human remains, together with the pottery and other utensils left there, have a greenish hue as a result of the oxidation of the ore. Hence the name. Archaeological excavation was undertaken by Dr Joan Maluquer towards the end of the 1950s. Some of the remains that he found and classified can be seen at the Museum of Navarre.

For an hour and a half the landscape is dull, broken up only now and again by the odd industrial or agricultural shed. However, after walking for almost four hours you will come across a bench to sit down on. In this bare terrain it comes as quite a surprise, but you will see a sign right away that explains that the bench faces the ruins of the old church of Yániz. Three menhirs also used to stand there until they were uprooted in 1959, and their whereabouts have been unknown ever since. Unfortunately, their disappearance destroyed the 'evidence' behind the legend that they were three maidens turned to stone when they failed to obey their mother's order to go to mass.

It will take a little over half an hour more to reach Los Arcos. You enter the town via what is described as a service area, although it is in fact nothing more than a garage which an enterprising citizen has turned into a refreshments shop, having realized that pilgrims arrive here thirsty and tired after a three-hour walk without shade.

## Los Arcos – Sansol

**6 h 30 min →** You cross Los Arcos along the Calle Mayor. It was already an important point on the Way in medieval times and reference to it appears in the *Codex Calixtinus* of Aymeric de Picaud. Even today you only have to see the church of Santa María (Saint Mary) to appreciate the importance of the place.

On leaving Los Arcos you will see a similar landscape. An hour later you cross a watercourse via a concrete ford and come to a sign explaining that this was the site of the old Melgar pilgrims' hospice (the term "hospice" is used here in its more general meaning of a lodging for travellers). The Way twists to the right and passes through a picnic area among vast vineyards. A little before reaching Sansol there is a stretch of road.

## Sansol – Torres del Río

**6 h 50 min →** Cross the town of Sansol, and after short walk along the main road take a well-prepared track that offers an easy descent, if steep, across the gully and into Torres del Río.

# From Torres del Río to Logroño

**20,2 km • 4 h 55 min • Elevation difference ▲ 360 m ▼ 440 m**

**Torres del Río – Virgen del Poyo**
**40 min** → Very few pilgrims will have heard of Torres del Río before coming to this part of the Way as it runs through Navarre. However, having seen the town they will forever remember it as being one of the most surprising places on the whole pilgrimage. At first sight it could just be one more small rural community through which the Way passes as it heads for La Rioja. When coming down from Sansol there is no reason to imagine that you will soon encounter a town which is in a constant process of urban restoration and provides, furthermore, a number of high-level services. It is, however, the Santo Sepulcro (Holy Sepulchre)

church that will leave the visitor truly astounded.

Hidden away in the network of streets that runs up and down the hill, the twelfth-century church has an octagonal base and south-facing doorway.

Its plan suggests that its origins lie with the Knights Templar, even though no documentation has been found to support this theory. It is, on the other hand, undeniable that its decoration has a Mudejar imprint and that there is a certain Cistercian air about it. The magnificence of the building lies in its simplicity. The nave is bare, without any benches, and services are held with the congregation standing throughout.

■ The Santo Sepulcro (Holy Sepulchre) church in Torres del Río

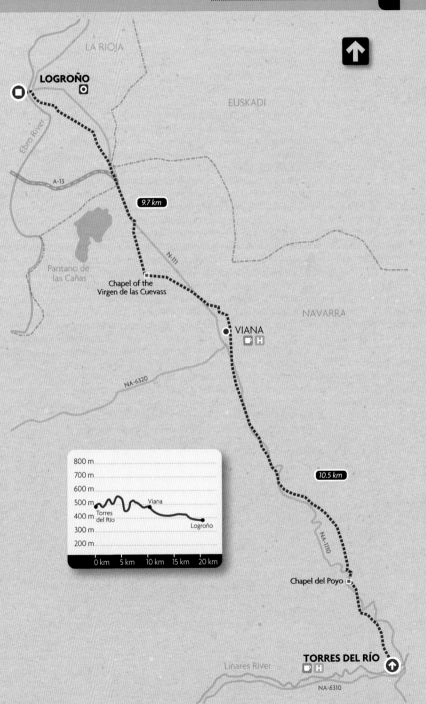

LA RIOJA

**LOGROÑO**

EUSKADI

Ebro River

A-13

9.7 km

Pantano de las Cañas

N-111

Chapel of the
Virgen de las Cuevass

NAVARRA

VIANA

NA-6320

10.5 km

NA-1110

800 m
700 m
600 m
500 m
400 m
300 m
200 m

Viana

Torres
del Río

Logroño

0 km    5 km    10 km    15 km    20 km

Chapel del Poyo

**TORRES DEL RÍO**

Linares River

NA-6310

The church has no fewer than 50 capitals decorated with flower and animal motifs. The most outstanding element, however, is the dome. Eight arches rise from the corbels, their ribs intersecting to form a star. Openings at the base of the ribs provide the dome with natural light, displaying a clear Moorish architectural influence. Advancing to the altar you will see the figure of a crowned Christ, unusual in that there are four nails, as the feet are separated, instead of the customary three. This confers a striking degree of realism to the scene.

The church is usually closed. To see the inside you need to phone one of the women who look after the key (the telephone number appears on a notice pinned to the main door) and pay one euro.

The deep impression left by the church and its contents still lingers on leaving Torres del Río through the upper part of the town, following the yellow arrows which now take you past one of the town's hostels and, now out of town, past the cemetery (where there is a drinking fountain outside). Once out of the built-up area, you immediately come to an earth track. There are some short, sharp inclines, with paving where the gradient is very steep. If you have an altimeter to hand, you can see that you are, in general, gaining height. After covering about two kilometres you reach the small church of the Virgen del Poyo. The construction remains solid, given that the church,

originally built in the sixteenth century, has been restored on various occasions. Experts rate its rococo altarpiece highly.

### Virgen del Poyo – Viana

**2 h 35 min →** This stretch calls for a degree of patience with the landscape, as it will be practically two hours before you reach the next centre of population – the only one you pass today – and the track meanwhile rises and falls constantly. It is not tiring, however, as the slopes are short. The Mataburros gully constitutes the only variation. Once you have passed through that, go gently down to the historic town of Viana, a stronghold of the Way and once a bastion on the disputed frontier between the old kingdoms of Navarre and Castile. The Baroque town hall is of interest, as is, particularly, the church of Santa María (Saint Mary), where Cesare Borgia, the son of Pope

### MONUMENT TO THE WAY

→ On entering La Rioja, walkers have to pass through an industrial area for a good while. But on reaching the Monument to the Way of Saint James at the entrance to the Puente de Piedra, reflected in the waters of the Ebro River you will see a typical image of Logroño. The sculpture is a mixture of avant-garde and traditional styles which not everyone likes, but it is certainly one of the most original you will see on all the journey.

■ Rioja Culture Centre in Logroño

Alexander VI, is buried. He died in these parts at the beginning of the sixteenth century following a duel. The church's southern portal, in Late Renaissance style, and the Baroque altarpiece are a feast of images and adornment.

The town centre of Viana is truly monumental, and it is worth having a leisurely stroll around it before setting off on the last stretch of this stage.

### Viana – Virgen de las Cuevas

**3 h 20 min →** The route out of the town is on surfaced local and secondary roads that are well marked by yellow arrows and have little traffic. After half an hour you come to a track which leads to the old chapel of Virgen de las Cuevas (Our Lady of the Caves). This cool, romantic place, with its shaded tables and benches and babbling stream, is an inviting spot for a picnic or siesta.

### Virgen de las Cuevas – Logroño

**4 h 55 min →** When you leave the chapel, although you are following a path bordering a

> 🍴 One of the culinary delights of La Rioja is truly worthy of recommendation: these are 'alegrías', fiendishly hot chillies packed in diminutive cans. They are easy to find and to carry and make a terrific souvenir.

fragrant pine wood, the noisy road is very close by. Cross the bridge over the motorway and the route becomes very pleasant, and soon becomes the cycle lane into the capital. Surrounded by factories, the border between Navarre and La Rioja is one of the least interesting places. The only pleasant feature is the house of Doña Felisa, who used to stamp the pilgrims' passes and make them presents of fresh figs. Now it is her daughter María who does so. Finally, you arrive at the downhill slope that goes through a lovely park alongside the Ebro River, leaving you at the Puente de Piedra (stone bridge). At the beginning of the slope you will find an information point for pilgrims.

# Logroño

**Distance behind you: 162.7 km**

→**Co-cathedral of Santa María la Redonda 1** The church of Santa María (Saint Mary) la Redonda, a co-cathedral, dominates the old town, its twin towers reaching skywards. It is the city's largest church and began to be built in the fifteenth century. It has a Romanesque doorway guarded by wrought-iron railings. The towers have long been a favourite nesting place for storks, although some of these have recently been frightened off by ongoing works on the side of the building. Inside there is a painting, attributed to Michelangelo, depicting the Crucifixion.

→**The old town 2** In the peaceful old town of Logroño, the visitor should not miss two streets in particular. The first, Portales, is full of traditional or more modern shops clustered under the arches which give the street its name. The locals traditionally use it for their walks in winter, given the shelter that those arches provide. The second, Laurel, crammed with bars and taverns, is the favourite haunt of those delighting in tapas and wine. The alleyways running between the Plaza del Mercado and the town hall are also worth exploring.

→**El Espolón 3** In Logroño they say that El Espolón is for the summer. Indeed, as mentioned already, locals out for an evening stroll preferred Calle Portales for its shelter during the cold, rainy season, leaving this park - whose official name is Paseo Príncipe de Vergara – for hot summer evenings. This never fails to surprise visitors, once they realise that the two avenues are barely 200 metres apart. Today the Espolón, with its gardens and statue of General Baldomero Fernández Espartero on horseback, is a green oasis of fountains and shade, where many evening concerts are held on the stage erected on the west side.

→**Bridges over the Ebro and riverside walk 4** The Ebro River has played a key role in the history and development of the city. The view of the river is at its best in the evening, when the lighting is on, from the south bank.

The Puente de Piedra is a work of engineering in which, it is said, the saints Domingo de la Calzada (Dominic of the Causeway) and Juan de Ortega (John the Hermit) were involved. It is a pleasure to walk by the riverbank and to cross the Ebro on that bridge or any of the others: Mantible, Sagasta, de Hierro (the iron bridge) or the footbridge, strengthened by new infrastructure, the GR-99. The GR-99 is a path, restored and marked, running for almost 1,300 km beside the river. The Logroño stretch, marked with red and white stripes, enters via the Cortijo quarter and subsequently moves on towards the neighbouring town of Agoncillo. It provides a perfect view of the river islets and the birds that inhabit the banks.

Map labels:
- Monumento al Camino de Santiago
- Ebro River
- Puente de Hierro
- Parque del Ebro
- C. DEL GENERAL URRUTIA
- Iglesia de Santiago el Real
- Camino del Ebro
- C. SAN FRANCISCO
- Puente de Piedra
- Albergue
- AV. DE GONZALO DE BERCEO
- Fuente de los Peregrinos
- C. BARRIO NUEVO
- C. RUAVIEJA
- C. NICOLÁS
- Iglesia Santa María de Palacio
- C. MARQUÉS DE
- CORREDERA MEDRANO
- C. DE PORTALES
- C. SAGASTA
- AV. DE NAVARRA
- Catedral La Redonda
- AYUNTAMIENTO
- Casco Viejo
- C. LAUREL
- AV. DE LA PAZ
- EL ESPOLÓN
- GRAN VÍA DEL REY DON JUAN CARLOS I
- C. DEL MARQUÉS DE MURRIETA
- C. REY PASTOR
- AV. PÉREZ GALDÓS
- C. DE COLÓN
- AV. DE JORGE VIGÓN
- Parque de la Laguna
- C. DE HUESCA
- C. GENERAL VARA DEL REY
- Estación de autobuses
- Parque San Miguel
- C. DE LOS DUQUES DE NÁJERA
- AV. DE LOBETE
- Estación de
- AV. DEL CLUB DEPORTIVO
- CARRETERA DE CIRCUNVALACIÓN

A short distance from the Way in the heart of the old quarter of Logroño is the Rioja Culture Centre, a space devoted to the world of Rioja wine and the gastronomy of the area. The centre is housed in a historically interesting building.

→City walls and Pilgrims' Fountain 5 Pilgrims most often stay at the hostel in Ruavieja, the street leading to the old quarter of the city. On the following morning they continue along that same street on their way out of Logroño. At a certain point they come to the Pilgrims' Fountain, where they may stop for water. You don't need much imagination to picture the thousands of pilgrims who have, over the centuries, descended the steps to that fountain in order to fill their water bottles or, formerly, gourds. The Puerta del Camino gateway marks the exit from the city.

→Churches of Santa María de Palacio and Santiago el Real 6 These are the two churches of which the citizens of Logroño are most proud. That of Santa María (Saint Mary) de Palacio is distinctive in that its pyramid-shaped tower, known locally as La Aguja (the needle), is a feature of the city's skyline. The church dates from the eleventh and twelfth centuries. The doorway of the church of Santiago (Saint James) el Real bears an image of Saint James the Moor-slayer. It is worth noting that Clavijo, the site of the battle where the saint intervened so decisively, is very close to Logroño.

# From Logroño to Nájera

**29 km • 7 h • Elevation difference ▲ 409 m ▼ 280 m**

**Logroño – Alto de la Grajera**
**2 h 10 min →**The way out of Logroño is easy and relaxed. On leaving the hostel, continue along Ruavieja and then take Calle Barriocepo, following the arrows.

Soon you come to the Pilgrim's Fountain, set a little below the level of the street. In accordance with tradition, go down the steps to the fountain and fill your water bottle, just as millions of travellers have done over the centuries. On the right side of the street is the imposing church of Santiago el Real and, if you pay attention, you will notice that the paving of the Plaza de Santiago is inset with a giant *juego de la oca*, a game closely associated with the Way (see page 40).

After passing through the gateway in the walls you come to an area of gardens with a round-about which is a little confusing. However, continue to head southwest and you come to the broad Marqués de Murrieta ave-nue, which you will be following for a good while.

The city stretches into the outskirts and you have to walk for some time before crossing the railway line and coming to a corner (Calle Portillejo) where various car dealerships are situated. Turn left here, leaving behind the sounds of the city, and follow a cycle lane through the San Miguel Park and on to

■ Pantano de La Grajera, just out of Logroño

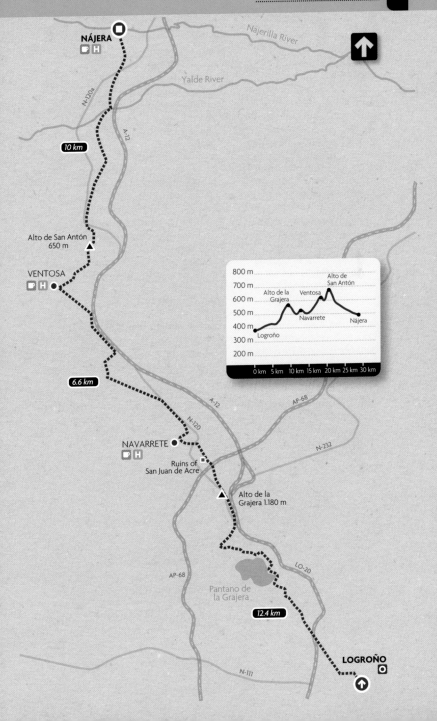

NÁJERA

Najerilla River

Yalde River

N-120a

A-12

10 km

Alto de San Antón
650 m

VENTOSA

6.6 km

A-12

N-120

AP-68

N-232

NAVARRETE

Ruins of
San Juan de Acre

Alto de la
Grajera 1.180 m

AP-68

LO-20

Pantano de
la Grajera

12.4 km

N-111

LOGROÑO

800 m
700 m                                    Alto de
600 m      Alto de la        Ventosa    San Antón
500 m       Grajera
400 m                        Navarrete       Nájera
300 m       Logroño
200 m

0 km  5 km  10 km  15 km  20 km  25 km  30 km

an underpass under the dual carriageway. Fifty-five minutes have gone by since the starting point. The noise of the traffic disappears and you will hear nothing more than birdsong and the rustling tracksuits of those who like to train in this area.

The walk through the parkland is very pleasant. You come to the La Grajera reservoir, protected by a low wall, and, following a well-marked path, you reach the bridge that takes you over a corner of the reservoir. Waterfowl abound in this area.

Once over the bridge you come to a steady but not particularly demanding climb up a concrete track, leading between picnic and other leisure facilities in the park. It will take almost an hour to cover this stretch. In the summer season there might be a kiosk or bar open where you can stop for a coffee or tea.

After a long ascent along the tarmac you reach Alto de La Grajera, which has a wire fence to which pilgrims have affixed little crosses made from sticks found on the ground. The dual carriageway is now below you and once again you will hear the roar of vehicles.

### Alto de La Grajera – Navarrete

**2 h 55 min** → Take a brief rest on the hill, with its pleasant oaks and holm oaks, before tackling a long descent along paths that are generally well surfaced, running between vineyards, to Navarrete. First you will see the ruins of the hospice of San Juan de Acre (see box on this page) and then come to the town, where it is worth spending a few minutes on a couple of visits. The old town is full of streets with imposing houses. One of these is Calle Mayor, along which the Way runs. Others include Calle Nueva, with its arches, and Cuesta del Caño.

Navarrete is well known for its pottery and there is a monument that pays tribute to its potters in the square by the church. About a dozen potteries are currently open to the public where you can see clay being worked in the traditional manner. You can also buy finished products, but since the material is both fragile and heavy this is not such a good idea while walking the Way. However, you might be able to find something small enough not to add to your burden.

In terms of monuments, it is well worth visiting the parish church of la Asunción (the

### RUINS OF SAN JUAN DE ACRE

→ The ruins of the monastery of San Juan de Acre lie just a few hundred metres outside the town of Navarrete. It was founded in 1185 as a pilgrims' hospice. Today all that remains is the base of some of the principal walls, but information panels have been erected so that the traveller may appreciate the historical importance of the site for the La Rioja section of the Way.

La Rioja style potatoes is one of the outstanding local dishes. You will find this energy-giving stew on every menu. Of humble origin, its main ingredients are potatoes, chorizo, and *choricero* pepper paste.

Assumption), which dates from the sixteenth century. Navarrete does not forget how important the Way has been for the town historically. Thus, every 25 July the association of local townswomen organizes a musical evening to which pilgrims are expressly invited. There is also a charming monument to the travellers who pass through on their way to Santiago.

### Navarrete – Ventosa

**4 h 35 min** → Leaving Navarrete, you will see the cemetery to your left. Its size is striking and so is its impressive twelfth-century Romanesque gateway. In fact, this used to be the entrance to the old hospice of San Juan de Acre before it was brought here. It is richly ornamented, particularly with geometrical figures. On an adjacent wall you can see a plaque to the memory of a cyclist pilgrim killed in an accident in 1986.

The walk to Ventosa takes little more than an hour and a half, surrounded by vineyards and then accompanied for a good while by the noise of the A-12. The '1 kilómetro de arte' (one kilometre of art) project invites pilgrims to make detour to arrive in Ventosa, a worthwhile alternative if only to move away from the motorway.

### Ventosa – Alto de San Antón

**5 h** → Between Ventosa and Alto de San Antón there is a short but very stiff climb. The shelter hitherto provided by the vineyards wanes at this point and the wind can often be troublesome. The good thing, however, is that when you reach the top you can see Nájera, no more than some eight kilometres away, all downhill.

### Alto de San Antón – Nájera

**7 h** → The last two hours before reaching Nájera are rather monotonous, with only vines for company, although you will pass a reconstructed *chozo* – a stone hut traditionally used locally for storing agricultural implements and similar purposes – very near Poyo de Roldán (Roland), where the legendary warrior defeated the giant Ferragut.

Further on the path passes by an aggregates quarry and the landscape suffers as a result. On approaching Nájera a series of bucolic little bridges spanning streams is visible, but the scene is marred by occasional mounds of rubble. Finally, you will enter the town, cross the Najerilla River and reach the hostel.

# From Nájera to Santo Domingo de la Calzada

**20.7 km • 5 h • Elevation difference ▲ 405 m ▼ 250 m**

## Nájera – Azofra

**1 h 20 min →**The monastery of Santa María la Real (Royal Saint Mary) is the pride of Nájera and one of the most beautiful buildings on the entire Way. It warrants more than a cursory visit.

The traveller enters through the Carlos I doorway, which leads almost straight to the cloister of the Caballeros (knights), so called because its walls house the tombs of numerous nobles from Rioja and the Basque Country who lived between the

sixteenth and eighteenth centuries. One of the most important is the mausoleum of Diego López de Haro, Lord of Bizkaia in the thirteenth century and founder of the city of Bilbao. The traceries of the arches are magnificent, resembling crochet work in stone, and each one different.

Once inside the monastery, the architectural style you can see is late Gothic with some Plateresque additions, such as the galleries. The royal pantheon, dating from around 1556, houses the tombs of some of the monarchs of Navarre of the Jimena or Abarca dynasties and that of King García Ramírez the Restorer.

In the crypt there is a cave where the Gothic figure of the Virgen de la Rosa (Our Lady of the Rose) may be seen. According to legend, the image was found in this precise spot by a noble falconer out hunting for partridge. A monastery was then founded on the spot, together with a pilgrims' hospice of which nothing remains.

You must also see the pantheon of the *infantes*, where the

### HISTORIC MONASTERIES

→Throughout the history of the Way, thousands of pilgrims have made a detour in order to visit the nearby monasteries at San Millán de la Cogolla. In that of Suso, which is troglodytic, were laid the remains of San Millán (Saint Emilianus). That of Yuso has one of the most beautiful sacristies in the whole peninsula. The twin monasteries have been a World Heritage site since 1997.

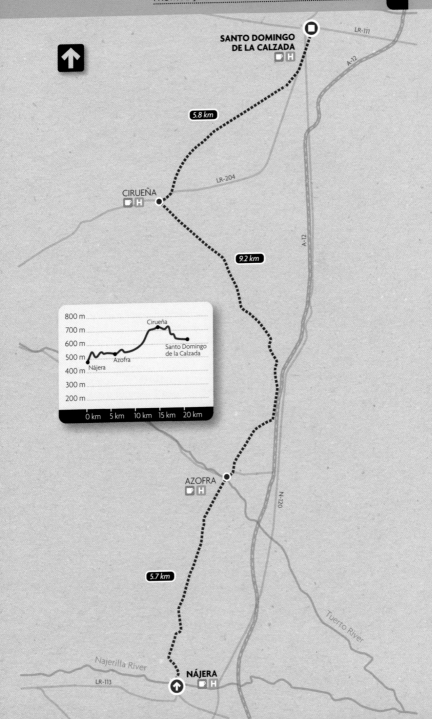

SANTO DOMINGO
DE LA CALZADA

LR-111

A-12

5.8 km

LR-204

CIRUEÑA

A-12

9.2 km

800 m
700 m                    Cirueña
600 m                         Santo Domingo
500 m                         de la Calzada
400 m    Nájera    Azofra
300 m
200 m
      0 km  5 km  10 km  15 km  20 km

AZOFRA

N-120

5.7 km

Tuerto River

Najerilla River

NÁJERA

LR-113

most famous tomb is that of Blanca of Navarre with its decorated sarcophagus, and the choir stalls. The ornate carving is a masterpiece of the florid Gothic style of the late fifteenth century, full of monsters and demons, of religious, geometrical and plant motifs and of scenes from the everyday life of the time.

Lastly, there is the great Baroque reredos of the main altar, depicting the Virgin with the child Jesus blessing the people.

Still marvelling at the beauty of the monastery, follow the yellow arrows out of Nájera. You will pass close by some old cave dwellings dug out of the soft rock of the outcrops to the north of the town. The Way is well marked and runs along trails through agricultural land. This stretch is rather monotonous and flat, except at the beginning where there is a steep slope about a kilometre in length. To the south you can see the Ezcaray mountains on the horizon. Snow generally covers their peaks until well into the year. The approach to Azofra is slightly uphill, but the ascent is barely perceptible.

### Azofra – Crucero

**1 h 40 min** ➔ Today Azofra is a small place you can walk through in no time. However, the ancestral houses on its Calle Mayor, which you will walk along from end to end, bear witness to the importance that the town has had over the centuries. In the square is a fountain with four

*Ahorcaditos are delicious sweet pastries from Rioja, made with almond cream and puff pastry. They were first made in the Isidro pastry shop (Calle Pinar, 52) in Santo Domingo de la Calzada.*

jets where you might pause for a moment to refresh yourself. The water is not drinkable, but there is a drinking fountain just behind it. You might also take a look at the parish church, where there is a statue of Santiago Peregrino (Saint James the Pilgrim).

To leave the town, go to the end of the Calle Mayor, walk along the main road for a few metres and then follow a broad gravel track through the forest. For about two hours the route goes gradually upwards, although the ascent is barely perceptible.

Some twenty minutes out from Azofra there is a well-restored medieval cross which was formerly a *picota*, a stone column to which wrongdoers were shackled to teach them a lesson, and where the heads of executed criminals were exhibited.

Further ahead, on crossing a main road, on the left is the turn-off to San Millán de Cogolla (the sign says Alesanco).

### Crucero – Cirueña

**3 h 20 min** ➔ After the junction there is a straightforward stretch of a couple of hours on which one of the few distractions is observing the flight of storks or other birds common to this region. A long upward stretch takes you to the outskirts of Cirueña; some recently built developments show you the impact that the golf course has had. The old town lies to the right of the Way and does not contain many buildings of note. There is no need to visit it, unless you simply wish to look around.

### Cirueña – Santo Domingo de la Calzada

**5 h →** Five minutes out from Cirueña you come to the high point of the stage at a little more than 700 metres above sea level. From here you can see the outline of Santo Domingo de la Calzada just eight kilometres away.

Continue along the same broad track. Although the going is easy, there is no shade. The only interruption is the occasional cairn left by pilgrims or the odd handmade cross. The stretch before Santo Domingo is a long descent along a broad, easy track; the transition from country to city has none of the usual intermediate waste ground or industrial areas.

You enter Santo Domingo de la Calzada via the Calle Mayor and pass the Centro de Interpretación del Camino de Santiago (Way of Saint James Interpretation Centre), with its display of technical wizardry and rather over-the-top theatricality intended to help the tourist experience the sensations of the pilgrim. Although admission is free for those in possession of a pilgrim's pass, true pilgrims do not seem to need the virtual; they are living the reality.

■ The Plaza Mayor (main square) and town council of Santo Domingo seen from the cathedral tower

# From Santo Domingo de la Calzada to Belorado

**22.4 km • 5 h 40 min • Elevation difference ▲ 382 m ▼ 250 m**

### Santo Domingo de la Calzada – Grañón

**1 h 40 min →**Known as 'the Compostela of Rioja', Santo Domingo de la Calzada is so closely linked to the Way and has so many monuments that a full visit is warranted. The old town is shady and pleasant. Centred around the Calle Mayor, by which you enter the city, it has an array of imposing houses bearing witness to the antiquity and nobility of the place. You will also find the modern, interactive Way of Saint James Interpretation Centre here. This is of greater interest to tourists than to pilgrims, but if you wish to visit it nevertheless, take your pilgrim's pass in order to get in for free.

### A HEN WITH A GRIP ON LIFE

→This local legend is so well known that the saying 'where the hen sang after being roasted' is even recorded as the town council's motto. When a young pilgrim was wrongly convicted for a theft he had not committed, Saint Dominic worked a miracle whereby a hen which had already been roasted rose and began to sing in proof of the innocence of the boy, whose life was thus saved.

The city's most outstanding building is without doubt the cathedral. Inside is the famous coop housing the cock and hen that symbolize the legend associated with the city (see box on this page). Construction of the cathedral commenced at the beginning of the twelfth century, precisely so that it could be the burial place of Saint Dominic. The main altarpiece, the choir, the saint's sepulchre and the chicken coop are four of the elements of most interest for tourists.

Visitors may climb the cathedral tower, which is separate from the main building, to enjoy an excellent view of the Plaza Mayor, a large part of the old town and the surrounding farmlands. Admission to the cathedral and to the tower costs 4 euros for pilgrims (tower only: 2 euros).

Other places of interest during a relaxed visit include the Plaza Mayor, where the town hall stands. The sides of the open square feature the typical arches so frequently seen throughout Castile. The walls of the city are the biggest in the whole of La Rioja and date from the fourteenth century. The bridge over the Oja River was the scene of several miracles performed by Saint Dominic. In the most

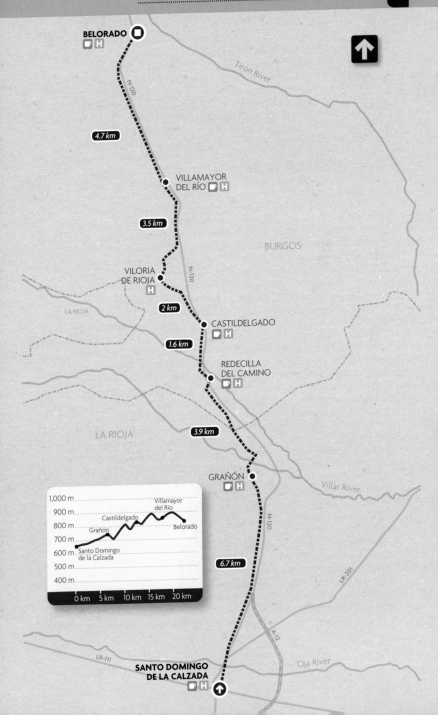

BELORADO

4.7 km

VILLAMAYOR
DEL RÍO

3.5 km

BURGOS

VILORIA
DE RIOJA

2 km

CASTILDELGADO

1.6 km

REDECILLA
DEL CAMINO

LA RIOJA

3.9 km

LA RIOJA

GRAÑÓN

Villar River

Tirón River

N-120

6.7 km

LR-201

1,000 m
900 m                                    Villamayor
                                         del Río
800 m          Castildelgado
700 m       Grañón                       Belorado
600 m    Santo Domingo
         de la Calzada
500 m
400 m
       0 km  5 km  10 km  15 km  20 km

LR-111

SANTO DOMINGO
DE LA CALZADA

Oja River

A-12

famous one, he brought a young man who had been run over by a cart back to life. Lastly, there are two convents worth seeing: that of San Francisco (Saint Francis), which now shares its extensive facilities with a *parador* (a state-run luxury hotel), a workshop where works of art are restored and a hospital; and the Cistercian nuns' abbey, dating from the seventeenth century.

From the cathedral, the yellow arrows guide you out of Santo Domingo and lead once again to earth tracks flanked by grain fields which in spring are green, in the early summer are yellow and in winter are the ochre of the dormant earth. A gentle ascent takes you to Grañón.

### Grañón – Redecilla del Camino
**2 h 40 min →**A good, broad track leads, in an almost imperceptible ascent through terrain practically devoid of shade, to Grañón, which you enter via its long Calle Mayor. This town, which has plenty of facilities, has a lovely viewpoint with tables and benches on the way out of the town centre. It is the last in the autonomous community of La Rioja.

You would never have known from the landscape, which is exactly the same, but the regional authorities ensure that you are aware of the boundaries. Thus, on a small bend to the right you come

to a huge metal sign marking the starting point of the province of Burgos and, therefore, of the autonomous community of Castilla y León. There are also some information panels with maps so that you can take an advance look at the stages you will be covering in the coming weeks, as it shows the entire course of the Way through this region of Burgos and the community of Castilla y León. On this stretch the pedestrian suffers a little on the bare, shadeless track. The cyclist, in contrast, can take advantage of the level terrain to keep up a steady speed.

### Redecilla del Camino – Castildelgado
**3 h 5 min →**Shortly after crossing the provincial border you come to the town of Redecilla del Camino. Cross the road here, taking even more care than usual because the monotony of the landscape may have dulled your senses a little, and you come to a little square where a fountain provides refreshment. Although small, the town has good facilities and therefore warrants consideration as a place to stop for lunch, bearing in mind, that you have by now covered more than half the day's journey. It is a good idea to

■ Ancient fountain in Redecilla del Camino

■ View of Grañón, last town on the Way in La Rioja

🍴 For those undertaking the Way in winter, one of the best options for recovering strength and raising body temperature is a stew made from *caparrones*, a red bean variety from the area known as the 'Riojilla burgalesa'.

have a rest here, given that in the course of the last three kilometres you have climbed over a hundred metres and that the stretch that lies ahead in turn has steep inclines and is therefore no less tough.

### Castildelgado – Viloria

**3 h 40 min →** Even at the speed of the foot pilgrim, so small is the village of Castildelgado that it seems to go by in a flash. The trail continues to climb until it reaches Viloria. This small town, with hardly any facilities for pilgrims, is famous in the area as the birthplace of Saint Dominic. The church of the Asunción (Assumption) houses the font where the saint was baptised in the year 1019 and a beautiful large altarpiece built around 1665, but these can rarely be seen by visitors as the church is closed for most of the year.

### Viloria – Villamayor del Río

**4 h 25 min →** Leave Viloria on a surfaced road which leads gently downward for some time, then link up with a path running parallel to the main road. This takes you to Villamayor del Río, which is quickly crossed.

### Villamayor del Río – Belorado

**5 h 40 min →** A rural track descends smoothly to Belorado, where you come to the first hostel before entering the town as such. On completing this stage take note (as your legs already may have done) that you have now covered a third of the Way.

# From Belorado to Agés

**27.5 km • 6 h 45 min • Elevation difference ▲ 530 m ▼ 332 m**

### Belorado – Tosantos

**1 h →** The walk from Belorado is on easy, level ground beside the road. The landscape at once takes on the familiar look of these past days: a rural track surrounded on either side by wheat and barley fields. After a few minutes the path starts to become steep, little by little at first, for about twenty minutes. You then come once again to level terrain until you reach Tosantos, which is small but has a bar and a hostel.

### Tosantos – Villambistia

**1 h 25 min →** From Tosantos you can see the chapel of the Virgen de la Peña (Our Lady of the Rock), clinging to a wall of rock.

The path runs along the back of the town and then out towards Villambistia, whose church you can see in the distance. Now the path ascends quite steeply and continues thus for a good part of the day as this stage includes going over the Montes de Oca hills.

If it is open, the church of San Esteban (Saint Steven) is worth a visit. It looks like an impregnable stronghold. Inside is its beautiful Baroque altarpiece. In the village you will pass by a pretty octagonal fountain with four jets surmounted by an iron cross. This used to be the source of the water supply for the villagers, but its water is no longer drinkable.

The route out of Villambistia

■ Oak wood in Alto de la Pedraja

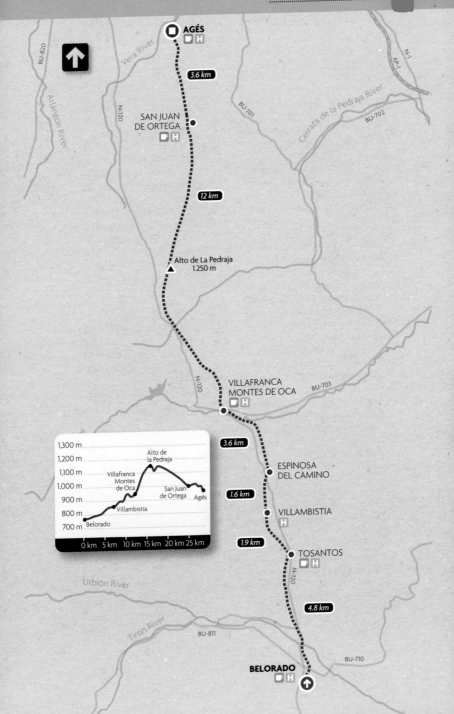

AGÉS

3.6 km

SAN JUAN
DE ORTEGA

12 km

Alto de La Pedraja
1.250 m

VILLAFRANCA
MONTES DE OCA

BU-703

3.6 km

ESPINOSA
DEL CAMINO

1.6 km

VILLAMBISTIA

1.9 km

TOSANTOS

4.8 km

BELORADO

1,300 m
1,200 m
1,100 m
1,000 m
900 m
800 m
700 m

Alto de
la Pedraja

Villafranca
Montes
de Oca

San Juan
de Ortega

Agés

Villambistia

Belorado

0 km  5 km  10 km  15 km  20 km  25 km

Vera River

Arlanzón River

BU-820

N-120

BU-701

Cerrata de la Pedraja River

BU-702

AP-1

N-1

N-120

N-120

Urbión River

Tirón River

BU-811

BU-710

is along a broad, smooth rural track.

### Villambistia – Espinosa del Camino

**1 h 50 min →** With the path becoming progressively steeper, you will reach the next town, Espinosa, in less than half an hour. The name of the town suggests that it was founded as a result of the passage of pilgrims a few centuries ago. Today it still has a hostel, but the rest of the town's business seems to be failing. Many of its houses look neglected and almost abandoned.

### Espinosa del Camino – Monasterio de San Felices

**2 h 15 min →** On leaving Espinosa you face the longest and steepest part of the day's route. Over the next five kilometres you will ascend by 200 m. Before that, however, you come to the ruins of the Hispano-Visigothic (sixth century) monastery of San Felices or San Félix. These stand very close to the side of the track and are identified by a sign. From the ruins you can just about work out where the main altar and the apse were situated. According to the history books, the founder of the city of Burgos, Diego Porcelos, may have been buried here.

### Monasterio de San Felices – Villafranca de Montes de Oca

**2 h 40 min →** Leaving the monastery behind, continue along the track and cross the Oca River. From here you will be walking uncomfortably close to the busy road. An alternative path avoids the road and crosses a small bridge.

The town of Villafranca, whose church is dedicated to Saint James, must have known better days, to judge by its current look. It is the last populated place you will pass through before reaching San Juan de Ortega, so this is an good moment to buy provisions – or to stop for lunch, since you are halfway through the day's journey.

From here you enter the oak woods of Montes de Oca, where there are no facilities of any kind.

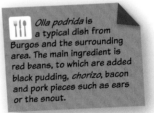

*Olla podrida* is a typical dish from Burgos and the surrounding area. The main ingredient is red beans, to which are added black pudding, *chorizo*, bacon and pork pieces such as ears or the snout.

### Villafranca de Montes de Oca – Alto de la Pedraja

**3 h 45 min →** Following a gentle ascent lasting just ten minutes, the path again starts to climb steeply. You will reach a viewpoint facing the San Millán mountains, and soon after there is an area with tables and benches where you can rest. This is a very good idea, as ahead lies the steepest stretch. The track is broad and smooth and you walk through a good-sized oak wood, dotted here and there with ash and juniper. It is the first wooded area of any size that you will have seen since leaving Navarre. It will also be the last for many days, as the rest of the route through Castile is practically devoid of trees.

Coming to Alto de la Pedraja, at 1,250 metres above sea level, you will see that the monument to the memory of Civil War dead, erected here decades ago, remains surprisingly undamaged. Next to it there is a picnic area with tables and benches at which you can rest. From here there is a good view of the Valbuena hill and the bottom of the valley. Although you will not have to walk along it, the road runs close by and you will constantly hear the hum of the traffic.

### Alto de la Pedraja – San Juan de Ortega

**5 h 55 min** ➜ You now come to a steep descent into the gully followed an equivalent ascent, beyond which the terrain remains flat for almost two hours' walking, although the overall trend is downward. The trail runs through an area of deforestation that is frankly ugly. The path is very wide and in very poor condition, littered with the debris of the extraction process, while heavy vehicles manoeuvre to take the timber away. There is a sharp descent to San Juan de Ortega.

### San Juan de Ortega – Agés

**6 h 45 min** ➜ San Juan de Ortega is worth a leisurely visit. Take

**IMPRESSIVE MONUMENTS**
➜ San Juan de Ortega is just a small village within the municipality of Barrios de Colinas. However, such was its historical importance on the Way of Saint James that it boasts a magnificent array of monuments including the group formed by the church, the chapel of San Nicolás de Bari (Saint Nicholas), the Hieronymite monastery and the building which is now the pilgrims' hostel.

off your backpack and enter the church to admire the capital where the 'miracle of light' occurs on the days of the spring and autumn equinoxes (21 March and 22 September), when a ray of light illuminates the image of the Annunciation, in which the Archangel Gabriel and the Virgin Mary may be seen. The mausoleum of San Juan (Saint John), with the canopy that surrounds it, the chapel of San Nicolás de Bari (Saint Nicholas) and the hostel building are all worth visiting too. The hostel was recently renovated and the inadequacies that so many pilgrims had complained about have now been fixed. Next to the hostel stands Casa Marcela, a bar where it is traditional to eat black pudding with fried eggs.

From San Juan to Agés there is a pleasant walk of three quarters of an hour through a pretty, shady oak wood.

# From Agés to Burgos

**22.5 km • 5 h 10 min • Elevation difference ▲ 160 m ▼ 270 m**

### Agés – Atapuerca

**35 min →** Agés is a small but pretty town and a pleasant place to take a stroll. In the old quarter are houses in a traditional style of architecture that you will be seeing more and more over the next few days. Wood and adobe are the basic elements of construction, although you will see that stone also has a role to play in the architecture of Agés. There are a couple of fountains with granite basins, the old public laundry and, particularly, the single-arched Roman bridge with its impressive cutwater over the Vena River. Although it generally appears to be little more than a stream, according to the locals when the level becomes high the Vena can cause severe flooding even in the city of Burgos. The church is also worth a quick visit.

The first section of the stage leads slightly downhill to Atapuerca along a tarmac road with very little traffic. You may want to go into the centre of the town, but the path takes you lower down, then to the left past the monument to the ancestor and out of the town. Atapuerca has become world famous for its archaeological sites, chief among which is the Sima de los Huesos (the pit of bones), where the remains of some of the human race's earliest forebears have been found. Be aware, however, the sites are three kilometres off the Way and the round trip, plus the time spent at the sites, would take up a large part of the day.

■ Monument at the Atapuerca archaeological site

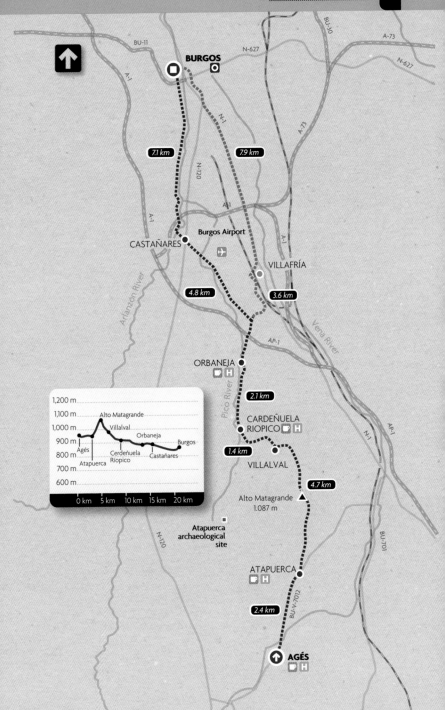

**BURGOS**

BU-11

N-627

BU-30

A-73

N-627

A-1

N-1

A-73

N-120

A-1

7.1 km

7.9 km

A-1

A-1

Burgos Airport

CASTAÑARES

VILLAFRÍA

Arlanzón River

4.8 km

3.6 km

AP-1

Vena River

ORBANEJA

Pico River

2.1 km

CARDEÑUELA
RIOPICO

N-1

AP-1

1.4 km

VILLALVAL

Alto Matagrande
1.087 m

4.7 km

BU-701

Atapuerca
archaeological
site

N-120

ATAPUERCA

BU-V-7012

2.4 km

**AGÉS**

**Elevation profile**

1,200 m
1,100 m — Alto Matagrande
1,000 m — Villalval
900 m — Agés        Orbaneja        Burgos
800 m —     Cerdeñuela   Castañares
700 m — Atapuerca  Riopico
600 m

0 km    5 km    10 km    15 km    20 km

### Atapuerca – Villalval

**1 h 40 min** →Leave Atapuerca along a broad, stony track which takes you steadily upwards to an unnamed hill marked by a large cross where, from a height of 1,050 metres above sea level, you can see the sparse oak wood through which you will descend towards the next town. More impressive is the view of the broad plain of Burgos down below. From the viewpoint a few metres from the cross you can make out the towers of the city's cathedral in the distance, and get a feel for the distance you still have to cover today. Leaving this windy spot behind, move sharply downwards between the trees along an awkward path strewn with large stones, and you come to Villalval. The town has no facilities or buildings of note, so carry on right through it.

### THE GRAPEVINE OF THE WAY

→ There is plenty of time to chat while walking or at the hostels and thus to keep a secret for the length of the pilgrimage is virtually impossible. This 'grapevine of the Way' ('el periódico del Camino') means that everybody knows that a certain Dutch girl is undertaking the pilgrimage after having been disappointed in love, that the chap from Valencia works for the gas company and that the bearded Austrian is partial to brandy. Be careful what you tell people.

### Villalval – Cardeñuela Ríopico

**2 h 5 min** →Descending little by little, it takes less than half an hour to Cardeñuela Ríopico, a village consisting of little more than a single street along which the Way runs. There is a bar and a pilgrims' hostel, but you are only 30 minutes away from Orbaneja, which is a good place to stop.

### Cardeñuela Ríopico – Orbaneja

**2 h 35 min** →From Cardeñuela Ríopico and Orbaneja you walk along a local tarmac road with no hard shoulder but, fortunately, practically no traffic. It is flat and therefore allows you to reach Orbaneja with fairly little effort. Once in the town, it may be a good idea to stop at a bar, study the guide and the map and perhaps seek the views of the locals on the various alternatives on offer.

### Orbaneja – Castañares

**3 h 35 min** →Of the many stages of the Way of Saint James, this one is likely to give you the most headaches. There are two main ways of getting to Burgos, the provincial capital. The traditional route goes from Orbaneja to Villafría along a local road but then, from Villafría, runs along the main N-1, where the vehicles roar by unpleasantly and, at times, dangerously close. This stretch is laborious. The noise is hellish and, although you are walking on the flat, the distance seems endless.

For the last few years an alternative route has been

■ Burgos, Santa María bridge and arch, with the cathedral spire behind

marked out. The distance is no shorter, but it is far more pleasant. We strongly recommend this one as it is much safer – at no point do you have to walk alongside the traffic or negotiate dangerous crossings.

On leaving Orbaneja, cross a bridge over the A-1 dual carriageway and you come to a small development with white houses. Follow the yellow arrows on the left down a muddy slope, around the development and towards the aerodrome. Here you have to walk beside the perimeter fence. There are few signs, but there is no risk of losing your way. After the runway you pass by an area of open ground, where you momentarily lose sight of the arrows, but there is only one possible way to go, leading straight to the town of Castañares.

### Castañares – Burgos

**5 h 10 min** →The landscape may not be any better, but the route is far less fraught. At Castañares, cross the N-120 and follow the signs past the church, turning right at a gravel pit. Go down to the Arlanzón River, cross it via the walkway and follow a path signposted 'Paseo de Fuentes Blancas a Castañares'. This is an attractive pathway that follows the river through a park dotted with huge trees and popular for sports activities, leading to the old quarter of Burgos.

The Way, with its two lanes, for cyclists and for walkers, respectively, follows the river past San Pablo (St Paul's) bridge, with the Museum of Human Evolution just opposite. On crossing the Santa María (St Mary's) bridge you will find yourself at the famous eponymous gateway next to the cathedral. You could hardly hope for a better end to a stage.

# Burgos

**Distance behind you: 284.9 km**

**→Cathedral 1** Work on the construction of Burgos cathedral began in 1221. In recent years the building has undergone in-depth restoration. Its two towers, dominating Plaza de Santa María, are very impressive. The visitor really needs a number of hours to appreciate all the marvels inside. There is the golden stairway, in Italian Renaissance style, the central nave and the chapel of San Nicolás (Saint Nicholas), which has a thirteenth-century altar and a still-older Romanesque tomb. In the area devoted to worship and prayer we find the chapel of the Santísimo Cristo de Burgos (Most Holy Christ of Burgos), with a fourteenth-century carving and the sixteenth-century clock known as Papamoscas

(flycatcher), and the Baroque-style chapel of Santa Tecla (Saint Thecla). In the central nave you will notice the tombs of El Cid and Doña Jimena (his wife), as well as the main altarpiece and the choir stalls. But it is the chapel of the Condestables (the Constables) that leaves visitors in awe. There, in addition to the tomb (see box) you can admire the central altarpiece, the starred vault, the painting of *Magdalena* by Gianpetrino and the *Christ Crucified* canvas.

**→Casa del Cordón 2** The palace of the Condestables de Castilla (the Constables of Castile) is a cultural centre belonging to a foundation run by a bank. Its name comes from the representation of a Franciscan cord which frames the main doorway. It is one of the finest examples of civil architecture in Burgos and it was here that the Catholic Monarchs received Columbus on his return from his first voyage to America.

**→El Castillo park 3** From this high point of the city you can see the ruins of the castle and parts of the old walls. From the surrounding park there are excellent views of a large part of the city and of the plain round about.

**→The city's arches 4** The Santa María arch is the most striking and ornate, but if you also take the time to visit that of San Esteban and the gate to the Hospital del Rey, a one-time pilgrims' hospice, you can get

## THE CONDESTABLES (CONSTABLES)

**→** Inside Burgos cathedral, one of the places which most impresses the visitor is the chapel of the Condestables (see main text). In the centre are the recumbent statues of the founders, Pedro Fernández de Velasco and Mencía de Mendoza. These marble statues of the couple are works of captivating realism, displaying exquisite detail in the representation of their features, hair, clothing and jewellery.

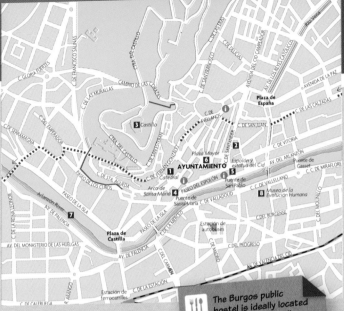

The Burgos public hostel is ideally located to check out the most well-known bars in the old part of town, as many of these places, famous for their tapas, are found around the cathedral.

an idea of what the old walls which surrounded the city must have looked like.

**→Plaza Mayor 5** This is a typical Castillian square, if a little irregular in shape, with arches on all sides. Together with the steep streets leading off to the north and west from the cathedral, it is the natural starting point for a walk through the old town.

**→Espolón and statue of El Cid 6** Right next to the Espolón and the Teatro Principal you will find the equestrian statue of El Cid pointing towards the battlefield with his famous sword, Tizona. It is worth taking a leisurely walk through the theatre itself and the Espolón with its magnificent trees, just as the people of the city do.

**→Arlanzón River 7** This river runs around the south side of the city and separates the old town from the new. A stroll along its banks and over its bridges affords a view of the waterfowl swimming tranquilly in its waters.

**→Museum of Human Evolution 8** This museum houses findings from the Atapuerca archaeological sites, granted World Heritage status by Unesco. On display are original fossils such as the 'Miguelón' skull or the 'Elvis' pelvis, and the remains of animals such as panthers or hippopotamuses.

# From Burgos to Hontanas

**31,5 km • 7 h 40 min • Elevation difference ▲ 305 m ▼ 290 m**

### Burgos – Villalbilla

**1 h 20 min →** The route out of Burgos is pleasant. The transition from town to country takes place swiftly, without disagreeable industrial estates or blighted suburban landscapes between the two. However, the Way is poorly marked, leading to confusion.

Start out up Calle Fernán González, go round the back of the cathedral and, following the rather inconspicuous yellow arrows, you end up at the San Martín arch. Here you leave the old, walled quarters of the city behind.

Now go down the hill on which the old town of Burgos stands and pass briefly through new neighbourhoods. You will come to the Malatos bridge, which takes you over the Arlanzón River. Next, walk into and through the El Parral park to the university square. There is no need to worry about losing sight of the river; for the first half of the day you will be walking along its valley, encountering beautiful wooded areas by the banks and delighting in the riverside scenery.

Cross the university campus area, with broad avenues where you need to pay attention to the yellow arrows, through to the neighbourhoods on the outskirts of Burgos. At present you are walking on the flat, but very shortly you will commence a gentle descent along a surfaced road to Villalbilla.

■ Burgos

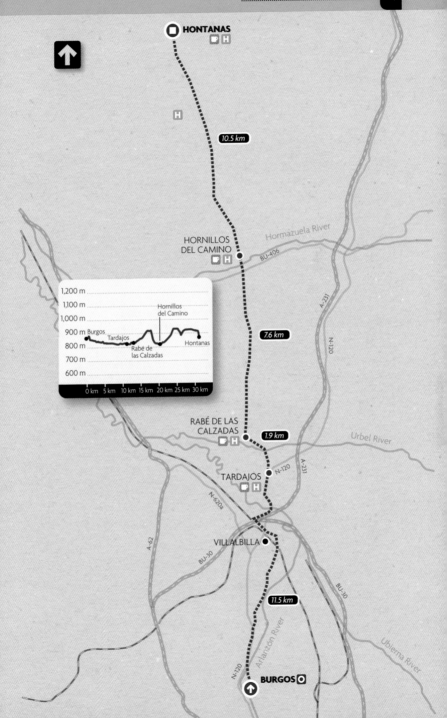

**HONTANAS**

10.5 km

**HORNILLOS DEL CAMINO**

BU-406

Hormazuela River

A-231

N-120

7.6 km

1,200 m
1,100 m
1,000 m
900 m  Burgos
800 m
700 m
600 m

Tardajos

Rabé de
las Calzadas

Hornillos
del Camino

Hontanas

0 km  5 km  10 km  15 km  20 km  25 km  30 km

**RABÉ DE LAS CALZADAS**

1.9 km

Urbel River

**TARDAJOS**

N-120

A-231

N-620a

**VILLALBILLA**

A-62

BU-30

11.5 km

BU-30

Arlanzón River

Ubierna River

N-120

**BURGOS**

### Villalbilla – Tardajos

**2 h 20 min →** You will see little of Villalbilla, as the Way goes around the outside of the town, although some pilgrims prefer to spend the night here (at a guest house or B&B) to avoid the more crowded conditions of the hostels in Burgos. On leaving the town of Villalbilla you take a rural track, which is flat and in very good condition.

### Tardajos – Rabé de las Calzadas

**2 h 55 min →** Although on this stretch you encounter awkward features in the form of railway lines and main roads, you will get around them with little difficulty. You also pass underneath a dual carriageway viaduct, which is a little intimidating. If you look closely you may see, on one of its concrete pillars, a small plaque apologising for the detour that the building of the new road obliges the pilgrim to make. It is true that the road has caused just such a detour; however, on the positive side, the path now passes close to the river, which looks magnificent here, bordered by poplars, alders and some ash.

One of the most highly valued dishes of Burgos's gastronomy is *lechazo*, or suckling lamb. In León there is a variant of *lechazo* that uses lambs of the Churra breed, fed only on their mother's milk.

You enter Tardajos passing beside the cross. This town has the best facilities of all those on the stage. There are bars and restaurants, grocery stores, a pharmacy and a bank with an ATM. The other villages through which you will be passing are very small and their facilities are limited.

From Tardajos you take a local road to Rabé de las Calzadas. There is very little traffic and this is therefore an easy walk, although it is said that this was once an area of swamps so terrible that the local people used to offer up prayers for divine protection.

### Rabé de las Calzadas – Fuente de Prao Torre

**3 h 45 min →** Rabé de las Calzadas, so called because it was the point where two Roman roads met, goes by in a flash, as it consists of little more than one long street with a fountain sporting long iron jets and decorated with scallop shells.

From this village onwards, the landscape changes dramatically. You will now be walking for several days across the broad, treeless plain of Castile, a lonely and monotonous landscape that can prove quite a tough psychological test for the traveller. There will be more of this is in the next stage, at Tierra de Campos in Palencia. Today not only is the landscape bare, it also incorporates some steep inclines, as there are two small plateaus to be crossed. Thus, on leaving

Rabé you face a sharp, two-kilometre ascent to Fuente de Prao.

### Fuente de Prao Torre – Hornillos del Camino

**4 h 55 min** → A picnic area, with tables, seats and a bin, has been set up by this fountain. Taking a rest here is not a bad idea, as you have further to climb before reaching the top of the first plateau. The track is broad and well prepared but walking is not easy, as there are deep ruts in it left by the wheels of tractors and other agricultural machinery. There are also pebbles the size of tennis balls which will have twisted the ankle of more than one pilgrim. At around kilometre 14 of the stage you start to go steeply downwards and follow that incline all the way to Hornillos del Camino.

### Hornillos del Camino – Arroyo San Bol

**6 h 35 min** → Hornillos has facilities for pilgrims and you may as well take advantage of them, as the stage is long and a couple of difficult stretches still lie ahead. The town has a pleasant corner in the little square of the church, where there is a fountain adorned with the figure of a cock.

On leaving Hornillos you at once face another climb as stiff as the last one. A large wind farm

**THE OMNIPRESENT VENDING MACHINES**
→ For the first two weeks of the pilgrimage you will find the Way full of vending machines. After that they become less common and finally disappear. It is not only drinks and snacks that they offer, however. Some also dispense first-aid material or even souvenir scallop shells. At some hostels, where breakfast is not served, they provide the only choice for the first meal of the day.

on the horizon will remain in sight for a good while. All around you will see a vast moor, with pilgrims trudging through a sea of wheat. As soon as you reach the top, you begin the descent to the stream called Arroyo San Bol.

### Arroyo San Bol – Hontanas

**7 h 40 min** → Some 200 metres to the left of the Arroyo San Bol is a hostel of the same name, simple, very clean and welcoming. It is in the middle of the countryside and is powered by solar panels. Some prefer to continue another four kilometres to Hontanas, a town whose existence you doubt until the last minute, as it lies in a hollow and is therefore not visible until you are practically on top of it.

# From Hontanas to Boadilla del Camino

**28.5 km • 6 h 25 min • Elevation difference ▲ 280 m ▼ 360 m**

### Hontanas –
### Convento de San Antón

**1 h 10 min →**On the previous stage you had to walk down into a hollow to get to Hontanas. It would seem only logical, therefore, that today you should expect to climb upwards. Yet the day's walking again begins with a gentle descent. The Way runs along an elevated track to the right of the road, past an ancient tower, joining the road itself shortly before reaching the Convento de San Antón. There is not much traffic, but you will generally be covering this section early in the day, so you should therefore be particularly careful and stick to the left-hand side.

### Convento de San Antón –
### Castrojeriz

**2 h →**The ruins of the monastery of Saint Anthony are one of the most pleasant surprises of the day on the architectural front. You approach along a tarmac road and come upon an enormous arch which once supported a roof, thus forming a porch which provided travellers with momentary shelter. Parts of the apse and of the façade of the church, together with some main walls of the central nave, are likewise still standing. You can also see the remains of the cupboards where the monks used to leave pilgrims a bite to eat.

The Order of Saint Anthony, which governed this monastery

■ Castrojeriz

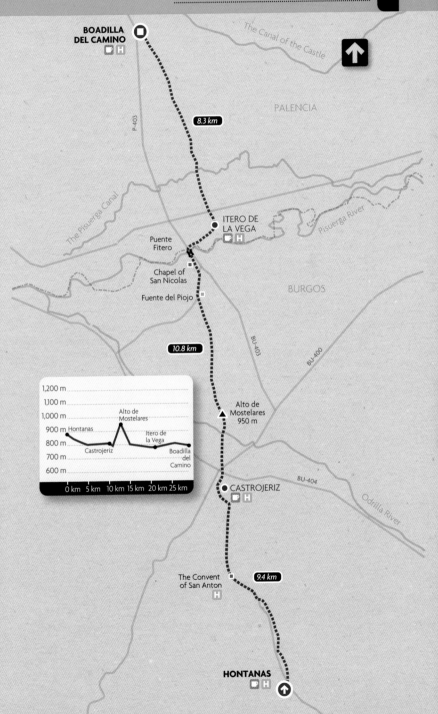

BOADILLA
DEL CAMINO

The Canal of the Castle

PALENCIA

P-403

8.3 km

The Pisuerga Canal

ITERO DE
LA VEGA

Pisuerga River

Puente
Fitero

Chapel of
San Nicolas

Fuente del Piojo

BURGOS

10.8 km

BU-403

BU-400

1,200 m
1,100 m
1,000 m
900 m   Hontanas
800 m
700 m
600 m

Alto de
Mostelares

Itero de
la Vega

Castrojeriz

Boadilla
del
Camino

0 km  5 km  10 km  15 km  20 km 25 km

Alto de
Mostelares
950 m

BU-404

CASTROJERIZ

Odrilla River

The Convent
of San Anton

9.4 km

HONTANAS

until it was dissolved at the end of the eighteenth century, was very powerful on the Way in its time. It was founded for the purpose of caring for those suffering from a disease similar to leprosy. The members of the community wore a habit bearing the Greek letter tau embroidered on the front. You will become very familiar with that letter, as you will see it repeatedly on T-shirts and other souvenirs.

Note that the road passes directly under the Gothic arch. For some this is a clear sign that on this section the Way in its present form continues to follow the medieval route exactly. There are still four kilometres of tarmac to go on this stretch.

### Castrojeriz – Alto de Mostelares

**3 h →** When you reach Castrojeriz it is a good idea, for various reasons, to call a brief

### THE START OF A TOUGH TEST

→ Although the last part of the preceding stage allowed you to form an idea of what lay ahead, it is on stage 14 that you come to the province of Palencia, where the Tierra de Campos subjects pilgrims to a tough psychological test: bleak uplands. The horizon is flat and there are no  visual references. For kilometres on end there are no towns, trees or even rocks that might serve as intermediate targets. It demands great mental strength.

halt. On the one hand, you have now been walking for a couple of hours. In addition, the town has a number of interesting monuments and it is worth taking off your backpack and having a look. Furthermore, upon leaving you face a tough 10-km stretch with a high point of some significance before coming to the next town.

The citizens of Castrojeriz boast of having the longest urban crossing on the whole Way. That may well be the case if you omit the cities. However, the churches of Nuestra Señora del Manzano (Our Lady of the Apple Tree) and San Juan (Saint John), the imposing civil buildings and the Plaza Mayor are more deserving of your attention, while the houses on Calle Mayor are fine examples of Castilian architecture.

### Alto de Mostelares – Fuente del Piojo

**4 h →** On leaving Castrojeriz you come immediately to a broad, earth track. It is in good condition, but entirely exposed. Initially you may not feel the wind, as you are still heading down towards the Odrilla River.

From there you see that the path ahead climbs and veers to the right. The ascent looks intimidating, with gradients of up to 12%, and you will gain some 140 metres in altitude in little more than a kilometre. It is, in a way, a pleasant change to head for a point that will give you a broad horizon. However, when

■ A pilgrim descending from the Alto de Mostelares

you actually reach the top (Alto de Mostelares), you may find the view a bit disheartening, as the endless plain stretches away to the town of Frómista and beyond.

Alto de Mostelares has an enormous trig point on the right and a rest area on the left. Being exposed to strong winds, however, this is not the most comfortable place for a pause. It is better to go on to Fuente del Piojo.

### Fuente del Piojo – Ermita de San Nicolás
**4 h 10 min →** At Fuente del Piojo, do take advantage of the little picnic area installed there. You have now descended the Alto de Mostelares by its west side and what remains, from here to the end of the stage, is a fairly gentle section without inclines of any significance.

### Ermita de San Nicolás – Itero de la Vega
**4 h 40 min →** Although in spring the ears of corn provide company of a sort, the landscape otherwise remains bare. Following the path you come to the Ermita de San Nicolás (Chapel of Saint Nicholas), a robust building to the left of the Way which was, in the golden age of the medieval pilgrimages, a noted hospice. It has been completely restored, but is closed. You are now very near to Fitero bridge, where you cross the Pisuerga River and enter the province of Palencia. Here the river is generally quiet and calm, but the seven arches and humped back of the bridge speak of powerful swells in times of heavy rain.

### Itero de la Vega – Boadilla del Camino
**6 h 25 min →** Between the village of Itero and the point of entry into Boadilla you will see just one tree. The terrain is endlessly flat, but before finishing the stage you at least come to a climb and a little pine wood which break up the monotony of the landscape. Today you have had your first taste of Tierra de Campos.

# From Boadilla del Camino to Carrión de los Condes

**24.7 km • 6 h 15 min • Elevation difference ▲ 130 m ▼ 95 m**

**Boadilla del Camino – Frómista**
**1 h 20 min** → The first five kilometres of this stage are the most beautiful of this stage in terms of landscape.

Leave Boadilla del Camino, still sheltered to some degree by trees, and at once you will notice that the terrain before you lies flat as far as the eye can see. Don't expect any significant changes of elevation or to see anything other than vast grain fields to either side of the Way. However, you soon come to a man-made feature which will make the rest of your walk to Frómista pleasant and interesting: the Canal de Castilla (Castile Canal). The purpose of this major work of engineering, begun in the eighteenth century, was to link the grain-growing lands of the plateau to ports

in the Bay of Biscay. It was only partly successful. Over 200 km of canals came into service, but unfortunately the goal of transporting the goods to the sea was never achieved. The walk along the towpath, bordered by elms, observing the birds in the reeds and hearing the slow movement of the water, goes all the way to Frómista. There, you cross a bridge over a system of locks which enables boats to overcome the significant change of elevation at that point. This is the only break from the monotony of the deserted landscape.

**Frómista – Campos**
**2 h 20 min** → While the Canal de Castilla represents a brief but welcome variation in the uniformity of the landscape,

■ Canal de Castilla between Boadilla del Camino and Frómista

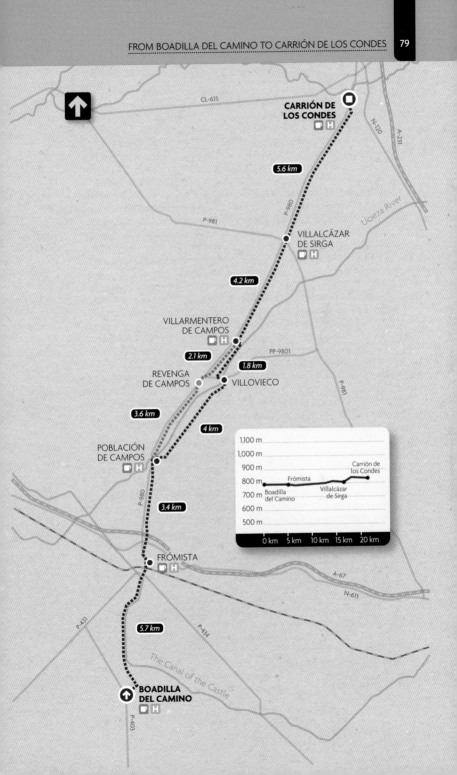

CL-615

N-120

A-231

**CARRIÓN DE
LOS CONDES**

5.6 km

P-980

Ucieza River

P-981

VILLALCÁZAR
DE SIRGA

4.2 km

VILLARMENTERO
DE CAMPOS

PP-9801

2.1 km

1.8 km

REVENGA
DE CAMPOS

VILLOVIECO

P-981

3.6 km

4 km

POBLACIÓN
DE CAMPOS

1,100 m
1,000 m
900 m
800 m
700 m
600 m
500 m

P-980

Carrión de
los Condes

Frómista

Boadilla
del Camino

Villalcázar
de Sirga

0 km   5 km   10 km   15 km   20 km

3.4 km

FRÓMISTA

A-67

N-611

P-431

5.7 km

P-424

The Canal of the Castle

**BOADILLA
DEL CAMINO**

P-403

the town of Frómista is one of the most attractive sights to be found along the Way in terms of religious architecture. The church of San Martín (Saint Martin) of Frómista, with its round towers flanking the main entrance, is a masterpiece of the Iberian Romanesque style. It stands apart in a rather graceless square, but this location at least means that you can admire the building from all four sides.

This church's exact name is San Martín de Tours (Saint Martin of Tours), and it is known to date back to the eleventh century, as it was mentioned in 1066. The restorations it underwent in the late nineteenth and early twentieth centuries have received as much criticism as its original structure has received praise. It has an octagonal cupola above the cross, while its cylindrical towers, acting as belfries, give it something of the appearance of a fortress. Inside there is a thirteenth-century figure of Christ. The naves are in general very sober, although on some of the columns there are capitals decorated with motifs that are biblical, such as the depiction of Adam and Eve, or relate to folk wisdom, like the fable of the fox and the grapes.

The church of San Martín is open to the public every day of the year, mornings and afternoons, except 1 January and 25 December and the afternoons of 24 and 31 December and 6 January. For pilgrims, admission is one euro.

It is worthwhile taking a look at the rest of Frómista while you still have the energy to do so. In addition to this flagship of Palencian Romanesque mentioned above, the churches of San Pedro (Saint Peter) and Santa María del Castillo (Saint Mary of the Castle) merit a visit, and the fine adobe-built houses are good examples of non-religious architecture. You will be coming across houses like these quite often during the rest of the day and on the stages which lie ahead.

Leaving Frómista, you immediately come to a comfortable, well-kept earth track running to the right of the road. Flanked by an over-abundance of marker stones, it takes you in long, straight stretches, with a barely perceptible incline, to Población de Campos, which you will cross by way of the main street.

**Campos – Revenga de Campos**
**3 h 15 min →** At this stage you can depart from the main route by

**THE WAY BY BOAT**
→ Palencia Council has put into operation an intriguing project that enables a few kilometres of the Way to be covered by boat along the Canal de Castilla. The boat, operating from Wednesday to Monday each week, covers the stretch between the lock at Frómista and the jetty where the Way and the Canal meet, near Boadilla del Camino (Tel. 673 368 486).

■ Villalcázar de Sirga

taking an alternative one to the left. It is quieter, as it takes us away from the noise of the traffic, but also a little longer. The last stretch before Villarmentero runs beside the Ucieza River in an area with a few trees, but it is muddy, so on rainy days it is best avoided.

If you follow the main route, upon leaving Población de Campos cross the bridge over the Ucieza River and return to the earth track. Now there is nothing on the horizon to distract your attention. If you were hoping to make an introspective journey, you will find such landscape very conducive to this.

### Revenga de Campos – Villarmentero de Campos
**3 h 50 min →** The section between Revenga and Villarmentero brings nothing new. Corn fields stretch away into the distance to left and right and there is nothing else to be seen.

### Villarmentero de Campos – Villalcázar de Sirga
**4 h 55 min →** At Villarmentero de Campos the track starts to ascend a little until shortly before reaching Villalcázar de Sirga. Here you will notice that you are coming to a gentle but rather long incline until shortly before the end of this stretch. The monumental size of the town's thirteenth-century church of Santa María la Blanca (Saint Mary the White) is rather surprising.

### Villalcázar de Sirga – Carrión de los Condes
**6 h 15 min →** After Villalcázar de Sirga the incline becomes sharper and the noise of the vehicles louder, as those heading downhill tend to do so at high speed.

On entering Carrión de los Condes you at once come to the convent of Santa Clara (Saint Clare) with its pretty courtyard. There is no need to hurry to find accommodation. It is worth taking a walk around the centre and considering the options before making a choice. Sometimes an ordinary-looking building proves to be more welcoming than a historic one.

# From Carrión de los Condes to Terradillos

**26.3 km • 6 h 30 min • Elevation difference ▲ 145 m ▼ 80 m**

### Carrión de los Condes – Abadía de Benevívere

**1 h 15 min →**At present Carrión de los Condes does not have even a fifth of the population it had in the Middle Ages, when it was one of the pillars of the Way of Saint James in Castile. Its heritage is immense, however, and it is well worth having a look around the town before starting the long stretch across the lonely plain.

The first monument you come to, upon entering the town, is the convent of Santa Clara. It has an magnificent courtyard and a museum housing some valuable works of art. It is one of the oldest Order of Saint Clare convents in Spain, dating from the mid-thirteenth century. The cakes made by the nuns who live there have become quite famous.

In the centre of the town you come to two imposing churches. Santa María del Camino (Saint Mary of the Way) is Romanesque and dates from the eleventh century. Its southern façade is porticoed and displays a representation of the tribute of the hundred maidens that the Christians were made to hand over to the Moors during the time of Muslim rule. It was precisely as a consequence of that tribute that in the year 844 the Christians fought the battle of Clavijo where, thanks to the miraculous intervention of Saint James on a white horse, they defeated the Moors. Inside the church there is a thirteenth-century figure of the Virgen del Camino (Our Lady of the Way).

■ Monument to the pilgrim in Carrión de los Condes

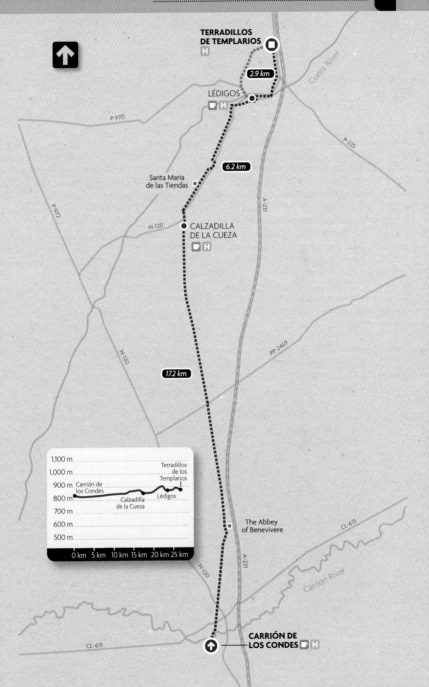

TERRADILLOS
DE TEMPLARIOS

2.9 km

LÉDIGOS

6.2 km

Santa María
de las Tiendas

CALZADILLA
DE LA CUEZA

P-970

P-972

P-225

A-231

N-120

N-120

PP-2469

17.2 km

1,100 m

1,000 m

900 m

800 m

700 m

600 m

500 m

Carrión de
los Condes

Calzadilla
de la Cueza

Lédigos

Terradillos
de los
Templarios

0 km  5 km  10 km  15 km  20 km  25 km

The Abbey
of Benevivere

CL-615

CL-615

Cueza River

Carrión River

A-231

CARRIÓN DE
LOS CONDES

Further along the Calle Mayor you find the church of Santiago (Saint James). This twelfth-century Romanesque church is one of the most important of its style in all Spain.

You will notice the richness of the frieze on the façade, depicting a seated Christ Pantocrator surrounded by the apostles and elders. Inside there is a museum of religious art which has several valuable pieces in various styles, including a fifteenth-century figure of the Piedad (Our Lady of Pity) and various figures of Christ on the cross.

Continuing up the street, you come to the door of the surprising Teatro Sarabia, a fine example of nineteenth-century architecture of its kind with a very well-kept interior. It has a regular programme of plays and performances and forms part of the network of historic theatres of Castilla y León.

**MIRAGES**
➜ To call this part of the plain of Palencia a desert would be an exaggeration. However, on stage 16 the straight stretch of over 17 km running from Carrión de los Condes to Calzadilla de la Cueza sometimes holds a surprise in store. Because of the intense heat and the refraction of light rays, objects ahead may seem to be floating on a liquid surface. This is an optical phenomenon which lasts only a few seconds.

There are many other buildings of architectural, artistic and historic value in the centre of Carrión, particularly the ancestral houses in the old town, but it is time to get going. The next monument to visit is outside the town. Arrows and signs indicating that Santiago lies 400 km ahead guide you up a gentle slope and out of the centre. Cross the bridge over the Carrión River and you come to the monastery of San Zoilo (Saint Zoilo), a building on an impressive scale dating from the mid-eleventh century. It belonged, over time, to various religious orders. Now most of the rooms have been restored and made into a luxury hotel. Although this is modern, its architects have endeavoured to respect most of the original elements of historic value. Nearby you may see some large marker stones displaying coats of arms of certain historic communities.

You now continue along a tarmacked road, although there is hardly any traffic. The land is entirely flat. You walk for about an hour before coming to the old abbey of Benevívere, founded in 1065. These days it is enclosed within private grounds, but it seems, from what you can see through the fence, that some practically unrecognisable remains are all that is left of the historic building.

### Abadía de Benevívere – Calzadilla de la Cueza
**4 h 15 min** ➜ Some 800 metres on from the abbey you come to a

■ Adobe architecture at Terradillos de Templarios

rather uncomfortable, stony path. This is the Cañada Real Leonesa and, at the same time, the original Way. You will come across some boulders on which information of interest to pilgrims has been carved. The Romans once trod these same stones, as this was originally part of the road they called Via Aquitania which ran between Astorga and Bordeaux.

There are occasional trees and streams, and now and then a solitary rest area, but in general the landscape is flat, monotonous and even hypnotic, and somewhat discouraging, given the absence of visual references on which to focus.

Three hours will go by before you see the tower of the cemetery of Calzadilla de la Cueza in the distance. It will then take almost another hour to reach that small town on the Way.

### Calzadilla de la Cueza – Lédigos
**5 h 45 min →** Pilgrims who have reached this point may subsequently find that the rest of the Way to Santiago seems to fly by, as they will have passed the toughest psychological test of the journey. The names of the streets in Calzadilla are a curious feature of the town: Travesía Mayor I, II, III. At least it is a very simple system. On leaving Calzadilla you take a very good track which leads to Lédigos.

### Lédigos – Terradillos de Templarios
**6 h 30 min →** The church at Lédigos has three images of Saint James: as apostle, as pilgrim and as Moor-slayer. As it is generally closed, you have to ask for it to be opened. From Lédigos to Terradillos de Templarios, instead of walking on the road you take the path alongside it that borders some farmlands. It is clearly marked.

# From Terradillos to El Burgo Ranero

**31 km • 7 h 30 min • Elevation difference ▲ 225 m ▼ 220 m**

### Terradillos de Templarios – Moratinos

**45 min ➔** There are two options at the start of this stage: continue along the track running beside the road or, instead, go for the alternative route via Moratinos and San Nicolás del Real Camino. The latter is better: it takes you away from the noise and the traffic, is more 'pastoral' and does not add to the total distance.

The going is easy along this wide, flat track and you reach Moratinos in just three quarters of an hour. The village, which is crossed in no time, stands in a dip and the locals say that this position makes it cooler than the majority of towns on the plain.

### Moratinos – San Nicolás del Real Camino

**1 h 20 min ➔** A gentle, barely noticeable slope leads upwards out of Moratinos. It is the last municipality in Palencia, within whose municipal area is also included the next town of San Nicolás del Real Camino, a major medieval enclave on the Way to Santiago. It was the site of a hospital founded at the end of the twelfth century where lepers were given refuge. Nothing remains of the building now. There is the odd bar in the village where you might want to take some refreshment, as there are practically no more facilities until you reach Sahagún.

■ First view of Moratinos. On the right, note traditional constructions in the hillside

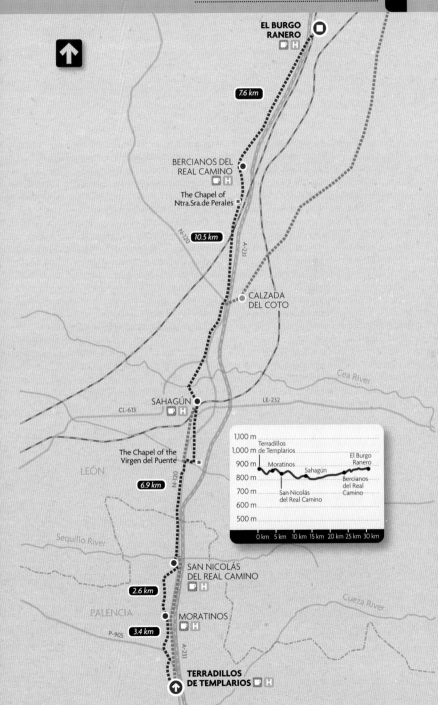

**EL BURGO RANERO**

7.6 km

**BERCIANOS DEL REAL CAMINO**

The Chapel of Ntra.Sra.de Perales

N-120

10.5 km

A-231

**CALZADA DEL COTO**

Cea River

LE-232

**SAHAGÚN**

CL-613

The Chapel of the Virgen del Puente

LEÓN

N-120

6.9 km

Sequillo River

1,100 m
1,000 m  Terradillos de Templarios
900 m  Moratinos                     El Burgo Ranero
800 m              Sahagún
700 m                                Bercianos del Real Camino
600 m       San Nicolás del Real Camino
500 m
0 km  5 km  10 km  15 km  20 km  25 km  30 km

**SAN NICOLÁS DEL REAL CAMINO**

2.6 km

PALENCIA

Cueza River

**MORATINOS**

3.4 km

P-905

A-231

**TERRADILLOS DE TEMPLARIOS**

### San Nicolás del Real Camino – Ermita Virgen del Puente

**2 h 30 min** →Cross the Sequillo River and follow the path that runs parallel to the N-120, with the tarmac to your right and vast grain fields to your left. You thus rejoin the main route from Terradillos de Templarios. After a series of long, monotonous stretches between the main road and agricultural fields you reach the Valderaduey River. Cross the road and turn to the right along a pathway that leads to the beautiful stone bridge over the river and so to the chapel called, appropriately, Virgen del Puente (Our Lady of the Bridge).

The chapel is closed and it is difficult to see anything inside. It has, however, been well restored outside. There is a picnic area with tables and benches and an 'artistic' arrangement of rusting metal seats propped against the walls of the chapel. From here you can see Sahagún not far away,

although the very pleasant 'official' pathway is rather roundabout compared to the road leading straight there. The choice is yours.

### Ermita Virgen del Puente – Sahagún

**3 h 15 min** →You have left the province of Palencia behind and are now in that of León. You will be crossing it from east to west at one of its broadest points. This section will take you a week.

About half an hour after leaving the chapel, you arrive in Sahagún. Pay attention to the arrows, which will lead you to the centre of the town.

### Sahagún – Calzada del Coto junction

**4 h 20 min** →Sahagún is typical of the towns which prospered greatly under the powerful order of Cluny, which at one time controlled as many as 300 enclaves along the Way. Numerous buildings survive to remind pilgrims of the splendour of that period. Two obvious examples are the churches of San Tirso (Saint Thyrsus) and San Lorenzo (Saint Lawrence), with their great bell towers full of windows. These will appeal particularly to lovers of the Mudejar style.

Another noteworthy building is the Benedictine monastery, which dated from the beginning of the twelfth century. All that remains of it today is the chapel of San Mancio (Saint Mancio), the tower and the arch of San Benito (Saint Benedict). This archway may look a little odd

### VOLUNTEER *HOSPITALEROS*
→Many of the *hospitaleros* who assist at the hostels on the Way are volunteers. They are people with a firm belief in solidarity who receive no payment for what they do and even have to bear some of the cost of getting themselves to the hostel. They nearly always stand out for their good humour and friendliness, qualities which are at times lacking in some of the paid employees.

■ The lake at El Burgo Ranero

since it stands alone, seemingly unconnected to anything, and nowadays an avenue, carrying traffic, passes beneath it. It was, in fact, once the south entrance to the monastery's church.

Also worth a visit are the Torre del Reloj (clock tower) and the pilgrims' hostel, located in the building of the former church of la Trinidad (the Trinity).

To leave Sahagún, you pass the church of San Lorenzo, Calle Antonio Nicolás, and follow the natural downward inclination of the streets. You will pass by a monument to the pilgrim consisting of a staff and bootprints in rusted iron beside a rock bearing a plaque. From that point on, large yellow arrows reappear and lead to Canto bridge over the Cea River. Follow the track until you come to Calzada de Coto junction. With the bridge over the dual carriageway to your right, follow an alternative route between the main road and the dual carriageway, passing by a cross and taking advantage of the old Roman road to Mansilla de las Mulas.

### Calzada del Coto junction – Ermita Nuestra Señora de Perales

**5 h 15 min →** On this stretch there is no traffic. Walk along close to the tarmac until you come to the pretty chapel of Perales.

### Ermita Nuestra Señora de Perales – Bercianos del Real Camino

**5 h 45 min →** The chapel is an ideal place for a picnic or a short rest. Bercianos is close by. There are a few trees, but otherwise the landscape is rather desolate.

### Bercianos del Real Camino – El Burgo Ranero

**7 h 30 →** After a walk of almost two hours on the plain, then passing under the dual carriageway and the railway line, you come to the pleasantly surprising town of El Burgo Ranero.

# From El Burgo Ranero to Arcahueja

**29 km • 7 h 15 min • Elevation difference ▲ 135 m ▼ 165 m**

**El Burgo Ranero - Reliegos**
**3 h 10 min** As is often the case in the desert, you need to take a closer look at El Burgo Ranero to appreciate its charm. At first glance, it may well look like a typical small town with nothing more to it than being somewhere to take the weight off your feet. But a short walk will soon rid your of this notion.

The hostel is the first surprise. This simple building stands at one end of the Calle Mayor (formerly known as the Calle del Camino Francés, proof of the Way's historical importance to the area). It is built using the traditional method of mixing clay and straw to form bricks, resulting in a warm brown colour that blends fully into the landscape. Inside, as well as a fireplace to warm up your conversations, there is an interesting view of the wooden structure that forms the roof. The rooms have no ceiling, so you can fully admire how the wood and vegetable fibres are interwoven.

This form of construction is by no means a rarity in El Burgo Ranero. Walking through the town, you will see many buildings of this type that have survived the passage of time. First and foremost is the church, crowned with a weathervane. In the golden evening light, it looks simply stunning. It is usually closed, but if you ask around in the vicinity you can generally find someone with a key. Inside, there is a multicoloured wooden altarpiece dating from the sixteenth century. There also used to be a valuable carving of the Virgen de las Nieves or Virgen Manca (Our Lady of the Snows), but this is now in the museum of León cathedral.

■ A traditional wine cellar in Reliegos, taking advantage of the hilly landscape

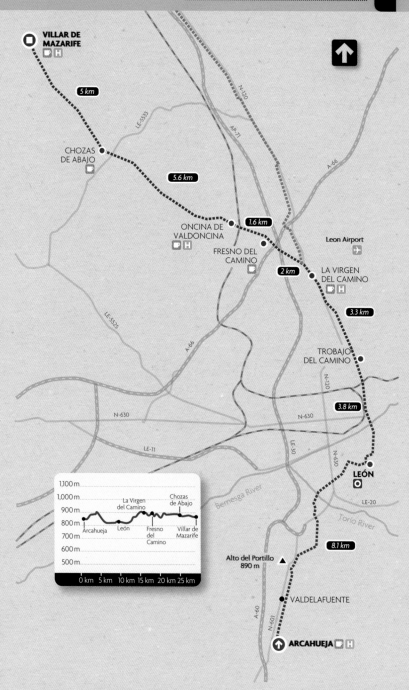

VILLAR DE
MAZARIFE

5 km

CHOZAS
DE ABAJO

5.6 km

ONCINA DE
VALDONCINA

1.6 km

FRESNO DEL
CAMINO

Leon Airport

2 km

LA VIRGEN
DEL CAMINO

3.3 km

TROBAJO
DEL CAMINO

3.8 km

LEÓN

LE-5593

AP-71

A-66

LE-5525

A-66

N-120

N-630

N-630

LE-11

LE-30

N-630

LE-20

Bernesga River

Torío River

1,100 m
1,000 m
900 m
800 m
700 m
600 m
500 m

La Virgen
del Camino

Chozas
de Abajo

Arcahueja

León

Fresno
del
Camino

Villar de
Mazarife

0 km   5 km   10 km   15 km   20 km   25 km

8.1 km

Alto del Portillo
890 m

VALDELAFUENTE

A-60

N-601

ARCAHUEJA

pine wood and then through open fields. At this point, the arrows disappear, but don't worry. Simply continue along the main track leading towards the blocks of flats on the horizon. To the right you can now make out the spires of León's cathedral: further confirmation that you are going in the right direction. Cross a bridge over the main road to arrive safely in the town of Puente del Castro. You will then see a fountain and arrows, in ever greater numbers, leading you along a pleasant urban path into the old town of León.

### León - Trobajo del Camino

**2 h 45 min** → If you have made an early start and it has only taken two hours to reach the doors of León cathedral, find a bar or a hostel where you can leave your backpack and take a leisurely look around the city's most famous sights (see the tourist guide on pages 98-99). Once you have ticked everything off your list, your route out of the city takes you past the historic basilica of San Isidoro (Saint Isidore) and monastery of San Marcos (Saint Mark) before crossing the Bernesga River and passing through the Parque de Quevado. Continue along the Avenida Quevado and Avenida Párroco Pablo Diez to leave the regional capital behind you. This entire stretch is urban, running between suburbs all the way to Trobajo.

**DISGRACEFUL COMPETITION**
→ On leaving La Virgen del Camino you can either walk to the left of the N-120 road on the alternative Way, through tranquil, rural surroundings (the route is signed), or take the footpath that runs alongside the N-120 to Villadangos del Páramo, which is more direct but noisy and less pleasant. We recommend the first of these routes, but the choice is, of course, up to you. However, at the junction a sort of turf war has broken out, with numerous signs painted on the road encouraging pilgrims to take one route or the other. It is a real shame, as nowhere else on the Way is this disgraceful fight for business so intense.

### Trobajo del Camino - La Virgen del Camino

**3 h 40 min** → You continue walking on tarmac, in an urban and somewhat industrial environment, for the hour that separates Trobajo from La Virgen del Camino. But while you have been walking on level ground since leaving León, you are now faced with a more testing uphill stretch. The highest point of the stage comes shortly before La Virgen del Camino, and what remains ahead poses little difficulty.

### La Virgen del Camino - Fresno del Camino

**4 h 15 min →** The main attraction of La Virgen del Camino is without doubt the sanctuary, built in the 1960s. Those familiar with the work of the sculptor Josep María Subirachs will instantly recognise the bronze figures adorning the façade as his. To leave the town, you will need to cross the road, go down a well-marked slope and pass a stretch with contradicting painted signs (see box opposite), following the signs for the alternative Way. The route to Fresno is part tarmac and part dirt track. Cross the village and then follow the route uphill.

### Fresno del Camino - Oncina de Valdeoncina

**4 h 35 min →** The plain of León is not as psychologically tough as that of Palencia. Although the terrain is barren, there are inclines and a few trees to liven things up. Onward to Oncina.

### Oncina de Valdeoncina - Chozas de Abajo

**5 h 55 min →** Passing by some of the oaks that pepper this plain, you come to the town of Chozas de Abajo with its peculiar iron bell tower.

### Chozas de Abajo - Villar de Mazarife

**7 h →** A straight, level stretch, which becomes rather tiring towards the end, takes you to Villar de Mazarife and the end of the day's stage.

■ Main façade of León cathedral

# León

**Distance covered: 459 km**

→ **Cathedral 1** According to the experts, León cathedral is the purest Gothic building in Spain. Work on its construction, atop the Romanesque church that previously occupied the site, began in 1205. Its architects drew their inspiration from Rheims cathedral, although León's is smaller. It has five portals. The most admired of these depicts the Last Judgement, with the scene carved in stone on its tympanum. There is also an image of Nuestra Señora de las Nieves (Our Lady of the Snows).

The most remarkable elements of the interior are the stained glass – which on sunny days is illuminated like a kaleidoscope – the retrochoir, the choir with its fifteenth-century carved walnut stalls, and the main altar. Also noteworthy are the cloister and the various chapels.

→ **Plaza Mayor and Barrio Húmedo 2** The old town of León is known as the Barrio Húmedo ('the wet quarter'). Besides its traditional architecture and its somewhat labyrinthine layout, it is noted for its lively atmosphere as this is the locals' preferred entertainment district. The Plaza Mayor, dominated by the old city hall, is magnificent.

→ **Basilica of San Isidoro (Saint Isidore) 3** Very near the cathedral (the Way takes you right past the front door) is the Basilica of San Isidoro, one of Spain's most prized Romanesque buildings. It dates from the tenth century and takes its name from the saint buried inside, although it is in fact dedicated to Saint John the Baptist. Its frescos are so outstanding that it has been called 'the Sistine Chapel of the Romanesque'. The main chapel has an altarpiece comprising 24 Renaissance panels.

→ **Monastery of San Marcos (Saint Mark) 4** The Way likewise leads you past the old monastery of San Marcos. Today it is a *parador* (state-run luxury hotel) but you can still peek into its main foyer. Measuring over a hundred metres in length, its enormous plateresque façade overlooks a large esplanade close to the Bernesga River. Over the main portal is a representation of Saint James the Moor-slayer mounted on his horse. The monastery was a pilgrims' hospice until well into the twelfth century, subsequently becoming the seat of the order of Saint James.

→ **Casa Botines 5** The Casa Botines, which has been classed as a National Historic Monument, was designed by Antoni Gaudí. The original owners of the fabrics warehouse that stood here were Catalans by the name of Botinàs. Their successors decided to commission the great architect to construct this new building. Gaudí created a neo-Gothic structure depicting some of his most beloved icons, including a large statue of St. George thrusting his sword at the dragon above

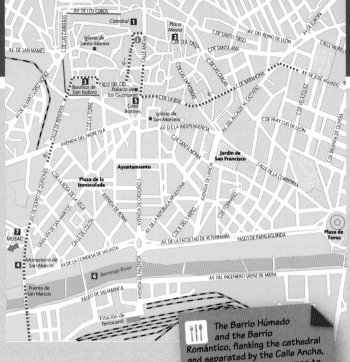

AV. DE LOS CUBOS

Catedral **1**

Iglesia de
Santa Marina

Plaza
Mayor **2**

AV. DE SAN MAMÉS

CALLE ANCHA

C DE STA. CRUZ

C DE SANTO TIRSO

AV. DEL REINO DE LEÓN

AV. EUROPA

CALLE MURILLO

C DE SANTA ANA

C DE LAS CARRERAS

C DE LAS CERCAS

C DE BARAHONA

AV. DE JOSÉ AGUADO

CALLE DEL CID

**3**
Basilica de
San Isidoro

**5**
Palacio de
los Guzmanes

Casa
Botines

Iglesia de
San Marcelo

C DE LA RÚA

AV. D E LA INDEPENDENCIA

C DE FRAY LUIS DE LEÓN

C DE VELÁZQUEZ

C DE BRAÑDA DE OLIVERA

AVENIDA DEL PADRE ISLA

AV. DE ÁLVARO LÓPEZ NÚÑEZ

CALLE DE RENUEVA

CALLE DE LA TORRE

AV. D E LA INDEPENDENCIA

C DE SANTA NONIA

AV. DEL ALCALDE M. CASTAÑO

Ayuntamiento

Jardín de
San Francisco

CALLE DE LA CORREDERA

Plaza de la
Inmaculada

C DE SUERO DE QUIÑONES

C DE LA ROSA DE LA VEGA

AVENIDA DE ORDOÑO II

AVENIDA DE ROMA

AVENIDA DE LANCIA

C DE TORIANO

AV. DE LA FACULTAD DE VETERINARIA

PASEO DE PAPALAGUINDA

AVENIDA DE REPÚBLICA ARGENTINA

AV. DE B. DEL CARRO

Plaza de
Toros

**7**
MUSAC

GRAN VÍA DE SAN MARCOS

CALLE DE COLÓN

Monasterio de
San Marcos

AV. DE LA CONDESA DE SAGASTA

**4**

**6** Bernesga River

AV. DEL INGENIERO SÁENZ DE MIERA

Puente de
San Marcos

AVENIDA DE PALENCIA

PASEO DE SALAMANCA

Estación de
ferrocarril

🍴 The Barrio Húmedo
and the Barrio
Romántico, flanking the cathedral
and separated by the Calle Ancha,
are León's most famous areas to
grab some tapas. The tapas come
free with your drinks in most bars.

the main portal. In 2017 it became
the Museo Gaudí Casa Botines, a
museum dedicated to the history
of the building, Antonio Gaudí, and
nineteenth- and twentieth-century
art and painting.

→**Bernesga River 6** The Bernesga
runs all along the west side of the
city. Its banks make the perfect
playground for locals who can step
across its bridges to take advantage
of the beautiful walks down both
banks. A few bars, restaurants and
cultural centres have also sprung
up, turning it into one of the city's
favourite leisure districts.

→**MUSAC 7** From the moment
the Museum of Contemporary
Art (MUSAC) was opened, the
flow of tourists towards León
increased spectacularly. Other cities
have witnessed the same effect
upon becoming host to cultural
institutions of similar importance.
The museum's colourful façade pays
tribute to the cathedral's famous
stained glass.

# From Villar de Mazarife to Astorga

**31 km • 7 h 40 min • Elevation difference ▲ 250 m ▼ 270 m**

### Villar de Mazarife - Villavante

**2 h 15 min →** You may well be relieved to hear that from Villar de Mazarife there are only 25 kilometres of the monotonous Tierra de Campos plain remaining. But you should also be warned that, during the first few hours of this section, you will be walking on completely flat terrain with no landmarks at all.

For the first hour you are on a local road with an almost eerie absence of vehicles. Subsequently, on reaching Milla del Páramo, you take a broad, stony track where progress is easier. Ignore the arrows that point you elsewhere, and instead carry on along the broad track until you come, an hour later, to Villavante.

### Villavante - Puente y Hospital de Órbigo

**3 h 30 min →** Walk through the streets of Villavante following the signs, which are very clear. You will pass the church and a series of traditional adobe-and-straw houses whose doors and frames are painted the classic blue to repel insects. You will soon see a track similar to the one that led you into the town. Everything is well marked. Walk on beside the railway line for about 300 metres and then take the bridge over the busy motorway. Ignore the left turn and carry on along the tarmac to cross the N-120 at a roundabout. Turn left near the water tower and continue until you reach the

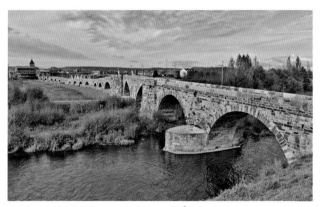

■ The long bridge that allows people to cross the Órbigo

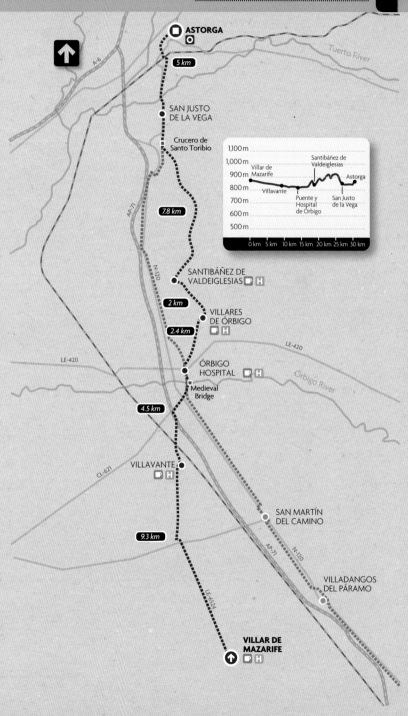

ASTORGA

5 km

SAN JUSTO
DE LA VEGA

Crucero de
Santo Toribio

1,100 m
1,000 m
900 m    Villar de
         Mazarife
800 m         Villavante
700 m
600 m
500 m

0 km  5 km  10 km  15 km  20 km  25 km  30 km

Santibáñez de
Valdeiglesias

Astorga

Puente y
Hospital
de Órbigo

San Justo
de la Vega

7.8 km

SANTIBÁÑEZ DE
VALDEIGLESIAS

2 km

VILLARES
DE ÓRBIGO

2.4 km

ÓRBIGO
HOSPITAL

Medieval
Bridge

4.5 km

VILLAVANTE

SAN MARTÍN
DEL CAMINO

9.3 km

VILLADANGOS
DEL PÁRAMO

VILLAR DE
MAZARIFE

Tuerto River

Órbigo River

LE-420

LE-420

CL-621

A-6

AP-71

AP-71

N-120

N-120

LE-6514

first cobblestones of the medieval bridge, which has its own wonderful story to tell.

### Puente y Hospital de Órbigo - Villares de Órbigo

**4 h 10 min →** Pause for a few minutes, take off your backpack and enjoy the sight of the magnificent bridge over the Órbigo River. The bridge may seem far too wide for the river, but before the Barrios de Luna reservoir was built, the river carried a much larger volume of water. It is in fact the longest bridge on the Way, with 19 arches and more than one change of direction along its length. The murmur of running water and the sound of the breeze in the poplars along the banks is particularly relaxing. But look carefully before crossing in case a knight in armour is barring your passage.

The story goes that in the year 1434, in accordance with a promise he had given to a lady, Suero de Quiñones mounted guard on the bridge from 10 July to 10 August and challenged anyone who wanted to cross to a joust. He found himself with plenty to do, as it is said that 166 opponents faced him and he defeated them all. The episode came to be known as *El Paso Honroso* (the Honourable Pass).

Having crossed the bridge, without a fight, you come to the town of Puente y Hospital de Órbigo, a pleasant place with many facilities for pilgrims.

On the way out of Puente y Hospital de Órbigo you come to a fork marked with a large sign. If you go left you will go in a more-or-less straight line along an easy path running close beside the main N-120 road. A better option, though, is to go right, where you will find a broad, level path with some loose pebbles, which also takes you to Astorga. The distance is very similar, but the landscape is more attractive and, above all, you do not have to listen to the traffic.

### Villares de Órbigo - Santibáñez de Valdeiglesias

**4 h 50 min →** Keeping an eye out for the irrigation channels and ditches that appear from time to time beside the path, you soon come to Villares de Órbigo.

The signs you see on leaving Villares can be a little confusing. If you take the local road that turns to the left, you will shortly find yourself on the very footpath you previously chose not to take. Instead, cross the road and continue up a fairly steep little hill. You then come gently down on the other side towards Santibáñez de Valdeiglesias.

### Santibáñez de Valdeiglesias - Crucero de San Toribio

**6 h 30 min →** You will at once notice that the landscape is changing. The plain is thankfully now behind you and, from Santibáñez de Valdeiglesias onwards, you will encounter a series of climbs. The terrain is not demanding, and is certainly more interesting. In addition, small oak woods, together with some holm

■ Detail of the façade of Astorga cathedral

and box trees, begin to dot the landscape. On leaving Santibáñez de Valdeiglesias, you will find an anonymous monument in a wood in the form of a dummy wearing traditional dress. A well-worn earthen track leads you past steep inclines and the odd 'altar' with votive offerings left by travellers. However, they are not particularly attractive and do nothing at all to improve on what nature has already provided.

You then come to another of the day's most notable features: the Crucero de Santo Toribio (Cross of Saint Turibius), where the Way's two different routes come together. From here you can see, on the plain below, the two towns that still lie ahead.

### Crucero de San Toribio - San Justo de la Vega
**6 h 50 min →**A rather steep slope leads downhill from the cross.

A concrete path has been laid, however, so that locals can walk here without having to traipse through mud, and there is a fountain with a sculpture of a pilgrim drinking. It is an easy walk to San Justo de la Vega. You have to cross the town and the Tuerto River.

### San Justo de la Vega - Astorga
**7 h 40 min →**It takes less than an hour to reach Astorga. The terrain is completely flat and you follow a very pleasant path through a poplar grove to the right of the road, with no industrial estates in sight.

Take the level crossing over the railway line, which brings you to a slope taking you up into Astorga. Here, you have four hostels to choose from.

# From Astorga to Foncebadón

**25.8 km • 6 h 30 min • Elevation difference ▲ 585 m ▼ 50 m**

**Astorga - Murias de Rechivaldo**
**1 h 5 min →**Before setting out, allow yourself a little time to look round Astorga. In the heart of the old town is the Plaza Mayor, overlooked by the magnificent town hall. Its façade dates from 1675 and the famous Maragatos clock from the eighteenth century. The square is typically porticoed, with bars and cafés that locals flock to on public holidays. There is also an interesting old-fashioned pharmacy with jars of traditional potions.

Standing practically side by side, the city's most prominent monuments are the episcopal palace and the cathedral.

The bishop's residence is the work of the Catalan architect Antoni Gaudí. The bishop in office at the time of its construction was, like Gaudí, from Reus and was familiar with the architect's achievements. Work on it began in 1887. Some of Gaudí's trademark features are evident, although this is without doubt one of his lesser works. The inside houses the Museo de los Caminos (museum of the pathways), bringing together a valuable collection of religious art. You can also learn more about the construction solutions and decorative ideas that Gaudí put into practice.

The cathedral has a mixture of styles that bear witness to the construction and remodelling that took place over the

■ The episcopal palace in Astorga, designed by Antoni Gaudí

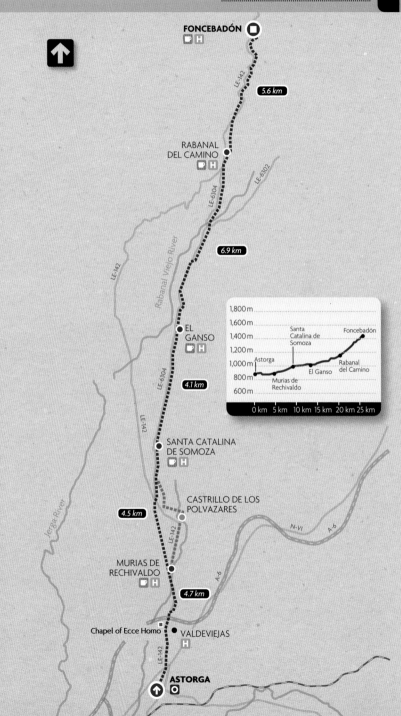

FONCEBADÓN

LE-142

5.6 km

RABANAL
DEL CAMINO

LE-6304

LE-6302

6.9 km

EL
GANSO

LE-6304

4.1 km

LE-142

1,800 m
1,600 m
1,400 m      Santa     Foncebadón
          Catalina de
1,200 m     Somoza
1,000 m   Astorga            Rabanal
800 m          El Ganso   del Camino
      Murias de
600 m   Rechivaldo

0 km   5 km   10 km   15 km   20 km   25 km

SANTA CATALINA
DE SOMOZA

CASTRILLO DE LOS
POLVAZARES

4.5 km

LE-142

N-VI

A-6

MURIAS DE
RECHIVALDO

4.7 km

A-6

Chapel of Ecce Homo   VALDEVIEJAS

LE-142

ASTORGA

Rabanal Viejo River

Jerga River

centuries. The main façade is clearly Baroque, but inside you can see some florid Gothic sections covering the earlier – and oldest – Romanesque parts. The cathedral dates from the mid-fifteenth century and has three altarpieces of great artistic value.

Between the Plaza Mayor and the cathedral lie the streets of the old town with their many shops selling the city's famous muffins and pastries. As there are steep climbs on the stages that lie ahead, you might want to stock up since you will soon need the energy.

### Murias de Rechivaldo - Santa Catalina de Somoza

**2 h 10 min** ➜ The route out of Astorga is well signed. Although you emerge from the close-knit streets of the old town only shortly after passing the cathedral, the comfortable, broad pavements keep you at a safe distance from the traffic. On the right you will pass the village of Valdeviejas while, beside the road on the left, you will see the renovated Ecce Homo chapel. A few hundred metres before reaching Murias de Rechivaldo you join a paved footpath.

You will have passed through Murias before you even realise it. The more ascetic pilgrims prefer to stay at the hostel in this small town rather than in Astorga in order to keep away from the city's bustling nightlife.

After Murias de Rechivaldo the path becomes progressively steeper – a trend that continues right to the end of the stage. The plain of Castile and León is well behind you now and a mountain range, the Montes de León, lies ahead. Although the climbs are not too demanding, they are the first that you have come to since the long-distant Montes de Oca.

Arrow markers made of stones and gravel point which way to go upon leaving Murias. A broad, well-maintained farm track takes you to Santa Catalina de Somoza. Here, if you wish, you can have a rest on some benches placed in front of a series of great iron crosses made from the ore mined in the area. A few that have not withstood the ravages of time have been replaced with wooden crosses.

### Santa Catalina de Somoza - El Ganso

**3 h 10 min** ➜ Ascending, gently but constantly, you come to El Ganso. You have reached what is, roughly, the halfway point of the day, and might want to take

### MESÓN COWBOY

➜ El Ganso is just one more of the many small towns along the Way without any monuments of note. However, every traveller stops to take a look at the Mesón Cowboy, a 'Wild West' bar so unusual that it appeared in one of the most amusing scenes of the French film *Peregrinos*, although this may have created the false impression that bars of this kind are common in Spain.

■ Drinking trough on the way up to Foncebadón

a rest stop and grab a bite to eat beside the church or at one of the taverns that is open during the summer season. From here on, you will have a steady climb until the end of the stage.

### El Ganso - Rabanal del Camino
**4 h 55 min →**On leaving El Ganso, you come to a very narrow pathway, but it opens out considerably after not too long. Before reaching Rabanal you come to an oak wood. At this point you walk by a wire fence festooned with little wooden crosses hand-made by pilgrims. You then enter the well-kept town of Rabanal del Camino and pass by the church of Santa María (Saint Mary). The town's other church, Our Lady of the Assumption, celebrates a Gregorian chant Mass each evening. Many pilgrims choose to spend the night here, as the town is so welcoming. While this cuts the stage rather short, it is tempting to save the remainder for the following day, when you will cross the Montes de León and reach the highest point of the Way at an altitude of 1,515 metres.

### Rabanal del Camino - Foncebadón
**6 h 30 min →**This section is perhaps the most mountainous since the Pyrenean stages. The path zigzags through a wood of oaks and holm oaks with plentiful gorse. It generally stays away from the road, but has to cross it numerous times. On the way out of Rabanal, you pass by the old public laundry and two well-made drinking troughs for livestock. The climb up to Foncebadón is constant and hard, with very few rest points.

# From Foncebadón to Ponferrada

**27 km • 6 h 30 min • Elevation difference ▲ 240 m ▼ 1,130 m**

**Foncebadón - Cruz de Fierro**
**30 min →** The climb out of Fonce-badón is tough. However, as you did most of the uphill work on the preceding stage and the track is good and broad, it will take barely half an hour to reach the Cruz de Fierro (Iron Cross). This is a major milestone as it marks the highest point on the Way, at an altitude of 1,515 m, although the slope is not the hardest one that travellers have to tackle.

The little iron cross mounted on a tall wooden post is not the original. It replaces another that may have been centuries older, as this was originally the site of a Roman altar dedicated to the god Mercury. At the base there is a mound of little stones left by pilgrims. It was a time-honoured custom for pilgrims to bring a stone from their hometowns and drop it here as a symbol of the pilgrimage delivering them from sin. In recent decades, however, the essence of that custom has been lost, as most of the stones now come from just a few metres away. In addition, travellers have begun to leave all manner of 'votive offerings', making the base of the cross rather untidy. It would be well worth reviving the original practice so that the site no longer looks like a second-hand goods stall.

The area around the cross has been nicely laid out, with a sundial on which the pilgrim is the gnomon (the stationary arm that projects the shadow). There is also a small chapel and an extensive rest and picnic area for car parties and ramblers.

You still have six hours' walk ahead until the end of the stage. On clear days, however, the city of Ponferrada can be seen from the Cruz de Fierro.

**Cruz de Fierro - Manjarín**
**1 h →** The Cruz de Fierro is revered to the extent that you may well see pilgrims praying on their knees beneath it. From here, the path leads downwards, but do not be fooled into thinking that the rest of the stage will all be downhill. There is still some climbing to do. A well-kept foot-path takes you to Manjarín in half an hour. The village is abandoned and in ruins, except for its pe-culiar hostel. Those with a keen interest in the Knights Templar will without doubt have noted this as a place to stop. The pen-nants and crosses bear witness to the efforts of the *hospitalero* to revive the tradition of this legendary order.

Another landmark in this village is the post bearing numer-ous signs indicating the distance

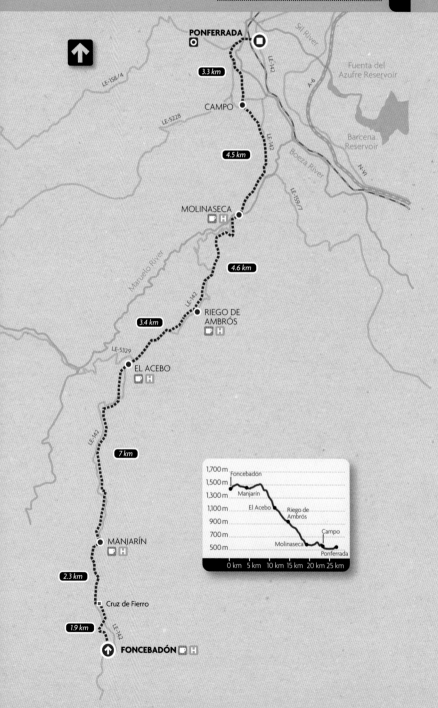

PONFERRADA

Sil River

Fuenta del
Azufre Reservoir

LE-158/4

3.3 km

LE-142

A-6

CAMPO

LE-S228

Barcena
Reservoir

LE-142

4.5 km

Boeza River

LE-159/7

N-VI

MOLINASECA

4.6 km

Maruelo River

LE-142

RIEGO DE
AMBRÓS

3.4 km

LE-5329

EL ACEBO

LE-142

7 km

1,700 m — Foncebadón
1,500 m
1,300 m — Manjarín
1,100 m — El Acebo
900 m                      Riego de
                            Ambrós
700 m                              Campo
500 m         Molinaseca
                                  Ponferrada
0 km  5 km  10 km  15 km  20 km  25 km

MANJARÍN

2.3 km

Cruz de Fierro

1.9 km        LE-142

FONCEBADÓN

to other points on the planet. The signs that generally arouse most interest are the ones marking 70 kilometres to Galicia, 255 to Santiago and 295 to Finisterre.

The local hostel offers a memorable experience if you are happy to keep things simple.

### Manjarín - El Acebo

**2 h 40 min** ➔From Manjarín you take a mountain path that leads steadily upwards to a pass forested with television and telephone masts. This might be just as high as the Cruz del Fierro, but it does not have the same mystique. The rest of the stage consists of a very lengthy downhill stretch that really punishes your knees, with just one short upturn.

### El Acebo - Riego de Ambrós

**3 h 30 min** ➔Although the profile of this stage shows a scary-looking descent, it is in fact gradual. That said, the track is very stony, making it uncomfortable and

**TRAVELLERS' IMPRESSIONS**
➔Many hostels keep guest books, in the tradition of mountain huts, where pilgrims are invited to jot down their impressions. Most just write the few customary words of thanks, but others give fuller accounts of their pilgrimage and even add drawings. The books are an interesting record of how pilgrims from different cultures and of different nationalities have experienced the Way.

liable to cause twisted ankles. It is worth taking care. El Acebo is a small but well-kept town. Most of the houses have been restored and some old agricultural implements, now disused, decorate the streets and fields. There is a bar and a grocery store.

As you leave the town you pass by a monument, painted in silver, to the memory of a bike pilgrim who died at this point. Cyclists may well be tempted to take this descent at speed, but the track is narrow and dangerous. If you are cycling to Santiago, you should exercise extreme caution on this tantalising stretch.

You do not need to be an expert to notice that the style of architecture is now changing significantly. Slate begins to take the place of terracotta, while the wooden balconies suggest a more wooded area and a cooler climate. You have just entered the region of El Bierzo. This is one of the most characterful sections of the Way and it makes a pleasant change from the austere Castile and the green and wooded Galicia.

You now have a half-hour-long, steep, downhill walk on the road before coming to a track that bypasses the long bends in the road to provide a more direct, if steeper, descent. This takes you to Riego de Ambrós.

### Riego de Ambrós - Molinaseca

**4 h 35 min** ➔The Way has breathed new life into Riego de Ambrós and, indeed, into this whole valley, which now has a

■ The old town of Ponferrada

buoyant atmosphere, particularly in the high season. On leaving the town you have to cross a small gully flanked by leafy chestnuts. At this point the track levels off and you again come to a short ascent. The path takes you through mountain scenery, with streams and woods. The arrows disappear at times, but if you come to an unmarked fork you should always take the path leading down towards the valley floor. Before reaching Molinaseca you occasionally find yourself walking down the dry bed of a stream, where the descent is very steep.

### Molinaseca - Campo
**5 h 40 min →**It is not until you reach the Maruelo River and see the magnificent bridge and old town that the day's great descent finally comes to an end.

The two-hour walk that still lies ahead is essentially on the flat.

For twenty minutes you walk along a pavement leading you out of Molinaseca before coming to a broad, well-kept farm track running between vines. It may descend a little at times, but this is nothing compared with the stretch you have left behind, where the descent was over a thousand metres in all. You will skirt Campo.

### Campo - Ponferrada
**6 h 30 min →**Before reaching Ponferrada the route is all on tarmac. Take the footbridge across the railway then take the stone bridge over the Sil River. It is a little difficult to follow the signs to the hostel, but they reappear at a traffic roundabout.

# From Ponferrada to Villafranca del Bierzo

**24.2 km • 5 h 45 min • Elevation difference ▲ 241 m ▼ 239 m**

### Ponferrada - Columbrianos

**1 h →** After leaving the hostel, head for Ponferrada's old town, where you will pass some of the city's most prominent monuments. Take the time to enjoy a few of the main sights before moving on. You can afford to do so as the stage that lies ahead is neither long nor difficult.

One of the most emblematic monuments of Ponferrada is the Renaissance-style Torre del Reloj (Clock Tower), which stands over one of the gates in the wall. Passing beneath it, you enter the rather dark, close world of the old town, although the Plaza Mayor provides a pleasant, spacious contrast. The city's most important place of worship is the Basilica de la Encina (Basilica of the Holm Oak), a Renaissance building dating from the end of the sixteenth century. It takes its name from a tree where the Knights Templar found a statue of the Virgin. According to legend, the statue had been hidden in the hollow of a large tree trunk centuries earlier to keep it safe from the invading Moors. There it remained, the hiding place forgotten, until one of the warrior monks, out cutting firewood, came across it. Other noteworthy buildings include the town hall and the Casa de los Escudos (House of Shields), beside the castle, which now houses the Radio Museum, a project promoted by the well-known radio journalist Luis del Olmo, who was born in Ponferrada. There is also the historic Real Cárcel (Royal Prison), which is now home to the Museum of El Bierzo.

But without doubt, Ponferrada's star attraction is the Templar castle. From the outside it has rather an artificial look and gives the impression of being only a small fortress. Yet once inside (there is an admission fee),

■ Monument to pilgrims in Villafranca

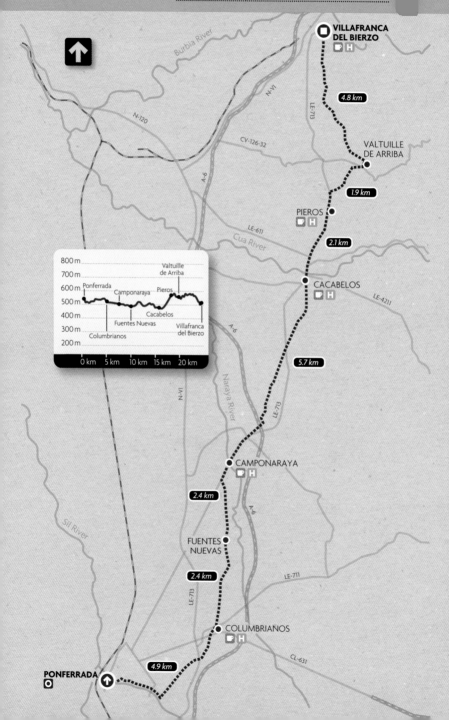

**VILLAFRANCA DEL BIERZO**

4.8 km

VALTUILLE DE ARRIBA

1.9 km

PIEROS

2.1 km

CACABELOS

5.7 km

CAMPONARAYA

2.4 km

FUENTES NUEVAS

2.4 km

COLUMBRIANOS

4.9 km

**PONFERRADA**

Burbia River

N-VI

N-120

CV-126-32

LE-713

LE-611

Cua River

LE-4211

A-6

Naraya River

IV-N

LE-711

LE-713

CL-631

Sil River

800 m
700 m
600 m — Ponferrada
500 m
400 m
300 m
200 m

Camponaraya
Fuentes Nuevas
Columbrianos
Cacabelos
Pieros
Valtuille de Arriba
Villafranca del Bierzo

0 km   5 km   10 km   15 km   20 km

you can more fully appreciate the construction, which dates from the twelfth century. When the castle was entrusted to the Knights Templar, they extended the original structure, which sits atop the hill and overlooks the Sil River and the nearby plain.

There are several churches and fortresses along the Way of Saint James that are attributed to the Templars, but in the case of Ponferrada castle their role is fully documented. The extensions that the castle underwent over the centuries and the new installations erected inside the walls are well explained on information panels placed at the relevant points. The coats of arms of the various noble families that played a part in managing the castle are displayed on one of the main walls.

The castle was declared a historic artistic monument in 1924. It is open to visitors from 11 am to 2 pm and 4 pm to 6 pm from Tuesday to Saturday. On Sundays and public holidays it opens in the morning only. It is closed on Mondays. Entry is free on Wednesdays.

Having taken in the sights of Ponferrada, it is time once again to take to the path. There are not many signs showing the way out of the city, but they are at least strategically placed. Keep an eye out for the park that runs alongside the Sil River, which will lead you on a pleasant stroll out of the town.

### Columbrianos - Fuentes Nuevas

**1 h 30 min** → If it were not for the road sign, you would not realise that you had left Ponferrada and entered Columbrianos. You will travel through various residential areas, with sports facilities appearing from time to time. The arrows pop up more regularly on this section. But you still have to be on the lookout for the yellow arrows as you come into Fuentes Nuevas. If you are in any doubt, remember that the Way crosses the town, leaving the road on which you entered to your right. Alternatively, ask a local for directions.

### Fuentes Nuevas - Camponaraya

**2 h 5 min** → Leave Fuentes Nuevas with the cemetery to your right and walk along a neighbouring tarmacked track that leads you to the local road. Although there is very little traffic, there is rarely any hard shoulder either. A small, passable path keeps you safe from the road.

### A VERY CHARACTERISTIC REGION

→ El Bierzo is one of the great discoveries of the pilgrimage. Its character makes itself felt from the moment you arrive; it is greener and more mountainous, with different architecture. In this region you also begin to see and hear signs of a different identity. *Gallego* (Galician) is the mother tongue of many of the inhabitants and is very common.

■ Villafranca castle is private and not open to visitors

### Camponaraya - Cacabelos
**3 h 25 min** →You cross Camponaraya via an avenue, leading slightly uphill, where most of the town's amenities are to be found. There is a fountain and some benches where you can rest, but the slight inclines you have encountered up to this point should not have tired you out much. You may be feeling the heat, however, as there is little shade on this stage. Next, you cross the Naraya River and, shortly after a service station, take a bridge over the A-6 motorway. From this point the landscape becomes more rural. On either side are vines whose grapes provide the increasingly valued wine of El Bierzo. The terrain is undulating, but the only difficulty for travellers is the dust that the path throws up and the absence of shade. The next port of call is Cacabelos.

### Cacabelos - Pieros
**4 h 15 min** →After three hours or more of fairly level ground, you come to a tough uphill stretch. The footpath is narrow and right beside the LE-713. You pass Pieros without entering the town as such and at once come to a fork. Go to the right, towards Valtuille.

### Pieros - Valtuille de Arriba
**4 h 45 min** →This stage crosses a rocky yet undemanding landscape of apple trees and vines. You pass by Valtuille.

### Valtuille de Arriba - Villafranca del Bierzo
**5 h 45 min** →A gentle ascent taking about an hour brings you to the Puerta del Perdón (Door of Forgiveness). You are now in Villafranca del Bierzo. You will find various hostels on the outskirts of town, with all the facilities you may need (restaurants, bank, shops and accommodation) in the town itself.

# From Villafranca del Bierzo to O Cebreiro

**29.3 km • 7 h 10 min • Elevation difference ▲ 942 m ▼ 143 m**

**Villafranca del Bierzo - Pereje**
**1 h 10 min →** The number of banks in Villafranca del Bierzo bears witness to the town's prosperity. Of more interest, however, are the outstanding buildings of the old quarter, such as the castle with its four round towers, the old convent of San Nicolás el Real (Saint Nicholas) and the church of Santiago (Saint James) with its well-known Puerta del Perdón (Door of Forgiveness), which you passed at the end of the previous stage.

The arrows leading you out of Villafranca are discreet. You go down a flight of steps from the centre and take the bridge over the Burbia River. Outside the built-up area the signs disappear, but if you keep to the road that follows the Valcarce River you will be going in the right direction. In three kilometres you come to a cross-roads. The hard shoulder, painted entirely in yellow, has faded with time and the scuffing of pilgrims' boots. It is separated from the main N-006A road by a concrete barrier. This should give you a well-founded sense of safety. For anyone seeking the metaphor of the Way – that it is always close to the real world but moves in an orbit of its own – they will find it here. When you reach Pereje, take the time to have a look at the town as it is a fine example of the traditional architecture of El Bierzo.

■ Walking through the rain in the woody area of Trabadelo

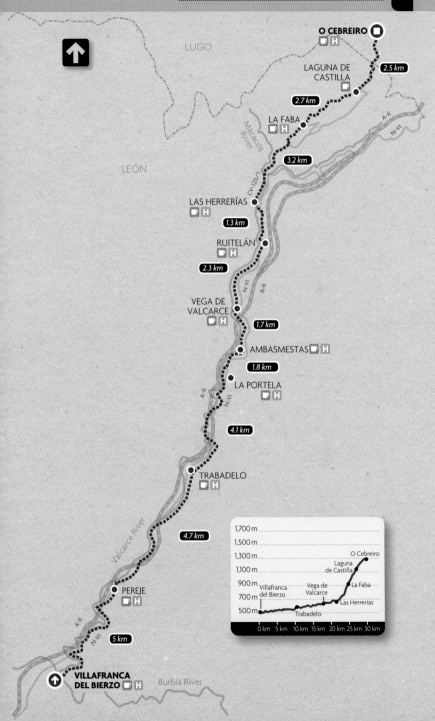

LUGO

O CEBREIRO

LAGUNA DE
CASTILLA

2.5 km

2.7 km

LA FABA

Mazacos River

3.2 km

LEÓN

CV-125/1

A-6

N-VI

LAS HERRERÍAS

1.3 km

RUITELÁN

2.3 km

VEGA DE
VALCARCE

N-VI

A-6

1.7 km

AMBASMESTAS

1.8 km

LA PORTELA

A-6

N-VI

4.1 km

TRABADELO

Valcarce River

4.7 km

1,700 m
1,500 m
1,300 m                                    O Cebreiro
1,100 m                              Laguna
                                     de Castilla
900 m   Villafranca        Vega de      La Faba
700 m   del Bierzo         Valcarce
500 m                          Trabadelo    Las Herrerías
        0 km  5 km  10 km 15 km 20 km 25 km 30 km

PEREJE

A-6

N-VI

5 km

VILLAFRANCA
DEL BIERZO

Burbia River

### Pereje - Trabadelo
**2 h 5 min** ➜ Cross the road, carefully, and return to the 'yellow footpath'. The ascent is gentler than it might look. Vehicles roar past, but you should feel well protected by the barrier. Imposing chestnuts welcome you to Trabadelo, where you will pass a sawmill with great piles of cut timber around it.

### Trabadelo - La Portela
**3 h 15 min** ➜ From Trabadelo the climb becomes steeper, although it is nothing compared with what awaits you during the second half of the day. The surroundings remain the same: you are close to the traffic but at the same time protected, while woods stretch out on either side.

### La Portela - Ambasmestas
**3 h 30 min** ➜ The yellow footpath disappears and you find yourself on a local road with no traffic or noise. You then come to Ambasmestas, a thoroughly rural village where, in high season, an enterprising local keeps a stall alongside the Way selling staffs for pilgrims.

### Ambasmestas - Vega de Valcarce
**3 h 45 min** ➜ Passing beneath rather intimidating viaducts, you next come to Vega de Valcarce, a large town and the main one in the valley. Ahead, you can see the next hill to be climbed.

### Vega de Valcarce - Ruitelán
**4 h 25 min** ➜ Vega de Valcarce has many amenities. You have now covered more than half the stage, but the hardest part for your legs is yet to come. Consequently, this is probably a good time to take a break, have something to eat or buy provisions, as you will need stamina on the steep, uphill stretch you come to in the last eight kilometres of the stage.

### Ruitelán - Las Herrerías
**4 h 45 min** ➜ It only takes a few minutes to walk from Ruitelán to Las Herrerías, yet the landscape changes dramatically. You are still in the region of Castile and León, but the surroundings have already taken on a markedly Galician look, with small villages where cattle and dairy farming are the main activities. You are entering a damp region with regular rainfall, in sharp contrast to the harsh, dry terrain of the past few weeks. Las Herrerías stands beside the Valcarce River, which has accompanied the route all morning.

### REINVENTED *PALLOZAS*
➜ O Cebreiro has witnessed a resurgence in recent years. As it is the first Galician town along the French Way, practically everybody has moved into the services sector. Even the traditional *pallozas*, round pre-Roman structures made of stone and thatch, formerly used for agricultural purposes, have in many cases been carefully restored and now form part of a museum complex.

■ A pilgrim with the view from O Cebreiro below him

### Las Herrerías - La Faba

**5 h 45 min** →Here you reach a leafy wood. As the trees cut off the horizon, it feels at first as though you are not advancing, but when the route begins to zigzag and the effort becomes harder you realise that you are climbing fast.

For a kilometre you walk on a steep tarmac track before coming to a marker stone where a path leads off to the left. While flat at first, it then climbs steeply through the chestnut wood (watch out for falling fruit in autumn). The route gives practically no respite all the way to La Faba, which in turn perches on the hillside. The village has a handy fountain.

### La Faba - Laguna de Castilla

**6 h 30 min** →The view from here is deceptive. You have now left the wood and are not far from Laguna de Castilla. The incline

At 1,300 m above sea level, O Cebreiro is a cold, windy place that you arrive at exhausted. You are now in Galicia, giving you your first chance to sample some delicious *caldo gallego* (Galician soup).

ahead may look less severe, but unfortunately that is not the case. Grit your teeth while climbing bare terrain with no shelter from the sun, wind or rain. Laguna de Castilla is the last town you will come across in León. At the last crossroads, keep going uphill.

### Laguna de Castilla - O Cebreiro

**7 h 10 min** →Behind the hill you find a sign telling you that you are entering the region of Galicia. Here the incline becomes gentler and in two kilometres you are in O Cebreiro, where there are splendid views over the valley.

# From O Cebreiro to Triacastela

**21.2 km • 4 h 55 min • Elevation difference ▲ 216 m ▼ 845 m**

### O Cebreiro - Liñares

**45 min →** If, at the end of yesterday's climb, you did not have time to take a look at O Cebreiro, try and do so today before leaving. The architecture is elegant, the houses and *pallozas* are well restored and the church, which marks the starting point for the many pilgrims who only walk the Galician section of the Way, is pretty. In summer you may well find pilgrims sleeping under the shelter of its porch, as there is not always enough accommodation available in the town.

In the church, where the pilgrim's pass is issued to those starting from here, there is a chalice associated with a miracle that occurred in the early fourteenth century. When a man who had travelled a long distance in hard weather to hear mass was treated with disdain by the local priest, the wine in the chalice turned to blood.

The route out of O Cebreiro is spectacular, providing views that extend for many kilometres all around. Green pastures and small villages dot the landscape below. Head straight downhill on the path below the council-run hostel, passing above but close to the road. This takes you practically to Liñares. The alternative path is more perilous, although they join up again shortly.

■ From now on, the signs are in Galician

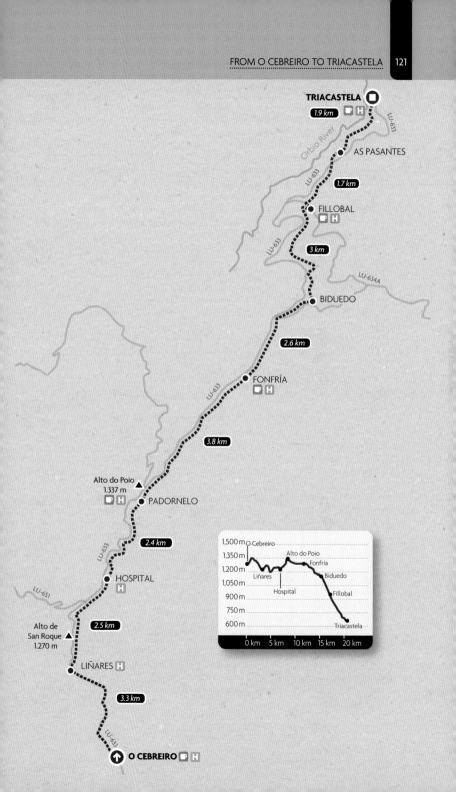

**TRIACASTELA**

1.9 km

AS PASANTES

1.7 km

FILLOBAL

3 km

BIDUEDO

2.6 km

FONFRÍA

3.8 km

Alto do Poio
1.337 m

PADORNELO

2.4 km

HOSPITAL

2.5 km

Alto de
San Roque
1.270 m

LIÑARES

3.3 km

O CEBREIRO

Orbio River

LU-633

LU-633

LU-633

LU-634A

LU-633

LU-633

LU-651

LU-633

1,500 m — Cebreiro
1,350 m — Alto do Poio
1,200 m — Fonfría
1,050 m — Liñares
900 m — Hospital — Biduedo
750 m — Fillobal
600 m — Triacastela

0 km  5 km  10 km  15 km  20 km

### Liñares - Alto de San Roque

**1 h** →Liñares is little more than a group of houses beside the road, but offers amenities for pilgrims.

After Liñares the markers take you to a track leading steeply uphill. For some minutes you walk through the edge of a wood where holly trees abound. You then come out at the pass of Alto de San Roque. You are 1,270 metres above sea level and the wind blows cold here. You have further climbs to face, however, before coming to the high point of the stage.

### Alto de San Roque - Hospital

**1 h 20 min** →On leaving the pass behind you come to a 20-minute stretch of alternating ascents and descents. None of them are very hard, but your legs may remind you of the demands of the previous day and of the hundreds of kilometres they have by now covered. At any rate, the earthen track is in good condition and

leads you to the village of Hospital, whose name is a reference to the medieval pilgrims' hospice that once stood here. There is a charming, solidly built church crowned with an iron cross.

### Hospital - Padornelo

**1 h 55 min** →From this point many pilgrims choose to follow the road to the next pass, as the distance is a little shorter. However, our recommendation is that you instead stay with the signs and take a path that loses a little height but leads you through a rural landscape of heather and rockrose. It crosses the village of Padornelo, where there is an elongated chapel, every part of which is made of stone. The little cemetery is also worth a look.

### Padornelo - Alto do Poio

**2 h 5 min** →The path turns steeply upwards and you have a hard ten-minute climb to the windy Alto do Poio, where there is an enormous monument depicting a pilgrim in medieval dress holding on to his hat. It is very exposed here and you should not dawdle; you are at a height of 1,310 metres and the temperature tends to be fairly low even in summer.

### Alto do Poio - Fonfría

**2 h 50 min** →This is today's summit, with views extending for several kilometres all around. You now face a 700-m descent, which will take over two hours and prove a hard test for the knees.

---

**A STEP BACK IN TIME**
→On stage 25, pilgrims walk through a rural world that has disappeared in other parts of the country. Many women, particularly older ones, dress entirely in black and cover their hair with a scarf. The villagers make their living raising cattle and dairy farming (the streets are full of the evidence of this!) and the people are friendly and eager to talk, happy to see new faces to break up their daily routine.

■ Traditional houses in Triacastela

The path runs three or four metres above the level of the road and is well marked.

### Fonfría - Biduedo
**3 h 20 min** →From here the path moves progressively away from the road and into pasture land, although the road always remains in sight. There is no shade or protection from the wind here, and the descent becomes steeper.

### Biduedo - Fillobal
**4 h 10 min** →From Biduedo to Fillobal the path is so good you could almost call it a magic carpet. Triacastela, lying on the floor of the valley, is now in sight.

### Fillobal - As Pasantes
**4 h 25 min** →As Pasantes is, like most, an agricultural village. Venerable old chestnut trees, like the Ramil tree, line the route here.

### As Pasantes - Triacastela
**4 h 55 min** →On emerging from the wooded area you come to the lowest point on the day's stage. The council-run hostel is just at the entrance to Triacastela. Others can be found in the centre and along the road.

■ Even the monument has to take precautions against the wind at Alto do Poio

# From Triacastela to Barbadelo

**28.7 km • 6 h 25 min • Elevation difference ▲ 334 m ▼ 577 m**

### Triacastela - Santo Cristobo do Real

**50 min →** This stage is a frequent topic of conversation in hostels the evening before, with travellers discussing whether to take the Samos or the San Xil route. The latter mainly follows the historic French Way to Santiago de Compostela. It is also the shorter by some five kilometres. However, those who take it will miss one of Galicia's most prominent religious monuments. It is for this reason that we recommend the Samos route. Even though it is the longer of the two, stage 26 is still very manageable in terms of both time and distance.

Furthermore, it is considerably flatter, as it avoids the Riocabo pass. Ultimately, you are free to change your mind as both routes are well signed. But you need to make your decision about five minutes after starting out as the path splits on the way out of Triacastela.

At the end of the main street of Triacastela, turn to the left and leave the houses behind. Walk alongside the LU-633 road for some time. You are well protected from the traffic, either by the side road or the crash barrier. An almost imperceptible descent leads you to Santo Cristobo do Real. There is a bar that is usually

■ The mighty monastery of Samos justifies parting company with the historic Way for a day

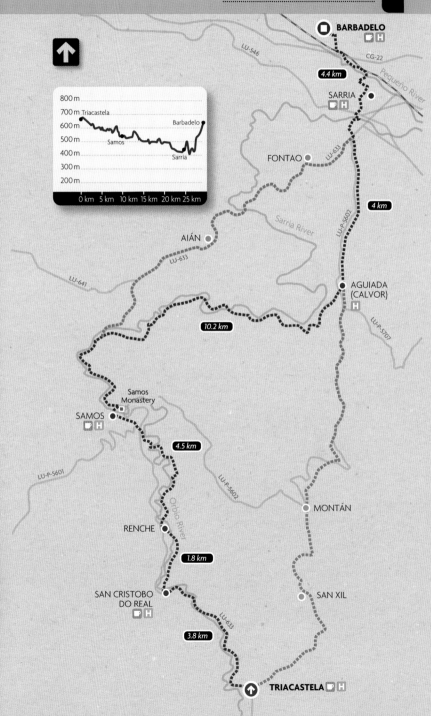

BARBADELO

LU-S46

CG-22

4.4 km

Pequeño River

SARRIA

FONTAO

LU-633

800 m
700 m Triacastela
600 m
500 m      Samos
400 m           Sarria
300 m
200 m
0 km 5 km 10 km 15 km 20 km 25 km

Barbadelo

LU-P-5602

4 km

Sarria River

AIÁN

LU-633

AGUIADA
(CALVOR)

LU-641

LU-P-5707

10.2 km

Samos
Monastery

SAMOS

4.5 km

LU-P-5601

LU-P-5602

Oribio River

MONTÁN

RENCHE

1.8 km

SAN CRISTOBO
DO REAL

SAN XIL

LU-633

3.8 km

TRIACASTELA

open during the high season. You then go back down towards the river and return to the path. The next five kilometres give you a taste of what is to come: woody landscapes with rivers and streams. You are entering the land of the *corredoiras*, pathways lined with stone walls that are typical of this part of Galicia.

### Santo Cristobo do Real - Renche

**1 h 20 min →** The terrain through this small village is reasonably flat.

### Renche - Samos

**2 h 20 min →** You now come to what is perhaps the most spectacular section of the Way on its passage through Galicia. It runs through a deep wood, with shady pathways carpeted with leaves and fallen chestnuts. The stone walls of the *corredoira* are covered with moss, and each turn is better than the last, with crystalline streams to marvel at.

**LAND OF WITCHES**

→ There are sensational landscapes to be enjoyed on each of the three days you spend walking through the province of Lugo, but stage 26 has particular charm, given that it runs through deep, leafy chestnut woods with babbling streams. The mists and shadows serve as an occasional reminder that you are in a territory where *meigas* (witches) traditionally hold sway.

The ground is soft, the terrain flat and the walking therefore easy all the way to Samos.

The first glimpse of Samos is rather dramatic. After a morning spent in the leafy forest, the path suddenly enters a clearing and the road and the top of the monastery's dome come into sight. Another 400 metres on and the splendid abbey comes is in full view. This is the perfect time to take your backpack off and explore the so-called "Galician Escorial".

With its almost fortified look, the group of buildings standing close beside the Sarria River is very imposing. A walk around the structure up to the main façade will leave you open-mouthed. There is a Baroque doorway with two horizontal and three vertical sections, which has the unusual characteristic of being finished horizontally at the top. The stairway leading up to it is reminiscent, on a smaller scale, of the one you will soon see in the Plaza del Obradoiro in Santiago de Compostela. One of the cloisters inside is among the most spacious in Spain, with sides over 50 metres long. A statue of Father Benito Feijoo presides over it.

There are also starred domes and exquisite frescos. The Benedictine monks take care of the upkeep and also provide accommodation for pilgrims If you can spare the time, it is worth spending the night to truly appreciate the architectural delights of Samos.

■ View from the hostel at Barbadelo

## Samos - Sarria

**5 h 25 min →** You leave Samos in the opposite direction to the monastery. Follow the official markers through the forest towards the Iglesia de Santa Uxia de Pascais, which takes about three hours to reach. You will pass several small settlements – Gorolfe, Aguiada and Souto de Perros – before arriving in Sarria, the second-largest city in Galicia after Santiago, where you will find everything you need.

## Sarria - Barbadelo

**6 h 25 min →** After crossing Sarria, walk sharply downwards past the cemetery and turn onto the pathway. You have to cross the railway line, walk through an old

The old town of Sarria is brimming with bars and pubs serving classic tapas dishes including padrón peppers, *lacón con grelos* (pork shoulder with local greens), and *filloas* (Spanish crepes). It is a highly recommended stop-off point before you carry on to Barbadelo.

wood and then climb a slope. When you again reach flat terrain, there is still a fair way to go before you get to the hostel. Extending this stage as far as Barbadelo means that the distance remaining to Santiago de Compostela is better distributed, with just four days' walk left.

# From Barbadelo to Gonzar

**27.7 km • 6 h 10 min • Elevation difference ▲ 496 m ▼ 474 m**

### Barbadelo - Rente
**10 min** → The hostel in Barbadelo is in a marvellous location. The small building, an old school-house, stands at the top of a sloping, grassy meadow where a great tree looks out over the surrounding countryside. It is worthwhile taking a walk over to the little church (which is only open when the priest, who looks after a number of parishes, is present) and the adjacent cemetery. The capitals of the church's Romanesque doorway are decorated with scenes from the Bible and of daily life in Lugo in the Middle Ages. The cemetery is an excellent place to discover interesting aspects of the traditional way of life.

### Rente - Brea
**1 h 35 min** → Once you have completed your mini tour, it is time to don your backpack again and walk up the track that leads to the "centre" of Barbadelo. As is common in this area, there are various small clusters of homes in the vicinity that all belong to the same village. You at once come to a local road that is rarely used. What traffic there is moves slowly and so you do not need

■ The Way in Brea

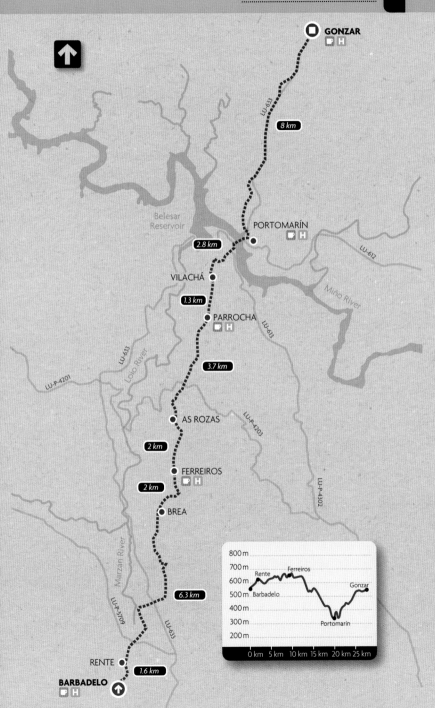

GONZAR

8 km

LU-633

PORTOMARÍN

2.8 km

Belesar
Reservoir

VILACHÁ

LU-612

Miño River

1.3 km

PARROCHA

LU-611

3.7 km

LU-633

Loio River

LU-P-4201

AS ROZAS

LU-P-4203

2 km

FERREIROS

LU-P-4302

2 km

BREA

6.3 km

Marzán River

LU-P-5109

LU-633

RENTE

1.6 km

BARBADELO

800 m
700 m          Ferreiros
          Rente
600 m
          Barbadelo          Gonzar
500 m
400 m
300 m          Portomarín
200 m
     0 km  5 km  10 km  15 km  20 km  25 km

to stay constantly on the alert. You will enjoy a calm walk through a landscape where cattle farming is clearly the main industry. Pastures and small herds are everywhere, with the odd oak tree here and there.

It takes no more than a quarter of an hour to cross Rente. From now until the end of the day you will come across *corredoira* after *corredoira* in an idyllic landscape of stone walls, moss and ancient trees. If you peek over the walls you will see rich pasture, although there seem to be fewer cows and horses here.

There are not many signs to help you identify the villages you pass through, which are generally deserted. However, if you check the map you will see that you have come through Mercado and are entering Peruscallo. You now literally walk across a little stream, where stepping stones have been laid to keep your feet dry.

### Brea - Ferreiros

**2 h 5 min →** It is easy to become confused at this point in the route as there are numerous signs pointing both right and left. Follow the ones to the right, which take you to the same place but along a shorter route. Not long after this, you will come across one of the most highly anticipated markers telling you that it is just 100 km further to Santiago de Compostela. That will take you barely three and a half days.

Some respectful pilgrims have placed pebbles on top

### THE MIÑO RIVER

Today's stage is highly symbolic. You will pass the 100 km marker stone (showing the distance to Santiago) and also cross the Miño River where the construction of the Belasar dam meant that the pretty town of Portomarín had to be relocated. The Galician landscape is inspiring and your legs may seem to gather renewed strength, despite the distance they have covered.

of the marker. Others, unfortunately, were unable to resist the temptation to daub it with scrawled messages of no interest to anyone.

### Ferreiros - Vilachá

**3 h 35 min →** The surroundings are so beautiful that you may not have noticed that you have been ascending constantly ever since leaving Barbadelo. It is at Ferreiros that you reach the high point of the stage, at 700 metres above sea level. You come first to a series of ascents and descents, and then to a steep downward slope entailing an abrupt 300-metre descent.

Half an hour before getting to Vilachá the landscape opens up and you have panoramic views of the rolling hills and the valley, together with the town of Portomarín. But before reaching it, you walk through yet more undulating *corredoiras* to the town of Vilachá.

### Vilachá - Portomarín

**4 h 5 min** →It is just half an hour from Vilachá to Portomarín, downhill and mostly on tarmac, with a whole host of not-very-helpful markers suggesting alternative routes, even though they all meet up at the bridge. You find yourself at the Belasar dam on the Miño River. Cross the bridge, go up a majestic flight of steps crowned with an arch into a pretty porticoed street lined with shops, and make your way over to the church.

Portomarín was relocated when the dam was built. You would never guess, though, as the town gives the impression of having always stood on this hill. The church of San Nicolás (Saint Nicholas) resembles a castle, more vertical than horizontal and crenellated at the top. The principal feature on the front of the building is a large rose window. Beneath it a short flight of steps leads up to a Romanesque doorway.

### Portomarín - Cortapezas

**4 h 45 min** →To leave Portomarín you have to walk back down the hill. The arrows guide you to a footbridge and, once on the other side of the Miño, along a woodland path.

### Cortapezas - Gonzar

**6 h 10 min** →On this stretch you find yourself walking close to the road some of the time and at other times through a fragrant pine wood from which vehicles can neither be seen nor heard. The route leads slightly upwards, following the arrows. You will pass a picnic area and will then see the first signs for the hostels at Gonzar.

■ The pretty, historic town of Portomarín

# From Gonzar to Melide

**31.6 km • 7 h 20 min • Elevation difference ▲ 491 m ▼ 631 m**

### Gonzar - Castromaior

**15 min →** The route out of Gonzar is easy as the hostel stands on the Way itself. Head out, turn left and advance up a steep local road with little or no traffic.

In fifteen minutes you come to Castromaior, where you find the first cluster of eucalyptuses. You will be seeing this tree, native to Australia, uninterruptedly from here on, as in the past decades it has been planted by the thousand to supply the paper industry. The ground is always littered with aromatic leaves and pieces of shed bark.

### Castromaior - De la Cruz Hospital

**50 min →** This is a stage with many climbs, but these first kilometres require the most effort. There is a fairly stiff climb up to Ventas de Narón. The footpath is stony and slightly uncomfortable but at least it is fairly separate from the road. You cannot see the cars, although you do hear the distant hum of traffic. The village of De la Cruz Hospital takes its name from an old pilgrims' hospice, which still stands. There is a hostel, but do not head towards it unless you need to,

■ A raised granary in Castromaior

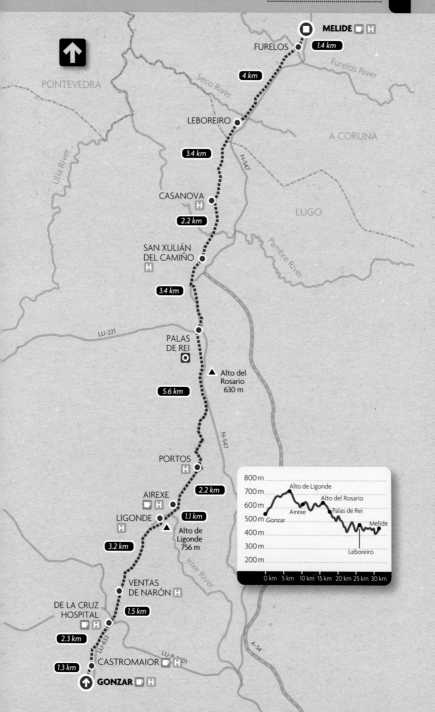

MELIDE 🍴 H
FURELOS
1.4 km
4 km
Furelos River

PONTEVEDRA

Seco River

LEBOREIRO

A CORUÑA

3.4 km

N-547

CASANOVA
H

LUGO

2.2 km

Pambre River

SAN XULIÁN
DEL CAMIÑO
H

3.4 km

LU-221

PALAS
DE REI
◎

▲ Alto del
Rosario
630 m

5.6 km

N-547

PORTOS
H

2.2 km

AIREXE
🍴 H

1.1 km

LIGONDE
H

▲ Alto de
Ligonde
756 m

3.2 km

Irixe River

VENTAS
DE NARÓN H

1.5 km

DE LA CRUZ
HOSPITAL
🍴 H

2.3 km

LU-P-3101

A-54

1.3 km

CASTROMAIOR 🍴 H

⬆ GONZAR 🍴 H

800 m
700 m — Alto de Ligonde
600 m — Airexe      Alto del Rosario
500 m — Gonzar         Palas de Rei    Melide
400 m
300 m
200 m                    Leboreiro

0 km  5 km  10 km  15 km  20 km  25 km  30 km

since you could lose sight of the markers, which are few and a little unclear.

### De la Cruz Hospital - Ventas de Narón

**1 h 10 min** → On this stretch the climb becomes steeper, testing your legs which, although by now very used to hard work, may be approaching their limit after four weeks of constant effort. Coming to the top of the earth track, you cross a bridge over the main road and take a pilgrim footpath — now leading down some of the climb you have just done — to Ventas de Narón.

### Ventas de Narón - Airexe

**2 h 10 min** → You now come to one of the prettiest and most interesting sections of the stage. On leaving Ventas de Narón you walk along the verge of the road and may feel like you are on or beside a pavement, as slabs of granite have been placed between the road itself and the path. The route leads steadily upwards to the pass of Ligonde. Descending from the summit, after passing through the unobtrusive little village of A Previsa, you see the impressive cross of Lameiros. The very worn base bears messages about death, while at the cross the figure of the Virgin symbolises maternity and the creation of life. Here pilgrims have left painted stones, together with a few messages. The cross is sheltered by a great oak, making it a pleasant place to pause for a few minutes.

### Airexe - Alto del Rosario

**3 h 10 min** → The 'pavement' continues to Airexe, where a cross greets you at the point of entry while behind there stands a Romanesque church. The setting is typically Galician.

On leaving the village you come to woodland paths. The trees are mainly eucalyptuses, but there are also some fine specimens of oak and beech that have withstood the invader from 'down under'.

A series of short, well-marked inclines takes you to Alto del Rosario, where there is a milestone. The main road runs close by, but dense gorse keeps the vehicles out of sight.

The Alto del Rosario pass marks a turning point on the stage. Although still walking on rolling terrain, you will now descend steadily until you come to the Pambre River and subsequently pass from Lugo into the province of A Coruña, through Casanova.

---

**GRANITE TO THE FORE**
→ You will notice that you have arrived in Galicia from the changes in landscape, language and agriculture, as well as from the constant appearance of granite. From here on, the stone can be seen in almost all civil and religious buildings, in traditional structures such as the raised granaries, and even in the distance markers.

■ A simple metal sign on a granite block

### Alto del Rosario - Palas de Rei
**3 h 45 min →** Walking downhill, cross the village of Avenostre, a small farming community similar to the many others you have seen on the way through the province of Lugo. Shortly afterwards you come to Palas de Rei which, in contrast, is a large town with many services. There you go past the church of San Tirso (Saint Thyrsus) then head sharply down towards the valley of the Pambre.

### Palas de Rei - San Xulián del Camiño
**4 h 35 min →** As Palas de Rei is a reasonably sized town with plenty of amenities, the route out of town takes on a slightly ugly urban character. Yet you soon find yourself back on very pleasant paths running gently up and down through eucalyptus-scented woods. The path leads you to the small but pretty village of San Xulián del Camiño.

### San Xulián del Camiño - Casanova
**5 h 10 min →** The route continues much the same, lined with some majestic chestnuts and oaks that give pilgrims a real carpet of crisp leaves to crunch through in autumn. You will shortly arrive in Casanova.

### Casanova - Leboreiro
**5 h 55 min →** It takes three quarters of an hour to reach Leboreiro, the first town in the province of A Coruña. Of particular interest are its paved street and the *cabaceiro*, a thatched raised granary

### Leboreiro - Melide
**7 h 20 min →** From this point onwards the surroundings become more industrial. Although you are walking on an earth track, there are sheds and factories on both sides practically all the way to the medieval bridge of Furelos. Finally, you come to the rather dull ascent to Melide.

# From Melide to Pedrouzo

**33.3 km • 7 h 50 min • Elevation difference ▲ 583 m ▼ 772 m**

### Melide - Boente
**1 h 10 min →**The route out of Melide is well signed. From the municipal hostel the arrows lead you sharply downwards to the San Martiño road. You pass by the cemetery and the Romanesque church of Santa María de Melide (Saint Mary).

Once out of the built-up area, you come to a wood of tall eucalyptuses interspersed with broader oaks.

The terrain rises and falls and will basically continue like this throughout the day. The first three kilometres of the stage are gentle, but the inclines will become steeper later on. You will constantly be going up and down, with little flat terrain. This stage is long and while the overall changes in height are not very significant, the gradients are taxing. Your body has already taken a lot of punishment and rushing to finish could have unfortunate consequences. It is actually better, on this stage, to pause for a rest more frequently than you may have done on recent days.

### Boente - Castañeda
**1 h 45 min →**Boente is very small and stands beside the road. The river of the same name is almost a hundred metres lower down. Descend to the river, cross it and then climb the other side. On this stretch, particularly, the climbs are very steep. Although it is only half an hour to Castañeda, a good deal of effort is required.

### Castañeda - Ribadiso da Baixo
**2 h 30 min →**From Navarre on, the Way runs from east to west. Given that on this last section the rivers run from north to south, you have no alternative but to cross them, which normally entails going down and up slopes. Although the watercourses are often in practice no more than unnamed streams, each one that has to be crossed calls for additional effort. The last half-hour's walk to Ribadiso da Baixo differs as it is on tarmac.

The village is very small, but it might be a good idea to pause a little here before taking on the steep incline leading to Arzúa.

■ A well-looked-after raised granary in Ribadiso da Baixo

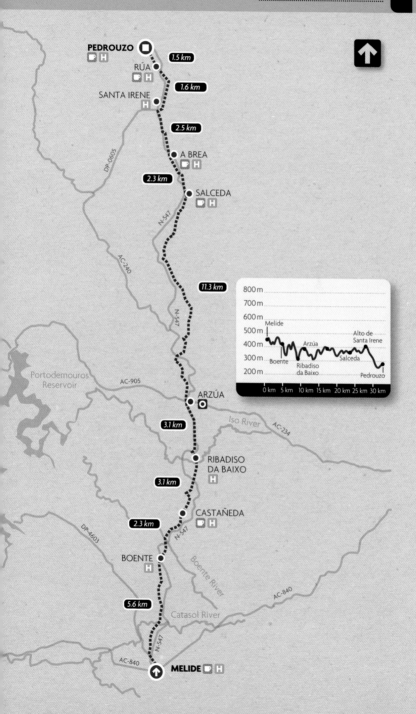

PEDROUZO

1.5 km

RÚA

1.6 km

SANTA IRENE

2.5 km

A BREA

2.3 km

SALCEDA

DP-0605

N-547

AC-240

N-547

11.3 km

800 m
700 m
600 m
500 m — Melide
400 m
300 m — Boente
200 m

Arzúa

Ribadiso
da Baixo

Alto de
Santa Irene

Salceda

Pedrouzo

0 km  5 km  10 km 15 km 20 km 25 km 30 km

Portodemouros
Reservoir

AC-905

ARZÚA

Iso River

AC-234

3.1 km

RIBADISO
DA BAIXO

3.1 km

CASTAÑEDA

2.3 km

N-547

BOENTE

DP-4603

Boente River

AC-840

5.6 km

Catasol River

N-547

AC-840

MELIDE

### Ribadiso da Baixo - Arzúa

**3 h 5 min →** It is a stiff climb all the way to the next town, as you will quickly realise. You are walking on tarmac, which makes the stretch doubly tiring as the soles of your boots will have less grip than they would on an earth track. At least the distance is short. Arzúa is a fairly large town with all the services you could need. One drawback, though, is that the built-up area is rather sprawling and for a full half hour you find yourself dealing with crossroads and traffic lights and stepping off and onto pavements. You also have to pay attention to the traffic.

You have not yet covered half the day's walking. But there are a few decisions to make in Arzúa. You have to choose whether to break the journey here and whether to pick up supplies. Bear in mind that, although you will be passing through typical farming hamlets, you will not see another amenities – save the

### CARRYING ON

→ On this penultimate stage, you know how many days you have taken so far and how much time you still have available. It is therefore not unusual to find people making plans to go further, whether to Finisterre or to more distant places such as Fatima in Portugal. Ever increasing numbers of pilgrims opt to walk back home along the Way in the opposite direction.

odd bar in the high season – for almost three hours once you leave Arzúa.

### Arzúa - Salceda

**5 h 55 min →** Getting out of Arzúa is a slow process. Once again you face a long and tedious series of crossings, traffic lights and avenues before finally leaving the buildings behind. The reward for this tedious section is the woodland path you then come to. Here the trail takes you up and down beneath the shade of the scented eucalyptuses. At times stone walls separate the path from pasture. At others it is bordered only by the vegetation. Almost without realising, you leave behind the little villages of Pergontuño, Calzada and Calle Boavista.

The road generally lies to the left, but at times the well-marked path moves so far away from it that you do not even hear the hum of the traffic.

Salceda stands at a height of close to 300 metres above sea level. There is a stretch of a few hundred metres where you have to walk along the hard shoulder. Take care not to stray onto the road itself: this is a particularly dangerous section where drivers are careless and the vehicles move at high speeds. In a kilometre and a half, you draw close to Alto de Santa Irene. You come to a crossroads that you have to negotiate with care and then continue along the edge of the road until the arrows lead you off it.

■ Mist around Pedrouzo

### Salceda - Alto de Santa Irene

**7 h →** This is a very risky stretch of the Way as you will need to cross the N-547 on more than one occasion. Although there are warning signs telling cars to slow down, safety is certainly lacking here.

### Alto de Santa Irene - Rua

**7 h 35 min →** Rua stands on the flat and your legs therefore have some respite while you are crossing the village. However, as soon as you leave the last house behind the climb begins afresh.

### Rua - Pedrouzo

**7 h 50 min →** It takes less than half an hour to cover the distance between Rua and the day's destination. You reach Pedrouzo

walking just beside the road, and must take care once again at the last roundabout. The town's main street has everything you need: plenty of hostels, restaurants, food shops, banks, a pharmacy, and more.

The official name of the town is Pedrouzo, but everybody calls it Arca, as that is the name of the parish to which it belongs. To make matters even more complicated, the name of the district is O Pino. As Pedrouzo has become the last stage destination prior to Santiago for almost everyone, its fame has grown throughout Galicia. In the evenings it is thronged with pilgrims making preparations for the big day. You are only 20 kilometres from your goal.

# From Pedrouzo to Santiago de Compostela

**20.1 km • 4 h 25 min • Elevation difference ▲ 347 m ▼ 359 m**

### Pedrouzo - Tunnel

**45 min →** To leave Pedrouzo you walk up the main street for three or four minutes until you come to signs pointing to the schools and the football ground. Very soon you leave the houses behind and enter a dappled wood where native species mingle with tall eucalyptuses that scent the area and cover the path with their leaves and shreds of bark. The route flattens out and remains that way for most of the stage.

The comfortable, earth path dives in and out of the wood and finally leads towards the main N-547. About a kilometre short of it you come to a tarmac surface and then to a tunnel that takes you safely under the road.

### Tunnel - Airport

**1 h 25 min →** Pass by two groups of houses with no name signs. Only by consulting the map do you learn that these hamlets are called San Antón and Amenal. In the second of the two you have to cross the watercourse of the same name, pass under the N-547 again and then cross the village of Cimadevila before heading up towards the pass of Lavacolla. Although lengthy, the climb poses no difficulty and only goes up about a hundred metres, shaded by groups of eucalyptus trees.

The path takes you to the left of an enormous traffic junction and then moves gradually away from the tarmac along a slope screened by high gorse bushes.

■ Monument erected on Monte do Gozo to commemorate the visit of the Pope in 1992

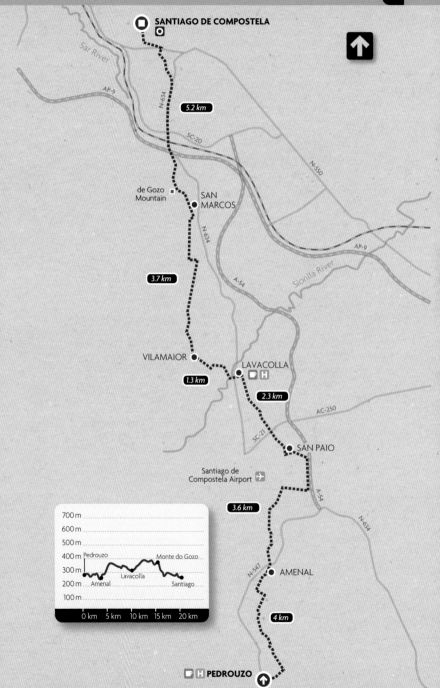

SANTIAGO DE COMPOSTELA

Sar River

AP-9

N-634

5.2 km

SC-20

N-550

de Gozo
Mountain

SAN
MARCOS

N-634

A-54

3.7 km

Sionlla River

AP-9

VILAMAIOR

LAVACOLLA

1.3 km

2.3 km

AC-250

SC-21

SAN PAIO

Santiago de
Compostela Airport

A-54

N-634

3.6 km

AMENAL

N-547

4 km

PEDROUZO

700 m
600 m
500 m
400 m  Pedrouzo                 Monte do Gozo
300 m
200 m   Amenal      Lavacolla          Santiago
100 m

0 km   5 km   10 km   15 km   20 km

The ground is clayey and tends to be a little slippery. Coming to a stretch that rises and falls gently, you pass by Lavacolla airport on your left and head for San Paio. Skirt the airport until you reach the village.

### Airport - San Paio

**1 h 40 min** ➜ The pretty church of San Paio, in a circular plaza surrounded by trees, welcomes you to this village, which you continue straight through before reaching Lavacolla a few hundred metres on.

### San Paio - Vilamaior

**2 h 25 min** ➜ From Lavacolla, you are back on tarmac, but this is not the main road (which has now become the N-634, to the right). You can hear the hum of the vehicles and at times even see them, but you are sheltered on this almost traffic-free local road leading to Vilamaior. The walk is pleasant, leading gently uphill.

### Vilamaior - San Marcos

**3 h** ➜ You will reach the other side of Vilamaior before you even know it. The climb is smooth but constant up to San Marcos, with its scattered clusters of houses.

### San Marcos - Monte do Gozo

**3 h 20 min** ➜ You will have barely entered the village when the yellow arrows indicate that you are nearly in Monte do Gozo. You pass just in front of a campsite with a bar.

---

**GALICIAN CEMETERIES**
➜ The cemeteries in Galicia are magnificent, just as they are in many other rural areas in Spain. From O Cebreiro on, you will stumble across these peaceful, well laid out, well kept graveyards often displaying impressive examples of funerary art. The last one you come to is at Lavacolla, where the stonework is outstanding.

---

On your way into Monte do Gozo, the vegetation screens you from the enormous concrete monument until you are almost on beside it. It is in the form of a truncated pyramid with allegorical scenes on each face. It is topped with an iron sculpture and a cross. There are a few spartan stone benches where you can catch your breath for a minute.

Leaving aside the question of the artistic merit of this work and its suitability to the site (it was built to commemorate the visit of Pope John Paul II in 1992), it is clear that Monte do Gozo is no longer the climactic place it was for medieval pilgrims. The Spanish word gozo means 'joy' and the hill was given this name because it was from here that pilgrims caught their first glimpse of the spires of the cathedral of Santiago de Compostela. Nowadays the view is obscured first by a wood and then by the urban sprawl of the Galician capital. Only from the edge of the earth platform on which the monument stands can you still see it. However, even though the circumstances have changed, many pilgrims still like to observe the old ritual, like their predecessors, of spending the night here, washing their clothes, and smartening themselves up before entering the city of the Saint well groomed. But we recommend you carry on, in the more modern fashion, downhill towards Santiago.

## Monte do Gozo - Santiago de Compostela

**4 h 25 min →** After the giant monument you come to the equally huge hostel complex built to cater for the needs of pilgrims in the summer. It is an eyesore, but its existence is understandable given how popular the Way has become in recent years. As you approach the city, you pass through outskirts that are more urban than industrial, before coming to the sign announcing that you are entering Santiago.

In Plaza de San Pedro you pass a cross telling you that you are just a stone's throw from the cathedral. As you walk downwards, following golden scallop shells encrusted in the ground, your emotions surge, reaching their height as you come finally to the great Plaza del Obradoiro. It is a stunning — and welcome — sight. The cathedral's Baroque façade towers above the clean esplanade. It is a moment for smiles and embraces.

The time has finally come to enter the cathedral (see page 144), see the Pórtico de la Gloria (which you are no longer allowed to touch) and embrace the statue of the saint. You have reached the end of a pilgrimage you will never forget.

■ The exquisite Baroque façade of the cathedral of Santiago with its staircase

# Santiago de Compostela

**Distance covered: 783.8 km**

→**Cathedral 1** There are certain rituals for pilgrims to perform inside the cathedral. Upon entering, look to the right, where you will see the Pórtico de la Gloria which depicts the story of salvation. In accordance with tradition, after their long journey, pilgrims used to kneel before the column depicting the Tree of Jesse and rest a hand on it. This went on for centuries, to the extent that the stone shows clear signs of wear. The portal has now been restored and can be viewed as part of a visit to the cathedral museum. Entry is ticketed and visits take place in small groups. The next thing is to go up the staircase leading to the chamber where the image of the apostle overlooks the main nave. Pilgrims embrace the statue from behind, thanking the saint for his protection during their long journey. Beneath the altar, in a silver reliquary, lies the tomb of the saint. If you set off early on the last stage, you might be in time to attend the pilgrim's mass (12.00). The compostela (certificate of accomplishment) is issued by the Pilgrim's Office, which is behind Plaza de los Caballos.

→**Plaza del Obradoiro 2** The great Plaza del Obradoiro is rectangular in shape and has an outstanding building on each of its four sides. To the east stands the cathedral with its Baroque façade and stairway; to the north is the Reyes Católicos parador, formerly a pilgrims' hospice; to the west is the Pazo de Raxoi, currently the seat of the presidency of the Galician regional government and also that of the city council; and to the south stands the San Xerome building, now the rectory of the university.

→**Old town 3** You could spend hours wandering around the old town, enticed by the porticoed calles Vilar and Nova, Rúa do Franco with its fish restaurants, the famous Azabachería and Praza de Praterías, which is pedestrianised and very pleasant.

→**Market 4** The market is housed in an enormous stone building standing between Rúa das Ameas and Rúa da Virxe on the ring road that runs round the old town on a lower level. Morning is the best time to visit, when it is bustling with activity. In the afternoons and evenings, only its souvenir stalls, bars and restaurants are open.

→**Pilgrimage museum 5** This little museum, hidden away in Praza de Praterías, houses some valuable works of art and explains the meaning that religious pilgrimages have for the different world cultures and where they have traditionally been undertaken.

→**Galician Centre of Contemporary Art 6** The Portuguese architect Álvaro Siza designed this outwardly austere building, with flat walls and few

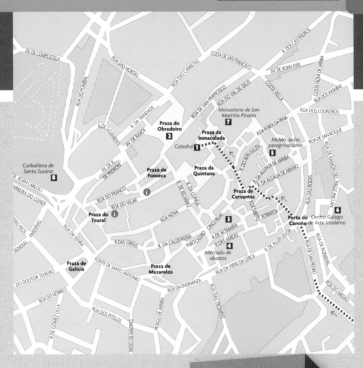

For pilgrims who have spent days eating a rather frugal diet, it is almost compulsory to treat themselves to a seafood platter at one of the old town's restaurants to celebrate their arrival in Santiago.

windows, which sits near the old monastery of Santo Domingo de Bonaval (Saint Dominic of Bonaval).

### →Monastery of San Martiño Pinario (Saint Martin Pinario) 7

The reredos of the main altar is the most admired feature in this centre of monastic power that traces its origins to the beginning of the tenth century. Nowadays it is a seminary. The ceilings and Baroque sculptures draw attention to the austere atmosphere.

### →Carballeira de Santa Susana 8

On ascending Rúa San Clemente, you come to an area of parkland known as La Alameda, part of which goes by the name of Carballeira de Santa Susana. It is a hill looking out over the old town where, according to locals, you get the best views of the cathedral's twin spires. It is an oasis of calm just a few minutes' walk from the bustle of the old town.

## 31 From Santiago de Compostela to Negreira
**21.2 km • 5 h • Elevation difference ▲ 635 m ▼ 668 m**

## 32 From Negreira to Olveiroa
**32.6 km • 7 h 10 min • Elevation difference ▲ 914 m ▼ 779 m**

**STAGE 31**

**Santiago - Sarela de Baixo**
**35 min →** You will find yourself
outside Santiago sooner than
you expect. The route takes you
along Rúa das Hortas, Poza de
Bar, Rúa San Lorenzo and Roble-
da de San Lorenzo. The yellow
arrows then guide you to a
wooded area called Ponte Sarela.
From there to Sarela de Baixo
you walk on soft ground under
a canopy of scented eucalyptuses on what is the pleasantest
stretch of the day. In less than
half an hour the noise of the
town will be long gone as you
stroll through the glade.

**Sarela de Baixo - Alto de Vento**
**1 h 55 min →** The path runs gently
up and down to the village of
Carballal, where the ascent to
the pass of Alto de Vento begins.

**Alto de Vento - Augapesada**
**2 h 30 min →** This section starts
with a long descent on tarmac,
although you soon have the
benefit of a sort of pavement
bordering the road. You end
up dropping down almost 100
metres practically in one go. It is
not much, but when you take a
look at the gradient on the map,
you will realise why your knees
are complaining.

■ The Pazo de Cotón, in Negreira

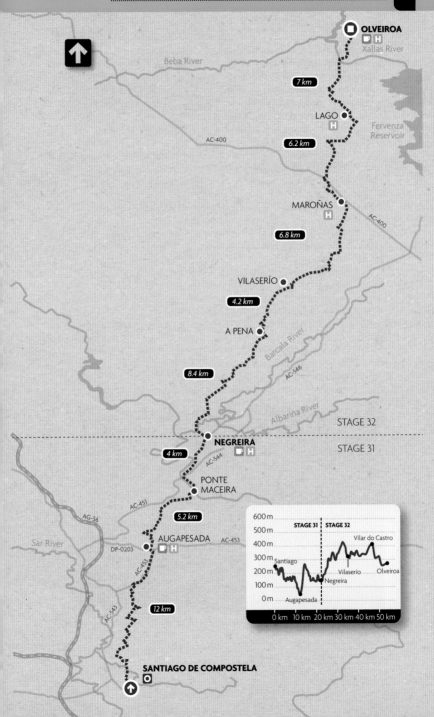

OLVEIROA

Xallas River

Beba River

7 km

LAGO

Fervenza Reservoir

AC-400

6.2 km

MAROÑAS

AC-400

6.8 km

VILASERÍO

4.2 km

A PENA

Barcala River

AC-546

8.4 km

Albariña River

STAGE 32

NEGREIRA

STAGE 31

4 km

AC-544

PONTE MACEIRA

AC-451

5.2 km

AG-56

AUGAPESADA

AC-453

DP-0203

AC-453

AC-543

12 km

SANTIAGO DE COMPOSTELA

Sar River

600 m
500 m    STAGE 31 | STAGE 32
400 m                        Vilar do Castro
300 m  Santiago
200 m                Vilaserío        Olveiroa
100 m                Negreira
0 m      Augapesada
    0 km  10 km  20 km  30 km  40 km  50 km

### Augapesada - Alto do Mar de Ovellas

**3 h 5 min →** After leaving Augapesada you come to a climb that is gentle at first but becomes gradually steeper. When you reach a fountain, you are less than 100 metres from the top. The pass is not marked, but you reach the top when you come out onto a larger road.

### Alto do Mar de Ovellas - Ponte Maceira

**3 h 50 min →** A gentle descent takes you to the pretty town of Ponte Maceira.

### Ponte Maceira - Negreira

**5 h →** This is a well-marked section running along the Tambre valley, which takes you through the town of Barca. On reaching Negreira you have to cross the town to find the hostel, which stands at the top of a rise. Negreira, which sits just to

No doubt you have enjoyed many a pie on your travels. If you have not yet tried one, fish and seafood fillings become increasingly common as you approach Finisterre.

the north of the Tambre River, is crossed by various routes and travellers are well catered for.

## STAGE 32

### Negreira - Zas

**40 min →** From the hostel in Negreira you return to the Way via a link that leads to the road. You then walk on to Zas through a eucalyptus wood.

### Zas - A Pena

**1 h 5 min →** Having now left the wood behind, you will be without shade almost right to the end of the stage. On summer days, make sure to stock up with plenty of water at the start of the day.

■ Wind turbines near Zas

■ The welcoming hostel in Olveiroa

### A Pena - Vilaserío
**2 h 45 min →** Once past the village of Portocamiño you come out onto the road and then walk on tarmac to Vilaseríoa.

### Vilaserío - Cornado
**3 h 10 min →** After Vilaserío you have to cross the DP5603 (take care!) to enter Cornado. You then pick up the Way again on a comfortable woodland track.

### Cornado - Maroñas
**4 h 15 min →** The land rises and falls but is not too difficult. From time to time you have to cross a road, although the route is well marked. A descent takes you to Maroñas.

### Maroñas - Abeleiroas
**6 h →** To get to Abeleiroas you have to do a brief stint on the AC-400 before heading due west. You are now close to your goal.

**THE POPULARITY OF FINISTERRE**
→ In recent years, it has become very popular to extend the pilgrimage as far as Finisterre. And while the number of council-run hostels along the route has increased, there are times of year when there is not enough room for everyone. It is worth giving them a ring in advance to book a bed for wherever you plan to stay the night. Other hostels and guest houses are available, but they certainly cost more and after more than a month of walking your wallet may be feeling rather light.

### Abeleiroas - Olveiroa
**7 h 10 min →** Still on tarmac and heading generally downwards, you cross the Xallas River and enter Olveiroa. The hostel there has a number of buildings.

## 33 From Olveiroa to Corcubión
**20 km • 5 h 30 min • Elevation difference ▲ 256 m ▼ 532 m**

## 34 From Corcubión to Finisterre
**15 km • 4 h 15 min • Elevation difference ▲ 303 m ▼ 197 m**

### STAGE 33
#### Olveiroa - Hospital
**1 h 35 min** → Return to the road and turn off to the left almost immediately. The turning is marked, but it is easy to miss if you are not careful. You then come to a track that leads quite steeply upwards and takes you close to a group of wind turbines. Cross a concrete bridge to the village of Hospital.

#### Hospital -
#### Crucero Marco do Couto
**2 h 15 min** → Go past the bar and up the road until you come to twin marker stones where a turning to Muxia is signed. Follow the sign to Fisterra. From this point, practically all the rest of the stage is downhill, with just the occasional short ascent.

#### Crucero Marco do Couto -
#### Nosa Señora das Neves
**2 h 40 min** → The stone cross of Marco do Couto stands on a kind of small plateau thick with scrub. Turn to the left, taking you parallel to the road, then turn to the right and descend towards the chapel. There you will find a visitor's book and a collection of votive offerings left by the faithful and by pilgrims.

■ The promenade at the end of the town of Cée

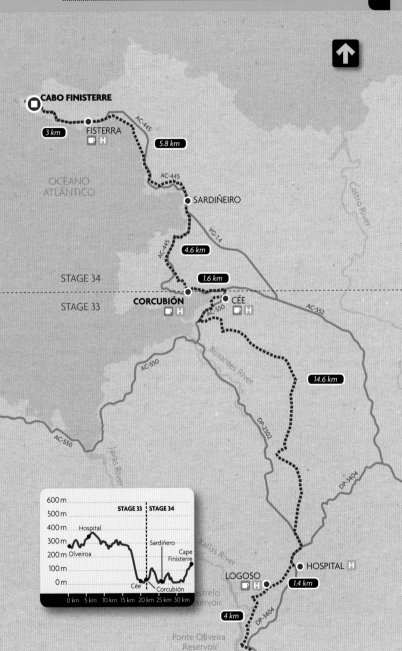

CABO FINISTERRE

3 km

FISTERRA

5.8 km

AC-445

OCÉANO
ATLÁNTICO

AC-445

SARDIÑEIRO

VG-14

AC-445

4.6 km

STAGE 34

1.6 km

STAGE 33

CORCUBIÓN

CÉE

AC-550

AC-552

AC-550

Buxantes River

14.6 km

AC-550

DP-2302

DP-3404

Xavas River

600 m
500 m
400 m          STAGE 33 | STAGE 34
300 m     Hospital
200 m   Olveiroa              Sardiñeiro
100 m                              Cape
0 m                       Cée    Finisterre
                                 Corcubión
        0 km 5 km 10 km 15 km 20 km 25 km 30 km

Xallas River

HOSPITAL

LOGOSO

1.4 km

Estrelo
Reservoir

4 km

DP-3404

Ponte Oliveira
Reservoir

OLVEIROA

Beba River

### Nosa Señora das Neves - Alto Cruceiro da Armada

**3 h 55 min →**Here the path leads upwards. Just before reaching the cross you have your first glimpse of the Atlantic Ocean.

### Alto Cruceiro da Armada - Cée

**4 h 50 min →**A very sharp downhill stretch takes you to the pretty town of Cée.

### Cée - Corcubión

**5 h 30 min →**To get from Cée to Corcubión you only need to cross the bay, but this entails a rather stiff ascent.

### STAGE 34
### Corcubión - Sardiñeiro

**1 h 25 min →**This stage may look very short on the map, but bear in mind that although it ends at the lighthouse of Finisterre, you will have to walk back to Fisterra afterwards. That adds almost an hour and a half to the journey time, unless you are fortunate

Sampling some *pulpo a feira* (Galician-style octopus) in Melide is almost a rite of passage. If you were too tired to do so during stage 28, you have another chance to enjoy it in Fisterra.

enough to hitch a lift on the return, in which case it will only take 10 minutes.

On this section the route has alternate stretches of road and woodland and runs parallel to the coast, meaning there are some steep inclines. Scented pines provide shade and distraction.

### Sardiñeiro - Fisterra

**2 h 55 min →**This section is fairly similar. At times you walk along the hard shoulder. At others the path takes you past splendid, unspoilt beaches. As this is the final stage and there are only a few hours still ahead, you may

■ The lighthouse (km 0)

■ Tribute to pilgrims

well be tempted to have a swim if the weather is right.

When you reach Fisterra, the best plan is to reserve a bed at the hostel and leave your backpack there, so you can go on to the cape carrying nothing more than a camera.

### Fisterra - Finisterre

**4 h 15 min** ➔ The stretch between Fisterra and the cape is unpleasant. It is road all the way and the hard shoulder is at best very narrow and at worst non-existent. The reward, however, is that you come to the end of the world, the Finis Terrae of the Romans. After passing the lighthouse you come to a humble but fitting tribute to pilgrims: a metal monument in the form of a boot (there were two, but one has disappeared).

**RITUALS TO AVOID**
➔ Some guide books are not always to be trusted. Many pilgrims will have read that a dip in the sea at Finisterre, to celebrate your arrival at the westernmost point of your odyssey, is a real thrill after having covered so many miles on foot. But beware of the hazardous cliffs, strong tide and big swell along this stretch of the Galician coast. It may not be as epic, but it is much safer to bathe at one of the beaches you passed along the way earlier. As for the tradition of burning the clothes you have been wearing, the authorities advise against it due to the risk of starting fires and because of the waste you end up leaving behind.

# MORE ABOUT THE WAY

A walking boot abandoned by a pilgrim and converted into a flower vase on one of the milestones that signpost the Way.

# History of the Way

The origins of Santiago de Compostela and of the ensuing pilgrimage towards it are to be found, as so often in Christian hagiography, in a supernatural occurrence. Early in the ninth century a mysterious glow appeared on Mount Libradón, which lies within the limits of the town of Padrón in the interior of Galicia. Some shepherds, seeing that the light came out from among the very rocks, informed the church authorities.

The bishop of the diocese of Iria Flavia, close to Padrón, promptly visited the spot and there found a sarcophagus with the remains of three humans. It was concluded that the marble coffin could be nothing less than the resting place of Saint James the apostle and two of his most loyal disciples, Atanasio and Teodoro.

King Alfonso II el Casto (the Chaste) was informed and ordered that a sepulchre and a small church be constructed at the place of the find.

So how was it that the remains of the apostle appeared on the Iberian Peninsula? Eight hundred years earlier, Saint James, who

some historians believe was directly related to Jesus of Nazareth, had witnessed the death of the Son of God and had then left for the Roman province of Hispania to preach His teachings. It was a short stay and took place somewhere between the years AD 34 and 41. It is known that Saint James died in Jerusalem, decapitated by the authorities, in AD 42.

At that time, it was a common practice for apostles to be buried where they had preached. It was here that a miracle occurred, since legend has it that a marble sarcophagus floated the length of the Mediterranean, crossed the Strait of Gibraltar, travelled northwards in the Atlantic Ocean and ran aground on the Galician coast. The stone coffin was escorted by the two disciples mentioned above, who would certainly have been the ones responsible for carrying it inland.

■ Alfonso II el Casto, the king who "paved the Way of Saint James" at the beginning of the ninth century

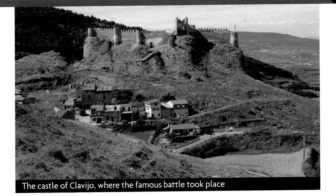

The castle of Clavijo, where the famous battle took place

### A miraculous warrior

Eight centuries later, the holy light emanating from the coffin with the remains of three people left no doubt as to the identity of its occupants. In the political context of the period, this event occurred at a time when the Christian kingdoms were under tremendous pressure, resisting as best they could in the north of the peninsula the unstoppable drive of the Moor hordes, well on their way to conquering the entire territory.

The miracle occurred at a time when the Christians, demoralised by repeated defeats and steady loss of territory, needed a supernatural, invincible leader. It had already become clear that the nobles were being beaten by the enemy on the battlefield.

The momentous date arrived. In 844 the battle of Clavijo took place, so called because it happened beside the hill of that name, on which there was a small military camp, to the south of where the city of Logroño now stands.

**PILGRIMAGE MUSEUM**
→ Pilgrims arriving in Santiago have usually had their fill of monuments and churches, pretty towns and introspective landscapes, wanting to have fun rather than more cultural fodder. However, they will do well to visit the unassuming museum that takes pilgrimage, specifically the Way of St James, as a universal phenomenon for the cornerstone of its exhibition and also the city of Santiago as a goal. It only takes a few hours but it is enough to enlighten the visitor about this way of travelling with spiritual aims that the main world religions adopt.

On an unequal footing, the Christians prepared to resist the demand for the yearly tribute of a hundred maidens, according to which they had to hand over that number of young women by way of a tax. When swords were crossed the desperate Christians realised how outnumbered they were. At that moment Saint James made his appearance. Mounted on a white horse, he helped win a conclusive victory for the Christians, who believed that the battle of Clavijo would be the turning point from which they would reconquer the peninsula.

King Ramiro I of Asturias swore that victory had been won thanks to the intervention of the apostle, who from that moment took on a new form, that of Santiago Matamoros (Saint James the Moor-slayer), depicted in murals and sculptures, although this portrayal is now regarded by many as politically incorrect.

To show his gratitude for the Saint's assistance, the king ordered that pilgrimage should be made to his tomb in Santiago. Over the following four centuries, the route to Santiago would become a true European highway for the passage of people, goods, languages and cultures. Many historians are convinced that it was on the strength of the Way of Saint James that Europe began to take shape.

From all ends of the continent the faithful set out on routes to make the pilgrimage, walking for months in order finally to kneel before the apostle's shrine. The more frequently travelled routes thus became well-worn and, even today more than a thousand years later, the very same paths from different starting points on the European continent to Santiago de Compostela continue to be used. The one most commonly used by today's pilgrims is the Via Francés (French Way) - to which this guide refers - but pilgrims also come together on the Via Podensis from Le Puy, the Via Turonensis from Chartres, the Via de la Plata (Silver Route),

Santuario de la Virgen Peregrina en Sahagún, León

running northward up the western side of the Iberian Peninsula, the Camino Aragonés (Aragonese Way), which crosses the Pyrenees at Somport, or the Camino de la Costa (Coastal Way), one of the routes most often used in the Middle Ages, which in the early years, although tortuous, ensured that pilgrims would be safe from Saracen attacks.

## Christian reference

Another important event in Christian history, which helped fuel the flow of pilgrims to Santiago, occurred towards the end of the ninth century. The Christians lost Jerusalem to the Muslims and were therefore deprived of what was, together with Rome, their primary pilgrimage destination in the world. As it was no longer possible to visit the holy places where Jesus of Nazareth had grown up, preached and suffered martyrdom, many eyes then turned towards Santiago de Compostela. It was in part also as a consequence of this situation that the shrine grew over the years, from a modest chapel to a large church and, later, to a great cathedral. The most significant refurbishment work was undertaken in 874, 997 and 1075, although it continued over decades. The shrine became a cathedral in the sixteenth century, although the spectacular Baroque façade which is so admired today was not finished until the eighteenth century.

By the start of the second millennium, Santiago de Compostela had become as important as Rome in the Christian calendar. The region was living a golden age and the more important monastic orders, such as Cluny or the Knights Templar, erected strongholds along the Way, in the form of monasteries or castles. Today you can visit the most striking of these, in Sahagún and Ponferrada. Moreover, the Way brought prosperity to towns that had the good fortune to be passed through by travellers. Churches were erected, taverns were opened and inns sprang up. Hospitals (for hospitality) began to proliferate, to the extent that there were dozens of them along the main pilgrim routes. Not only that, new towns appeared. These are still easily recognisable by their names: Boadilla del Camino, Espinosa del Camino, Fresno del Camino, Rabanal del Camino, Redecilla del Camino, San Martín del Camino, San Miguel del Camino, San Nicolás del Real Camino, La Virgen del Camino, and so on. These communities were not always small. Some, like Santo Domingo de la Calzada and Puente la Reina-Gares, grew in size and importance in the shade of the pilgrims' route.

In 1179 Pope Alexander III gave yet greater importance to the pilgrimage by decreeing that a plenary indulgence would be gained by all those who travelled the Way in years when Saint James's Day (25 July) fell on a Sunday. We now refer to these as Jacobean or Holy Years, in which the already large number of visitors to Santiago de Compostela swells threefold.

These measures encouraged not just ordinary folk to undertake the pilgrimage to Santiago. It was also made by monarchs and aristocrats of the time. While they sought to secure themselves a certain degree of comfort, they still had to endure the hardship of many long days of travelling. By the twelfth century the counts of Barcelona had set up a system to enable their most distinguished guests to make the pilgrimage suitably escorted. Even the Catholic monarchs King Ferdinand II of Aragon and Queen Isabella I of Castile undertook the journey in 1488, although by then the Way was very much in decline.

Fuelled by the flow of travellers, the towns located on the main routes grew large and prosperous, becoming major trading centres. However, the endless wars that shook Europe from the sixteenth century (above all the Hundred Years War), the spread of the plague and the disappearance of the relics of the saint (the whereabouts of which were unknown from 1588 to 1879) caused the Way to fall largely into disuse.

## Rebirth

A refurbishment of the cathedral in 1879 coincided with the appearance of some bones. Pope Leo XIII declared that they were the relics of the saint and, little by little, the pilgrimage gained a new lease of life. However, it was only in the last century that a genuine rebirth was witnessed. Various factors played a part but two had a decisive impact: in 1987 the Way was declared the first European cultural itinerary and, in 1993, UNESCO awarded it World Heritage status. The journeys that Pope John Paul II made to Santiago de Compostela from 1982 encouraged Catholics to follow his example. The Way of Saint James is now a cultural journey in a continuous state of growth. The next Jacobean years will be 2021, 2027 and 2032. All those involved in the conservation and improvement of the Way have time enough to consider how best to maintain the high current level of interest without impairing the unique essence of the pilgrimage, the risk of which is palpable.

**OFFICIAL PILGRIM'S PASSPORT**
→ To take advantage of the official hostels and enjoy benefits in restaurants and other services, you need to have your pilgrim's passport stamped at least twice a day at various locations. It will not come as a surprise to you that trickery had arisen even in this little document, with forgeries, photocopies, etc. Now the pilgrim's passport has been standardised and is approved. You need to obtain it before starting the Way from the authorised site: www. elcaminoasantiago.com.

# Pilgrimage by bike

To travel the Way of Saint James by bike is easy. Indeed, it might almost be termed relaxing. All the recommendations given in the preceding pages concerning equipment, nourishment, rest and behaviour are similarly valid for cyclists. However, cyclists should also give consideration to certain additional factors relating specifically to their chosen means of transport.

## The bike

It is possible to cover the whole of the French Way by road. To do so, however, is not only dangerous but also boring. It is better to follow the yellow arrows and to pedal along tracks, unmade roads, paved ways and, on some (very few) occasions, narrow paths. When this second course is chosen, the bike needs to be versatile with a robust frame. Mixed-surface tyres are the best for this varied terrain. There is no need for mountain bike tyres, which have a lot of grip and are slow, while road tyres would without doubt suffer frequent punctures. In some places the route that is the most favourable for cyclists is even well indicated with panels. Unless you are sure that you know the area, it is better to follow the recommendations. The climb to O Cebreiro, for example, is torture for someone on a bike if they take the route for hikers.

Cyclists looking for a hostel

## The stages

In a day the average cyclist can easily cover three times the distance walked by a pilgrim on foot. Planning to complete the journey in twelve days (see box on page 165) is therefore by no means unrealistic. However, it is necessary to bear in mind that adverse circumstances may be encountered. There is, for example, the wind, which can be especially harsh in the Castilian desert and which on the Iberian Peninsula tends to blow from the west. It is therefore in the pilgrim's face.

The guidelines previously provided about what to expect and how to behave at hostels apply to cyclists too. In their case, it is also important to remember that the wheels of their bike may be dirty. Consequently, for the same reason that, at many hostels, pilgrims are required to remove their boots before setting foot in the facilities, cyclists should take care that their bikes are not trailing mud and leaves into the building.

Many hostels have parking facilities or areas where bikes may safely be left for the night (generally free but some places charge). Others, however, do not have enough space and there is consequently no option but to leave the bike in the street. When that is the case any loose parts which may be stolen should first be removed, as the next mor-

---

**WHAT TO TAKE AND HOW**

➜ Given the speeds they reach, cyclists may feel the cold more acutely than walkers, especially on rainy or snowy days. It is advisable to bear this in mind when packing. While the weight to be carried should always be kept as light as possible, it is important to ensure that the hands and feet will be adequately protected, as those are the parts of the cyclist that suffer most.

➜ The bike, not the cyclist, should carry the gear. The bike should therefore be equipped with waterproof pannier bags and everything that has to be carried should be stowed in these bags or fastened to the luggage rack. It is not advisable for cyclists to carry a backpack, however small, as it will tire them and impede their natural movement on the bike, above all on uphill stretches.

➜ In addition to the standard gear, cyclists should carry a basic repair kit comprising spare tubes, puncture patches, a chain tool, a screwdriver and a multi-purpose wrench. Many towns along the Way have garages that work specifically with bicycles. If one of these is not to be found, however, any other garage dealing with cars or motorbikes may be able to help out.

➜ It is also a good idea to carry a decent lock for use when there is no place for the bike inside the hostel.

**Rainy day in Trabadelo**

ning you might otherwise find yourselves without the means to continue the journey.

### The first stage, a test

As it starts out from Saint-Jean-Pied-de-Port (in Basque: Donibane Garazi), the first stage of the French Way puts the pilgrim to the test. If it is hard for the walker, it can be tougher still for the cyclist. So be wary of overconfidence and warm up well before starting. The route is steeply uphill from the outset and remains thus almost until you reach the Ibañeta pass. To start out cold could therefore result in muscular injury and put a very early end to the journey.

The best plan is to spend half an hour pedalling along the flat terrain in the valley in order to work up a sweat first. Then, when the muscles of the legs and arms have warmed up, you will be in

**ADVANTAGES OF THE CYCLIST**
→ It can be extremely hard for a walker, upon reaching the end of a stage, tired out, to be told that the hostel is full and that the next one is three kilometres away. For the cyclist it is much less so. That said, cyclists should plan their stages of such a length (60-70 km) that an unexpected extension does not tax them to the limit. After a stage of 100 km or more, they may find it difficult to cope with an additional section.

better shape to take on the tough climb over the Pyrenees.

You should take great care when subsequently riding down into Roncesvalles (Orreaga) and, for that matter, on all the other downhill stretches along the Way. You may encounter other

A good track approaching Burgos

pilgrims on foot, local people doing agricultural work, flocks of sheep, herds of cows, or simply other vehicles. Breakneck descents are therefore never a good idea. Make sure your brakes are in good working order and be ready to use them at all times.

At all times of the year, it will be more important to be well hydrated than to carry solid foods. These are necessary, of course, but with good planning they can be acquired just before consumption and so lighten the load of saddlebags. Pieces of fruit, biscuits and a sandwich immediately weigh a couple of kilos. It is better if you conserve them. Conversely, you should always keep a handful of dried fruit, candied fruit or energy bars to hand, to draw upon the moment you start to feel weak. It is important to eat before the "tank is empty", because it is not then possible to recover before the dreaded hunger pains kick in.

In the coldest months it is a good idea to fill water bottles with tea or other hot drinks or even soup. They are a perfect tonic.

**MINIMUM GEAR**
→ Like the walker, the cyclist should tend towards being minimalist. It is better to wash frequently - there are washing machines and dryers in many hostels - than carry too many changes of clothes. In terms of reading, there is no contest between an e-reader and a conventional book. Above all, leave out the "just in case". In many towns there are shops where you can buy spare parts and workshops where serious faults can be fixed. All the gear should be packed in plastic bags inside the panniers.

## THE WAY IN TWELVE DAYS

The number stages on the Way depends on many variables, such as physical condition and pedalling speed. Something reasonable would be 12 stages.

**STAGE 1** → 8 h 30 min • 70 km
• elevation ▲1,850 m ▼1,600 m

◉ **SAINT-JEAN-PIED-DE-PORT → PAMPLONA**

**STAGE 2** → 5 h 0 min • 52 km
• elevation ▲1,000 m ▼950 m

● **PAMPLONA → AYEGUI**

**STAGE 3** → 5 h 15 min • 62 km
• elevation ▲900 m ▼870 m

● **AYEGUI → NAVARRETE**

**STAGE 4** → 5 h 15 min • 61 km
• elevation ▲930 m ▼640 m

● **NAVARRETE → BELORADO**

**STAGE 5** → 5 h 0 min • 54 km
• desnivel ▲650 m ▼540 m

● **BELORADO → BURGOS**

**STAGE 6** → 7 h 0 min • 87 km
• elevation ▲610 m ▼625 m

● **BURGOS → CARRIÓN DE LOS CONDES**

**STAGE 7** → 5 h 40 min • 88 km
• elevation ▲400 m ▼380 m

● **CARRIÓN DE LOS CONDES → ARCAHUEJA**

**STAGE 8** → 6 h 20 min • 83 km
• elevation ▲820 m ▼520 m

● **ARCAHUEJA → RABANAL DEL CAMINO**

**STAGE 9** → 5 h 45 min • 59 km
• elevation ▲725 m ▼1,300 m

● **RABANAL DEL CAMINO → VILLAFRANCA DEL BIERZO**

**STAGE 10** → 6 h 40 min • 75 km
• elevation ▲1,450 m ▼1,530 m

● **VILLAFRANCA DEL BIERZO → SARRIA**

**STAGE 11** → 6 h 20 min • 64 km
• elevation ▲1,170 m ▼1,100 m

● **SARRIA → MELIDE**

**STAGE 12** → 4 h 30 min • 55 km
• elevation ▲ 850 m ▼1,050 m

◻ **MELIDE → SANTIAGO DE COMPOSTELA**

# Hostels and services

## SYMBOLS USED IN THIS GUIDE

🅞 All services

🅗 Health centre
🅐 A&E
🅟 Pharmacy

🖵 Bar/restaurant
🍺 Bakery
🍰 Patisserie
🛒 Shop
🛒 Supermarket
🔧 Bike workshop
💆 Massages/physiotherapy

🅗 Hostel*
🅐 Accommodation*

🚕 Taxis
🚌 Buses
🚆 Train
✈ Airport

🏧 ATM
✉ Post office
☎ Telephone booth
🚔 Police

🏊 Swimming pool
🏞 River beach
📖 Library
@ Internet
ℹ Information for pilgrims

\* 🅗 refers to hostels which feature showers, dining rooms and community bedrooms, fixed closing hours at night and are often specifically for walkers.

\* 🅐 refers to general accommodation such as hotels and B&Bs.

## A

### A BREA
🅗
→**Albergue El Chalet** c/. A Brea. 5 • Tel. 659 380 723 • elchaletalbergue@gmail.com • Open from April to October (working days only, every day in August). 12 beds. €12 shared dormitory. Double rooms available: €40. Space for bikes. Reservations accepted.

### AGÉS
🅐🖵🅗
→**Albergue Municipal La Taberna de Agés** c/. del Medio, 21 • Tel. 947 400 697 and 660 044 575 • info@alberguedeages.com • WiFi • Open all year. 36 beds. €9 per person (€10 in winter, for the heating). Games room. Bike room. Bar/restaurant (Breakfast €3 and menus €10). Reservations accepted.
→**Albergue El Pajar de Agés** c/. Paralela del Medio, 12 • Tel. 947 400 629 and 699 273 856 • info@elpajardeages.net • Open from 1 March to 15 November. 34 beds. €10 per person. Bar (breakfast €3 and menu €10). Reservations accepted.
→**Albergue San Rafael (private)** c/. Camino de San Juan de Ortega, s/n • Tel. 947 430 392 • alberguesanrafael2010@hotmail.com • WiFi • Open all year. 16 beds. €10 bunk bed and €45 double room. Restaurant (breakfast €2.80 and menu €10). Gluten free menu (€12) and vegetarian menu (€12.50). Card payments accepted. Reservations accepted.

## AGUIADA
H
→**Albergue de peregrinos de Calvor** • Tel. 660 396 812 • www.xacobeo.es • Open all year. 22 beds. €6 shared dormitory. Kitchen. Reservations not accepted.

## AIREXE
H
→**Albergue de peregrinos de Airexe-Ligonde** Airexe, 7 • Tel. 982 153 483 • Open all year. 20 beds. €6 shared dormitory. Kitchen. Camping area. Reservations not accepted.

## AMBASMESTAS
H
→**Albergue Das Ánimas** c/. Campo Bajo, 3 • Tel. 987 543 077 • info@das-animas.com • www.das-animas.com • Open all year. 20 beds. €6-9 according to dormitory. Kitchen. Space for bikes. Reservations accepted.
→**Albergue-hostal Camynos** Ctra. antigua N-VI, 43 • Tel. 609 381 412 • camynos@gmail.com • www.camynos.es • Open from April to November. 10 beds. €10 according to dormitory. Single and double rooms available: €35-45. Space for bikes (chargeable). Reservations accepted.
→**Albergue Casa del Pescador** Ctra. antigua N-VI s/n • Tel. 603 515 868 • casitadelpescador@gmail.com • www.casadelpescador.eu • Open from 15 March to 15 November. 24 beds. €10-12 according to dormitory. Single and double rooms available: €22-30. Kitchen. Space for bikes (chargeable). Reservations accepted.

## ARCAHUEJA
H
→**Albergue La Torre** c/. Juan Carlos I, 19 D • Tel. 987 205 896 • info@alberguetorre.es • www.alberguelatorre.es • Open all year, except Christmas and February holidays. 27 beds. €10 in hostel, double room €35, triple €50, quadruple €60, quintuple €70 and octuple €80. Menus at €9, two-course menu at €5 and value menu at €6. Reservations accepted.

## ARZÚA
O
→**Albergue de peregrinos de Arzúa** c/. Cima do Lugar, 6 • Tel. 660 396 824 • Open all year. 56 beds. €6 shared dormitory. Kitchen. Space for bikes. Reservations not accepted.
→**Albergue da Fonte** c/. Carmen, 18 • Tel. 604 002 380 • alberguedafonte@hotmail.com • www.alberguedafonte.com. Open all year (winter, on request). 20 beds. €10-12 according to dormitory. Kitchen. Reservations accepted in low season only.
→**Albergue de Camino** c/. Lugo, 118 • Tel. 678 758 296 • info@decaminoalbergue.com • www.decaminoalbergue.com. Open from March to November. 46 beds. €10-12 according to dormitory. Kitchen. Space for bikes. Massages. Reservations accepted.
→**Albergue Don Quijote** c/. Lugo, 130 • Tel. 696 162 695 • alberguedonquijote@hotmail.com • www.alberguedonquijote.com • Open all year (winter, by reservation). 48 beds. €10 shared dormitory. Kitchen. Space for bikes. Reservations accepted.
→**Albergue Vía Láctea** c/. Xosé Neira Vilas, 26 • Tel. 616 759 447 • vialacteaalbergue@hotmail.com • www.alberguevialactea.com. Open all year. 60 beds. €10-12 according to dormitory. Kitchen. Space for bikes. Reservations accepted.
→**Albergue Ultreia** c/. Lugo, 126 • Tel. 626 639 450 • info@albergueultreia.com • www.albergueultreia.com • Open all year. 39 beds. €10 shared dormitory. Kitchen. Space for bikes. Reservations accepted.

→**Albergue Santiago Apóstol**
c/. Lugo, 107 • Tel. 660 427 771 •
santiagoapostolalbergue@hotmail.
com • www.alberguesantiagoapostol.
com • Open from April to October. 72
beds. €10-12 according to dormitory.
Kitchen. Space for bikes. Reservations
accepted.

→**Albergue Los Caminantes** c/.
Santiago, 14 • Tel. 647 020 600 •
info@albergueloscaminantes.com
• www.albergueloscaminantes.com
• Open from Easter to October.
28 beds. €10 shared dormitory.
Kitchen. Space for bikes. Massages.
Reservations accepted.

→**Albergue-pensión A Conda**
c/. Calexa, 92 • Tel. 687 926 604 •
hostalvilarino@gmail.com • www.
pensionvilarino.com • Open from
March to November. 18 beds.
€10 shared dormitory. Single and
double rooms available: €30-40.
Reservations accepted.

→**Albergue de Selmo** c/. Lugo,
133 • Tel. 981 939 018 • info@
alberguedeselmo.com • www.
oalberguedeselmo.com. Open from
Easter to October. 46 beds. €10-12
according to dormitory. Kitchen.
Space for bikes. Reservations
accepted.

→**Albergue-pensión Cima do Lugar**
c/. Cima do Lugar, 22 • Tel. 661 633
669 • acimadolugar@gmail.com •
www.cimadolugar.com • Open all
year. 14 beds. €10-12 according to
dormitory. Single and double rooms
available: €35-45. Space for bikes.
Reservations accepted.

→**Albergue Casa del Peregrino** c/.
Cima do Lugar, 7 • Tel. 686 708 704 •
Check opening dates. 14 beds. €10-12
according to dormitory. Kitchen.
Reservations accepted.

→**Albergue** O Santo c/. Xosé
Neira Vilas, 4 • Tel. 981 500 957 •
info@albergueosanto.com • www.
albergueosanto.com • Open from
April to October. 22 beds. €12 shared
dormitory. Single rooms available:
€35. Kitchen. Space for bikes.
Reservations accepted.

→**Albergue-pensión Arzúa** c/.
Rosalía de Castro, 2 • Tel. 608 380
011 • pensionarzua@gmail.com •
Open all year (winter, by reservation).
12 beds. €10 shared dormitory.
Double rooms available: €30-40.
Kitchen. Space for bikes. Reservations
accepted.

## ASTORGA

→**Albergue de Peregrinos Siervas de
María** Pza. San Francisco, 3 • Tel. 987
616 034 and 618 271 773 • asociacion@
caminodesantiagoastorga.com •
www.caminodesantiagoastorga.
com • WiFi • Pilgrims only. 156 beds.
€5 per night. Kitchen. Dining room.
Pilgrim's passport issued. Bike room.
Reservations not accepted.

→**Albergue San Javier** c/. Portería, 6
• Tel. 978 618 532 • WiFi • Open from
April to November. Pilgrims only. 95
beds. €10 per person. Kitchen. Bike
room (extra charge). Breakfast €4.
Reservations not accepted.

→**Albergue Ecce Homo** Located on
the outskirts of Astorga, in Valdeviejas,
200 metres from the Ecce Homo
hermitage • Tel. 620 960 060, 626
733 658 and 618 445 910 • Open
from March to October. Priority for
pilgrims on foot. 10 beds. €5 per night.
Reservations accepted.

## ATAPUERCA

→**Albergue La Hutte** c/. de
Enmedio, 38 • Tel. 947 430 320 •
42 beds. €10 per night. Kitchen.
Menus at €9 and breakfast at €4.
Reservations accepted.

## AUGAPESADA

→**Albergue casa Riamonte** Hamlet
of Castelo, 51 • Tel. 981 890 356 •
riamonte@telefonica.net • www.
riamontes.com • Open from March
to October. 4 beds. €12 shared
dormitory. Double rooms available:
€49. Space for bikes. Reservations
accepted.

## AZOFRA

🔲🚿🅿🍴🛏🗍

→**Albergue Municipal de Peregrinos de Azofra** c/. Las Parras, 7 • Tel. 941 379 325 (hostel), 638 261 432 (manager) and 941 379 049 (town hall) • WiFi • Open all year. 60 beds, increasing to 96 counting other premises that operate together and that open according to requirements. It closes in winter and the Herbert Simon parish hostel, with 16 beds, next to the church, is open. €10 per person. Kitchen. Reservations not accepted.

## ÁZQUETA

🗍🏠

→**Albergue La Perla Negra** c/. Carrera, 18 • Tel. 627 114 797 • laperlanegra67@gmail.com • https://alberguelaperlanegra. business.site • Open all year. Reservations accepted. 5 beds. €25 with dinner and breakfast.

**B**

## BARBADELO

🏠❌🍴🚲🗍🔳

→**Albergue de la Xunta Barbadelo** Former school buildings, right beside the Way on leaving the village • Tel. 660 396 814, 982 530 412 and 686 744 048 • Open all year. 18 beds. €6 per night. Dinner and breakfast available in the bar/restaurant located just 200 metres away. Reservations not accepted.

→**AAlbergue A Casa de Carmen** San Silvestre Barbadelo, 3, close to the Albergue de la Xunta • Tel. 982 532 294 and 606 156 705 • WiFi • Open all year. 30 beds. €10 per night (€30 in double room). Bike room. Reservations accepted.

→**Albergue O Pombal** 100 metres from the public hostel • Tel. 686 718 732 • albergueopombal@gmail. com • www.albergueopombal. blogspot.com • Open from April to November. 12 beds. €10. Large garden. Kitchen. Bike room. Reservations accepted.

→**Albergue-Pensión Casa Barbadelo** Vilei, s/n • Tel. 982 531 934 • info@ barbadelo.com • www.barbadelo. com • Open from April to October. 70 beds. Hostel with bunk beds for 8 people. €10 shared dormitory. €45 double room. €55 triple room and €60 quadruple room. Bar/restaurant. Massage service. Taxi. Swimming pool. Pilgrims' passports stamped. Reservations accepted.

→**Albergue-Pensión 108 to Santiago** Vilei s/n • Tel. 634 894 524 • pension108tosantiago@hotmail. com • www.pension108tosantiago. com • Open all year (winter, by reservation). 14 beds. €8-15 according to dormitory. Single, double and quadruple rooms available: €25-29-40. Space for bikes. Reservations accepted.

## BELORADO

🏠❌🔲🚿🍴🗍🗍🅰🔳🔵🅲

→**Albergue A Santiago** Camino Los Paules, s/n. Located right beside the Way, 400 metres from the centre • Tel. 677 811 847 • albergueasantiago@ hotmail.com • www.barbadelo. com • Open from April to October. 98 beds. Shared dormitories (€5-7) and single rooms (€30), doubles (€40) and triples (€55). Garden with swimming pool. Bar/restaurant. Serves breakfasts (€3) and menus for pilgrims (€10). Small workshop and bike washing. Reservations accepted.

→**Albergue Municipal El Corro** c/. Mayor, 68 • Tel. 947 581 419 and 629 507 470 • albergueelcorro@gmail. com • WiFi • Open all year. 45 beds. €10 shared dormitory and €30 double room. Kitchen. Menu €9 and breakfast €3. Reservations accepted.

→**Albergue El Caminante** c/. Mayor, 36 • Tel. 656 873 927 • g.caminante@hotmail.com • www. alberguecaminobelorado.es • Open from March to October. 26 beds. €5 per night. Hostel and breakfast €8. There are also rooms with full board from €25 up to €46. Restaurant. Bike room (extra charge). Reservations accepted.

→**Albergue parroquial de Belorado** Pza. San Francisco, 7, next to the church of Santa María • Tel. 947 580 085 • Open from April to October. Pilgrims only. 20 beds in shared dormitories. Reservations not accepted.

→**Albergue Cuatro Cantones** c/. Hipólito López Bernal, 10 • Tel. 947 580 591, 686 906 492 and 650 436 464 • info@cuatrocantones.com • www.cuatrocantones.com • WiFi • Fully refurbished in 2016. Open from March to October. 65 beds. €8 and €12 depending on room. Restaurant. Garden with covered swimming pool. Bike room. Buffet breakfast for €5 and menus for €12. During the summer, free yoga classes, stretches and relaxation are available to pilgrims staying there. Reservations accepted.

→**Albergue El Salto** Camino extramuros sur, s/n. On leaving the village, 500 metres from the Way and 1.2 km from the centre • Tel. 669 415 639 and 669 415 636 • elsalto@ elsalto.eu • www.elsalto.eu • It is a restored old house, in the heart of the countryside, with garden and kitchen garden. It runs on solar and biomass energy. Open all year. 24 beds. €10 per night. Workshop, sale and hire of bikes and accessories. Breakfast at €3 and dinner at €10. Reservations accepted.

## BERCIANOS DEL REAL CAMINO

→**Albergue parroquial Casa Rectoral** c/. Santa Rita, 11 • Tel. 987 784 008 • Open from April to October, reservations not accepted, with 44 beds in 5 shared dormitories. Runs on voluntary donations for accommodation, dinner and communal breakfast. Occupies a large 17th century building, with chapel.

→**Albergue Santa Clara** c/. Iglesia, 3 • Albergue Santa Clara c/. Iglesia, 3 • Tel. 605 839 993 and 987 784 314 • alberguesantaclara@hotmail.com • Open all year, reservations accepted, with 16 beds, rooms for 4 and 6 people (€8), twins (€25) and one double (€30). Buffet breakfast €5.

→**Albergue Bercianos 1900** c/. Mayor, 49 • Tel. 669 282 824 and 987 784 244 • hello@bercianos1900.com • www.bercianos1900.com • Hostel opened in 2017, open from March to November, reservations accepted, with 20 beds in shared dormitories. Price: €15 in dormitory with 16 beds and €15 in dormitory with 4 beds. Bar/restaurant with à la carte menu and breakfast for pilgrims at €4.

→**Albergue La Perala** Camino Sahagún, s/n, on leaving the village • Tel. 685 817 699 • alberguelaperala@ hotmail.com • Open all year, reservations accepted, with 58 beds. Shared room €10, single room €28, double with bath €38 and triple €48. Bar/restaurant with menu for €10.

## BOADILLA DEL CAMINO

→**Albergue Putzu** c/. Las Bodegas, 9 • Tel. 677 225 993 • inconformista1@ hotmail.com • Open all year except Christmas holidays. 16 beds. €8 per night. Kitchen. Dining room. Terrace. Bike room. Reservations not accepted.

→**AAlbergue Municipal Boadilla del Camino** c/. Las Escuelas, s/n • Tel. 979 810 390 • WiFi • Open all year. 12 beds. €5 per night. Bar/restaurant. Breakfast €4. Reservations not accepted.

→**Albergue En el Camino** Pza. El Rollo • Tel. 979 810 284 and 619 105 168 • albergue@boadilladelcamino. com • www.boadilladelcamino. com • WiFi • Open from March to early November. 48 beds. €8 per night. Garden with swimming pool. Fireplace. Personal lockers. Breakfast €3 and dinner €10. Reservations accepted.

→**Albergue Titas** c/. Mayor 7 • Tel. 979 810 776 • alberguetitas@hotmail. com • www.alberguetitas.com • Open all year. 12 beds. €10 per night. Breakfast €2.50, lunch and dinner €10. Reservations accepted.

## BOENTE
🄷

→**Albergue Os Albergues** Boente • Tel. 629 146 826 • os_albergues@ hotmail.es • Open from March to November. 30 beds. €11 shared dormitory. Space for bikes. Reservations accepted.

→**Albergue El Alemán** Boente de Arriba s/n • Tel. 981 501 984 • info@ alberguealeman.com • www. alberguealeman.com • Open from 15 March to 30 October. 40 beds. €12 shared dormitory. Swimming pool in summer. Space for bikes. Reservations accepted.

→**AAlbergue Boente** • Tel. 638 321 707 • info@albergueboente.com • www.albergueboente.com • Open all year (winter, please check). 40 beds. €12 shared dormitory. Single, double, triple and quadruple rooms available: €35-50-65-80. Swimming pool in summer. Space for bikes. Reservations accepted.

## BURGOS
◉

→**Albergue Municipal de Burgos** c/. Fernán González, 28 • Tel. 947 460 922 • asociacion@ caminosantiagoburgos.com • www. caminosantiagoburgos.com • Open all year. Pilgrims only. 150 beds. Payment by voluntary donation (€5 per night suggested). Meeting room. Dining room. Terrace. Bike room. Reservations not accepted.

→**Albergue de la Divina Pastora** c/. Laín Calvo, 10 • Tel. 947 207 952 • Open from Easter to October. Pilgrims only. 16 beds. €6 per night. Reservations not accepted.

→**Albergue Casa de Peregrinos Emaús** c/. San Pedro de Cardeña, 31 • Tel. 947 252 851 • peregrinosemaus@gmail.com • Open from Easter to October. Pilgrims only. 20 beds. €5 per night. Reservations not accepted.

**Other options.** In summer, the youth hostel is open (Tel. 947 220 362). Around the Plaza Mayor and in the old quarter you can find other accommodation at affordable prices: Pensión Peña (c/. Puebla, 18, Tel. 947 206 323), Pensión Victoria (c/. San Juan, 3, Tel. 947 201 542), Hostal Acacia (c/. Pérez Ortiz, 1, Tel. 947 205 134). Campsite (Fuentes Blancas, Tel. 947 486 016), 4 km from the city, although there are buses that stop right outside.

## C

## CACABELOS
🗌🛏🄷🖳

→**Albergue de peregrinos de Cacabelos** Pza. Santuario s/n • Tel. 987 547 167 • Open from April to November. 70 beds. €5 shared dormitory. Massages. Space for bikes. Reservations not accepted.

→**Albergue-hostal La Gallega** c/. Santa María, 23 • Tel. 987 549 476 • hostalgallega@gmail.com • www.hostalgallega.com • Open all year (except a fortnight in February). 29 beds. €10 shared dormitory. Single, double and triple rooms available: €25, €40 and €50. Space for bikes. Reservations accepted.

→**Albergue-Pensión El Molino** • c/. Santa María, 10 • Tel. 987 546 979 • abelelmolino@hotmail.com • www.elmolinoalbergue.com • Open all year (except Tuesdays and a fortnight in September). 16 beds. €9 shared dormitory. Single and double rooms available: €22 and €30. Space for bikes. Reservations accepted.

## CALZADILLA DE LA CUEZA

🔲 🔲 🔲 🔲 🔲

→**Albergue Municipal** c/. Mayor, 1 • Tel. 670 558 954 • municipalcalzadilla@outlook.es • Open all year, reservations not accepted, with two communal dormitories with a total of 34 beds. Price €5.

→**Albergue Camino** Real Located at the end of and behind the Calle Mayor • Tel. 979 883 187 • cesaracero2004@yahoo.es • Open all year, reservations not accepted, with 80 beds in two shared dormitories. Price €8. Has a pretty courtyard with swimming pool and a food shop next door. The owners also run the Camino Real hotel, where the town's bar/restaurant is located.

## CAMPONARAYA

🔲 🔲 🔲 🔲

→**Albergue Naraya** Av. Galicia, 506 • Tel. 987 459 159 • alberguenaraya@gmail.com • www.alberguenaraya.es • Open from April to November. 26 beds. €9 shared dormitory. Space for bikes. Reservations accepted.

→**Albergue La Medina** Av. Camino de Santiago, 87 • Tel. 987 463 962 • info@alberguelamedina.com • www.alberguelamedina.com • Open all year (winter, by reservation). 18 beds. €10 shared dormitory. Single and double rooms available: €18 and €30. Space for bikes. Reservations accepted.

## CARDEÑUELA RIOPICO

🔲 🔲 🔲

→**Albergue Municipal de Cardeñuela Riopico** c/. Real, 28, above the La Parada bar • Tel. 661 438 093 / 660 050 594 • laparadacardenuelariopico@gmail.com • WiFi • Bar/restaurant. Pilgrims only and open all year, except the last two weeks of December. €5. 12 beds in two shared dormitories. Reservations not accepted.

→**Albergue Vía Minera** c/. La Iglesia, 1 • Tel. 652 941 647 • viaminera@gmail.com • http://albergueviaminera.blogspot.com • WiFi • Open from March to October. Pilgrims only and reservations accepted. Bar/restaurant: breakfast €2.50; menus and dinner €9. 26 beds. €8 per person.

→**Albergue Santa Fe** c/. Los Huertos, 2 • Tel. 626 352 269 / 947 560 722 • info@baralberguesantafe.com www.baralberguesantafe.com/peregrinos • WiFi • Open all year. Bar/restaurant: communal dinner €8, breakfast €2. Pilgrims only, reservations accepted. 15 beds. €8 per person.

## CARRIÓN DE LOS CONDES

🔲 🔲 🔲 🔲 🔲 🔲 🔲 🔲

→**Albergue El Espíritu Santo** Pza. de San Juan, 4 • Tel. 979 880 052 • espiritusanto@hijasdelacaridad.org • WiFi • Open all year. Pilgrims only. 90 beds. €5 per person. Kitchen. Pets accepted in the inner courtyard. Reservations not accepted.

→**Albergue parroquial de Santa María** c/. Clérigo Pastor, 2, behind the church of Santa María • Tel. 979 880 768 • viastellarum@gmail.com • www.viastellarum-comunidaddelaconversion.blogspot.com.es • The hostel is run by nuns. Open from March to October. Pilgrims only. 52 beds. €5 per night. Kitchen and dining room. Reservations not accepted.

→**Albergue del convento de Santa Clara** c/. Santa Clara, 1 • Tel. 979 880 837 • Open from March to November. Pilgrims only. 31 beds. €5-7 shared dormitory. As well as the hostel, the monastery has guest quarters with single rooms (€22) and double rooms (44€) with bath. Reservations accepted.

→**Albergue Río Carrión** Pza. Marcelino Champagnat, 1 • Tel. 979 88 10 63 and 686 96 12 82 • info@alberguariocarrion.com • WiFi • http://alberguariocarrion.com • Open all year. Reserved for large groups. 421 beds. Prices on request.

## CASANOVA
**H**

→**Albergue Casa Domingo** Ponte Campaña • Tel. 630 728 864 • info@alberguecasadomingo.com • www.alberguecasadomingo.com • Open from Easter to October. 18 beds. €10 shared dormitory. Space for bikes. Reservations accepted.

→**Albergue de peregrinos de Casanova** • Tel. 982 173 483 • Open all year. 20 beds. €6 shared dormitory. Kitchen. Space for bikes. Reservations not accepted.

## CASTAÑEDA
**H**

→**Albergue Santiago** Castañeda • Tel. 699 761 698 • alberguesantiago@hotmail.com • Open all year. 4 beds. €10-11 according to dormitory. Double rooms available: €35. Space for bikes. Reservations accepted.

## CASTILDELGADO

→**Albergue Bideluze** c/. Mayor, 8 • Tel. 616 647 115 and 616 503 150 • info@alberguebideluze.com • www.alberguebideluze.com • WiFi • Open from March to November. 18 beds in two communal rooms (€10) and one double room with shared bathroom (€30). Bike room. Coffee service. Dinner €11 and breakfast €3. Reservations accepted.

## CASTROJERIZ

→**Albergue de San Esteban** Plaza Mayor • Tel. 947 377 001 • sanestebancastrojeriz@gmail.com • www.castrojeriz.com • Municipal hostel. Open all year, reservations not accepted, with a communal dormitory of 35 beds (mattresses provided if full in summer). Price €5. Breakfast served. The hostel is an old church, which was built in 1220, fell into ruin in 1864 and was acquired by the town council and refurbished as a cultural centre and hostel.

→**Albergue Camping Camino de Santiago** c/. Virgen del Manzano s/n • Tel. 947 377 255 • info@campingcamino.com • www.campingcamino.com • Located in the campsite on entering the village. The hostel has 32 beds and the price is €6 per night. It also has a country house with rooms from €30 and bungalows for 2 to 6 people.

→**Albergue Rosalía** c/. Cordón, 2 • Tel. 947 373 714 and 637 765 779 • info@alberguerosalia.com • www.alberguerosalia.com • Open from April to October, reservations accepted, with 30 beds in communal rooms (€10-12) and double rooms (€26-30). Communal dinner €9 and buffet breakfast €3. It is located in the Casa de Cordón, a building over 500 years old, refurbished as a hostel.

→**Albergue Orión** Av. de la Colegiata, 28 • Tel. 649 481 609 and 672 580 959 • albergueorion2016@ hotmail.com • Open from the mid-March to mid-October, reservations accepted, with 29 beds: shared dormitory €11, single room €30, double €40 and triple €50. Communal dinner €10 and breakfast €3.

→**Albergue A Cien Leguas** c/. Real de Oriente, 78 • Tel. 947 562 305 and 619 289 476 • info@acienleguas. es • www.acienleguas.es • Open all year, reservations accepted, with 18 beds in shared dormitories (€10) and 6 double rooms with bath (€35-55). Has a bar/restaurant that serves breakfast, lunch and dinner. Accessible for people with reduced mobility.

## CASTROMAIOR
□ℍ

→**Albergue Ortiz** Castromaior, 2 • Tel. 625 668 991 • info@ albergueortiz.com • www. albergueortiz.com • Open from March to November. 18 beds. €10 shared dormitory. Kitchen. Space for bikes. Reservations accepted.

## CÉE
□□□□Ⓒℍ

→**Albergue A Casa da Fonte** c/. Rúa de Arriba, 36 • Tel. 699 242 711 • guzmanroget@gmail.com • www. albergueacasadafonte.blogspot. com.es • Open from 15 March to 15 November. 42 beds. €11 shared dormitory. Kitchen. Space for bikes. Reservations accepted.

→**Albergue O Bordón** Camiños Chans-Brens • Tel. 655 903 932 • albergueobordon@gmail.com • www.albergueacasadafonte. blogspot.com.es • Open all year. 24 beds. €12 shared dormitory. Kitchen. Space for bikes. Reservations accepted.

→**Albergue Moreira** c/. Rosalía de Castro, 75 • Tel. 620 891 547 • info@alberguemoreira.es • www. alberguemoreira.es • Open from mid-March to October. 14 beds. €12 shared dormitory. Double rooms available: €30. Kitchen. Space for bikes. Reservations accepted.

→**Albergue Tequerón** c/. Rúa de Arriba, 31 • Tel. 666 119 594 • hostelalberguetequeron@hotmail. com • Open all year. 8 beds. €12-15 according to dormitory. Kitchen. Space for bikes. Reservations accepted.

→**Albergue O Camiño das Estrelas** Av. Finisterre, 78 • Tel. 981 747 575 • reservas@grupoinsua.com • www.alberguecaminodasestrelas. com • Open all year. 32 beds. €12 communal dormitory. Double rooms available: €30. Space for bikes. Reservations accepted.

## CIRAUQUI / ZIRAUKI
▣□Ⓦ⬇ℍ⊟◻

→**Albergue Maralotx** c/. San Román, 30 • Tel. 678 635 208 • albergueci018rauqui@gmail.com • WiFi • Open from March to October. 28 beds. €12 in communal rooms and €42 in double rooms. Bike room. Reservations accepted.

## CIRUEÑA
✚▣□ℍ

→**Albergue Virgen de Guadalupe** c/. Barrio Alto, 1 • Tel. 638 924 069 • virgendeguadalupe1@gmail.com • www.albergue-virgendeguadalupe. webnode.es • WiFi • Open from mid-March to mid-October. 35 beds. €7 per person. Tea service. Lunch and dinner €7 and breakfast €3. Reservations accepted.

→**Albergue Victoria** c/. San Andrés, 10 • Tel. 941 426 105 and 628 983 351 • Open from March to October (rest of the year, please check). 16 beds. €10 in shared dormitory, €35 for double room with shared bathroom and €40 for double room with bathroom. Reservations accepted.

## CIZUR MENOR / ZIZUR TXIKIA

→**Albergue de peregrinos de la Orden de Malta** Encomienda Sanjuanista, right on the Way, on entering the town, opposite the Romanesque church of San Miguel. • Tel. 616 651 330 • Open from June to September. 27 beds in a shared dormitory. €7 per person. Kitchen. Bike room. Reservations not accepted.

→**Albergue de Maribel** Paseo de Lurbeltzeta,1 • Tel. 670 323 271 and 948 183 885 • maribelroncal@jacobeo.net • www. elalberguedemaribel.com • Open from March to October. 52 beds. €12 per night. Garden. Dining room. Internet. Reservations accepted.

## COLUMBRIANOS

→**Albergue San Blas** c/. San Blas, 5 • Tel. 675 651 241 • reservas@ alberguesanblas.es • www. alberguesanblas.es • Open all year (in winter, by reservation). 20 beds. €10 shared dormitory. Double rooms available: €25-30. Kitchen. Reservations accepted.

## CONVENTO DE SAN ANTÓN

→**Albergue Hospital de peregrinos de San Antón** Convento de San Antón. Between Hontanas and Castrojeriz • campoovidio@ gmail.com • Open from May to September, reservations not accepted, with a shared dormitory of 12 beds. Runs on voluntary donations. No electricity or hot water, although in summer the climate is usually temperate. Communal dinner and breakfast by candlelight, also by voluntary donation.

## CORCUBIÓN

→**Albergue San Roque. Campo San Roque** s/n. Located in the hamlet of Vilar, 1 kilometre from Corcubión in the direction of Fisterra • Tel. 679 460 942 • info@amigosdelcamino. com. Open all year. 20 beds. Relies on voluntary donations. Reservations not accepted.

→**Albergue Camiño de Fisterra** c/. Cruceiro de Valdomar, 11 • Tel. 981 745 040 • Open all year. 14 beds. €10 shared dormitory. Kitchen. Space for bikes. Reservations accepted.

**Other options.** On arriving at the coast, the options for accommodation aside from the hostels of the Xunta are more varied. In Corcubión, Hotel El Hórreo (Santa Isabel, s/n. Tel. 981 749 185), the Casa da Balea rustic B&B (Rafael Juán, 44. Tel. 981 746 645 and 655 130 485) and Hotel Las Hortensias (Praia de Quenxe, s/n. Tel. 981 747 584).

**E**

## EL ACEBO

→**Albergue parroquial Apóstol Santiago** Plaza de la Iglesia • peregrinosflue@terra.es • Open from Easter to October, reservations not accepted, with 23 beds in a communal dormitory. Relies on voluntary donations and there are prayers after dinner. Communal dinner and breakfast.

→**Albergue La Casa del Peregrino** Carretera de Compludo, s/n • Tel. 987 057 793 • alberguelacasadelperegrino@ gmail.com • www. alberguelacasadelperegrino.es • Open all year, except from 22 December to 8 January, reservations accepted, with 103 beds in 12 rooms of 8 beds and several double rooms that can be converted into single and triple rooms. Price: €10, double €45 and double with bath €50. Dinner €10 and breakfast €4. The hostel is located in a large, modern complex on leaving the village, with a large swimming pool and organic garden.

→**Albergue Mesón El Acebo** Camino Real, 16 • Tel. 987 695 074 and 615 500 408 • mesonelacebo@ hotmail.com • www.mesonelacebo. es • Closes from 15 December to 15 January, reservations accepted, with 23 beds in a room with bunk beds (€7), a double room (€24) and a triple room (€36). The hostel is in fact an annex of the Mesón El Acebo restaurant, which serves the typical sausage of El Bierzo.

## EL BURGO RANERO
🌟 🚲 🍴 Ⓗ Ⓐ

→**Albergue El Domenico Laffi** Pza. Mayor, s/n • elburgoranero@gmail. com • WiFi • Open all year. Pilgrims only. 30 beds. Relies on voluntary donations. Kitchen. Parking for bikes in the outside area.  Reservations not accepted.

→**Albergue El Nogal** c/. Fray Pedro, 42, on entering the town • Tel. 667 207 454 and 627 229 331 • jelnogal@ yahoo.es • Open from Easter to October. €7 bunk bed and €10 bed. Kitchen and bike room.

→**Albergue La Laguna.** c/. La Laguna, 12 • Tel. 603 178 627 • Open from March to November. 18 beds. €9-12 shared dormitory. €30 single room and €40 double room. Garden and log cabins. Reservations accepted.

→**Albergue municipal de Calzadilla de los Hermanillos** c/. Mayor, 28. Located in the village of Calzadilla de los Hermanillos, which is part of El Burgo Ranero • Tel. 987 330 013 and 987 337 610 • elburgoranero@ gmail.com • WiFi • Open all year. Pilgrims only. 22 beds. Relies on voluntary donations. Kitchen. Reservations not accepted.

→**Albergue Vía Trajana** c/. Mayor, 55. Located in the village of Calzadilla de los Hermanillos, which is part of El Burgo Ranero •Tel. 987 337 610 and 600 220 104 • albergueviatrajana@gmail.com e info@albergueviatrajana.com • www.albergueviatrajana.com • Open from April to October. 20 beds. €15 shared dormitory. €35 double room. Garden. Restaurant. WiFi. Third-party transport (taxi, backpack pick-up and bus). Reservations accepted.

## EL GANSO
🍴 🚲 🍴 Ⓗ Ⓐ

→**Albergue Gabino** c/. Real, 9 • Tel. 625 318 585 • gabinoelganso@gmail. com • Open from March to mid-November, reservations accepted, with 24 beds in shared dormitories and double rooms. Price: €8 in shared room, €45 for the double room (with kitchen and bath) and €50 for the double room, with space for extra beds. Bar/cafeteria.

## ESPINAL (AURIZBERRI)
🍴 Ⓗ Ⓐ

→**Albergue Haizea** c/. Saroiberrin, 2 • Tel. 948 760 379 • iralepo@ hotmail.com • www.irugoienea. com • Open all year except second fortnight of November. 40 beds. €12 shared dormitory. Single, double and triple rooms available: €45, €60, €75. Space for bikes. Reservations accepted.

→**Albergue Irugoienea** c/. Ohianilun, 2 • Tel. 622 606 196 • info@irugoienea.com • www. hostalhaizea.com • Open from Easter to October. 26 beds. €12 shared dormitory. Single, double and triple rooms available: €37, €52, €67. Space for bikes. Reservations accepted.

## ESTELLA / LIZARRA

→**Albergue Municipal de Peregrinos de Estella** c/. La Rúa, 50 • Tel. 948 550 200 • caminodesantiagoestella@gmail.com • Open all year (except from 15 December to 15 January). Pilgrims only. 96 beds. €6 per night. Pilgrim's passport issued. Kitchen and bike room (extra charge). Reservations not accepted.

→**Albergue parroquial San Miguel** c/. Mercado Viejo, 18 • Tel. 635 866 009 and 948 550 431 • j.miguelarellano@gmail.com. Open from Easter to October. 32 beds. Relies on voluntary donations. Bike room. Reservations not accepted.

→**Albergue de la fundación ANFAS (Navarra Association for people with intellectual or developmental disabilities)** c/. Cordeleros, 7 • Tel. 639 011 688 and 948 554 551 • albergue@anfasnavarra.org • www.alberguenfas.org • WiFi • Open from May to September. 34 beds. €7 per night. Kitchen. Bike room (extra charge). Reservations not accepted.

→**Albergue Juvenil Municipal Oncineda** c/. Monasterio de Irache, 11 • Tel. 948 555 022 and 666 199 939 • info@albergueestella.com • www.albergueestella.com • WiFi • Open all year. In winter it only caters for large groups. It is a youth hostel open to all ages and not exclusive to pilgrims. 180 beds. €10 in multi-bed room, €14 for pilgrims in sole use room. Breakfast €5 and dinner €10. Bar/cafeteria. Computers for public use. Kitchen. Laundry service. Reservations accepted.

→**Albergue Capuchinos Rocamador** c/. Rocamador, 6. On leaving the town • Tel. 948 550 549 and 948 550 013 • reservas.estella@albergescapuchinos.org • www.albergescapuchinos.org • Open all year (closes from 22 December to 6 January). 30 beds. €13 bunk bed, €16 bed, both with shared bathrooms. Rooms with en-suite bathroom from €16 to €40. Breakfast, lunch and dinner available. Reservations accepted.

→**Albergue Agora Hostel** c/. Callizo Pelaires, 3 • Tel 948 546 574 and 681 346 882 • info@dormirenestella.com • www.dormirenestella.com • Open from February to December. Opened in 2017. 26 beds. €20 per night. Kitchen. Bike room (advance reservation required). Reservations accepted.

→**Albergue La hostería de Curtidores** c/. Curtidores, 43 • Tel. 948 550 070 and 663 613 642 • curtidores@alberguestella.com • www.lahosteriadelcamino.com • WiFi • Open all year. 45 beds. €15 shared dormitory. €45 double room. Breakfast €5. Bike room. Kitchen. Reservations accepted.

## F

## FERREIROS

→**Albergue de peregrinos de Ferreiros** s/n • Tel. 660 396 815 • www.xacobeo.com • Open all year. 22 beds. €6 shared dormitory. Kitchen. Reservations not accepted.

→**Albergue Casa do Rego** A Pena, 4 • Tel. 626 970 788 • casadoregopena@gmail.com • www.casadorego.com • Open from May to October. 10 beds. €10 shared dormitory. Double rooms available: €40. Space for bikes. Reservations accepted.

→**Albergue Casa Cruceiro de Ferreiros, 2** • Tel. 639 020 064 • casacruceirodeferreiros@gmail.com • www.casacruceirodeferreiros.com • Open from March to November. 24 beds. €10 shared dormitory. Double and triple rooms available: €40-60. Reservations accepted.

## FILLOBAL

→**Albergue Fillobal** • Tel. 666 826 414 • alberguefillobal@yahoo.es • www.alberguesanblas.es • Open all year (may close a few days in winter). 18 beds. €10 shared dormitory. Single and double rooms available: €25-35. Kitchen. Space for bikes. Reservations accepted.

## FISTERRA

→**Albergue de Fisterra.** Rúa Real, 2 • Tel. 981 740 781 • alberguefisterra@hotmail.com • Open all year. 36 beds. €6 per night. Kitchen. Bike room. The Fisterrana is issued in this hostel, which certifies completion of the pilgrimage to Finisterre (if closed, in the town hall). Reservations not accepted.

→**Albergue de Paz** c/. Víctor Cardalda, 11 • Tel. 981 740 332 and 628 903 693 • enrike.33@hispavista.com. WiFi. Open all year (closes in winter according to demand). 28 beds. €12-15 per night. Bike room.

→**Albergue pensión Finistellae** c/. Manuel Lago País, 7 • Tel. 637 821 296 • reservas@finistellae.com • www.finistellae.com • WiFi • Open from Easter to 31 October. 20 beds. €12 in hostel. €35 single room. €45 double room. €45 triple room. €60 quadruple room. Breakfast €3.50. Bike room. Reservations accepted.

→**Albergue Cabo da Vila** c/. A Coruña, 13 bajos • Tel. 607 735 474 and 981 740 454 • alberguecabodavila@gmail.com • www.alberguecabodavila.com • WiFi • Open from March to November. 28 beds. €12 bunk bed. €40 double room. €70 quadruple room. Breakfast €4. Kitchen. Dining room. Computers with Internet access. Bike room. Reservations accepted.

→**Albergue Mar de Rostro** c/. Alcalde Fernández, 45 • Tel. 637 107 765 and 981 740 362 • alberguemarderostro@hotmail.com • WiFi • Open from March to November. 23 beds. €10-12 per night. Kitchen. Bike room. Reservations accepted.

→**Albergue Do Sol e da Lúa** c/. Atalaya, 7. Located 200 metres from the centre • Tel. 881 108 710 and 617 568 648 • alberguedosol@hotmail.com • www.alberguedosol.blogspot.com • WiFi • Open all year. 18 beds. €11 shared dormitory. €20 single room. €27 double room. Kitchen. Meditation room. Reservations accepted.

→**Albergue Mar de Fora** c/. Rúa Potiña, 14. Located 3 kilometres from the lighthouse • Tel. 648 263 639 and 981 740 298 • alberguemardefora@gmail.com • www.alberguemardefora.com • WiFi • Open all year. 38 beds. €10 shared dormitory. €35 double room. €40 quadruple room. Garage service. Breakfast. Reservations accepted.

→**Albergue de Sonia-Buen Camino** c/. Atalaya, 11 • Tel. 981 740 771 and 619 529 343 • reservas@alberguedesoniafinisterre.com • www.buencaminofinisterre.com • WiFi • Open all year. 50 beds. €12 per night. Bike room. Sauna. Kitchen. Reservations accepted.

→**Albergue La Espiral** c/. Fonte Vella, 19 • Tel. 607 684 248 and 678 390 928 • alberguelaespiral@hotmail.com • WiFi • Open all year. €12 per night. €30-38 double room. Kitchen. Alternative therapies such as reiki and different types of massage. Reservations accepted.

→**Albergue-Pensión Fin da Terra e do Camiño** c/. Alfredo Saralegui, 15 • Tel. 675 361 890 • alberguefindaterra@gmail.com • www.alberguefindaterra.wixsite.com • WiFi • Open from Easter to October. Pilgrims only. 12 beds. €10 shared dormitory. €20 single room. €40 double room. Kitchen. Bike room. Reservations accepted.

→**Albergue-pensión O Encontro** c/. Rúa do Campo s/n • Tel. 696 503 363 • Open from April to November. 5 beds. €10-12 according to dormitory. Double rooms available: €34-45. Kitchen. Space for bikes. Reservations accepted.

→**Albergue Por Fin** c/. Federico Ávila, 19 • Tel. 636 764 726 • Open from Easter to November. 11 beds. €12 according to dormitory. Double rooms available: €26. Kitchen. Space for bikes. Reservations accepted.

→**Albergue Ara Solis** c/. Ara Solis, 3 • Tel. 638 326 869 • Open all year. 16 beds. €10-12 according to dormitory. Kitchen. Space for bikes. Reservations accepted.

## FONCEBADÓN
◻️Ⓗ

→**Albergue Domus Dei** c/. Real, s/n. In the same building as the church • peregrinosflue@terra.com • Open from April to October. Pilgrims only. 18 beds. Relies on voluntary donations. Offers breakfast and dinner. Reservations not accepted.

→**Albergue Monte Irago** c/. Real, s/n • Tel. 695 452 950 • alberguemonteirago@hotmail.com • Open all year. Pilgrims only. 34 beds. When the hostel is full, a room with mattresses on the floor

is made available. €8 per night with breakfast included. €9 for dinner. Small grocery shop. Massages and yoga exercises. Pilgrim's passport issued. Bed reservations accepted only for older people.

→**Albergue Roger de Lauria** c/. Real, s/n • Tel. 625 313 425 • alberguerogerdelauria@gmail.com • Closes in December and January. 20 beds. €5 per night. Breakfast and pilgrim's menu. Bar/restaurant. Reservations accepted.

→**Albergue Cruz de Fierro** c/. Real, s/n • Tel. 628 257 160 • fonfierro@gmail.com • WiFi • Open from March to November. 34 beds. €10 per night. Kitchen. Reservations accepted.

→**Albergue La Posada del Druida** c/. Real, s/n • Tel. 696 820 136 • Open from March to October. 20 beds. €7 per night. Reservations accepted.

## FONFRÍA
◻️🍴Ⓗ▱🏠

→**Albergue-pensión A Reboleira** Fonfría • Tel. 659 061 196 • alberguefonfria@yahoo.es • www.albergueareboleira.com • Open all year (may close a few days in winter). 70 beds. €€ shared dormitory. Single, double, triple and quadruple rooms available: €32-40-54-68. Space for bikes. Reservations accepted.

## FRÓMISTA
◻️🍴◻️◻️◻️ⒽⒶ▱🚕▱Ⓒ🖐️

→**Albergue Municipal de Frómista** Plaza de San Martín • Tel. 979 811 089 and 686 579 702 • carmen-hospitalera@live.com • Closes from Christmas to the end of January, reservations accepted, with 56 beds in shared dormitories. Price €8 and breakfast €3.

→A**Albergue Luz de Frómista** Av. Ejército Español 10 • Tel. 635 140 169 and 979 810 757 • gmag@live.nl • www.alberguluzdefromista.com • Opened in September 2018. Open all year, reservations accepted, with 26 beds in communal dormitories (€9) and one room with 2 single beds (€25 for two people and €17.50 for one person). Breakfast €3.50 from 6.30am.

→**Albergue Estrella del Camino** Av. Ejército Español s/n, next to the medical centre • Tel. 653 751 582 and 625 687 045 • albergueestrelladelcamino@ hotmail.com • www. albergueestrelladelcamino.com • Located in the refurbished outbuildings of an old inn on the Way, it stays open from March to November. Reservations accepted, with 32 beds in communal dormitories. Price €9, communal dinner €9 and breakfast €3. Pretty gardens to relax in.

→**Albergue Canal de Castilla** c/. La Estación, 2 • info@ albergueperegrinosfromista.com • www.albergueperegrinosfromista. com • Tel. 693 465 737 and 979 810 193 • Open from March to November. Reservations accepted, with 32 beds (16 in bunks and 16 in private rooms). Prices: in bunk bed with dinner €17, single room with bath €20, double room with bath €30 and triple room with bath €40. Communal dinner €10 and breakfast €4.

→**Albergue Betania** Av. Ejército Español, 26 • Tel. 638 846 043 (best to call the day before to confirm) • betaniafromista@gmail.com • Open in winter and intermittently the rest of the year. You are advised to check availability and make a reservation. Has 9 beds spread across two well-equipped apartments. Price: voluntary donation.

## G

### GRAÑÓN

→**Albergue Municipal Nuestra Señora de Carrasquedo** Camino de la Ermita, 45. Located 1.5 km from the Way, attached to the hermitage of Nuestra Señora de Carrasquedo • Tel. 627 341 907 and 665 284 685 • WiFi • Open all year. 42 beds. €6 per night. Bar/restaurant. Bike room with workshop. Lunch. Breakfast €3. Reservations accepted.

→**Albergue parroquial San Juan Bautista** c/. Mayor, 1 • Tel. 941 420 818 • Open all year. Pilgrims only. 40 beds. Relies on voluntary donations. Communal breakfast and dinner. Kitchen. Bike room. Prayers after dinner. Reservations not accepted.

→**Albergue La Casa de las Sonrisas** c/. Mayor, 16 • Tel. 687 877 891 and 630 823 767 • lacasadelassonrisas. albergue@gmail.com • WiFi • Open all year, except for the Christmas holidays. Pilgrims only. 27 beds. Relies on voluntary donations. Dinner and breakfast by voluntary donation. Lounge. Guitar. Games. Reservations not accepted.

→**Albergue Ave de Paso** c/. Caño, 18 • Tel. 666 801 051 • info@ albergueavedepaso.com • www. albergueavedepaso.com • WiFi • Open all year (off-season for groups and by reservation). 14 beds. €10 per night. Communal breakfast and dinner. Garden. Reservations accepted.

### GONZAR

→**Albergue de peregrinos de Gonzar,** s/n. Next to the main road • Tel. 982 157 840 • www. caminodesantiago.gal • WiFi • Open all year. Pilgrims only. 30 beds. €6 per night. Kitchen. Bike room. Reservations not accepted.

→**Albergue Casa García** Gonzar, 8. Next to the church • Tel. 982 157 842 • Open from Easter to November. Pilgrims only. 26 beds. €10 shared dormitory. €35 double room. Bar/restaurant. Menu €10. Bike room. Reservations accepted.

**H**

## HONTANAS
🏠🛏️♿🅰️🚕🚲

→**Albergue Municipal de Hontanas** c/. Real, 26 • Tel. 686 908 486 • hospitalsanjuan.hontanas@gmail.com • www.alberguemunicipal.negocio.site • Open all year. Pilgrims only. 44 beds. €6 in summer season and €10 in winter. Kitchen. Dinner. Breakfast. Reservations not accepted.

→**Albegue San Bol** Arroyo de San Bol (municipality of Iglesias, 4 km before Hontanas) • Tel. 606 893 407 • reservas@alberguesanbol.com • www.alberguesanbol.com • Open from April to mid-October. Pilgrims only, reservations accepted. Communal dinner €7. 12 beds. €5 per person.

→**Albergue Santa Brígida** c/. Real, 15 • Tel. 628 927 317. • reservas@alberguesantabrigida.com • www.alberguesantabrigida.com • WiFi • Open from 15 March to mid-October. Pilgrims only. 16 beds. €7 bunk bed. Kitchen. Lounge/dining room. Bike room with washing area. Bar/restaurant. Reservations accepted.

→**Albergue El Puntido** c/. Iglesia, 6 • Tel. 947 378 597 and 636 781 387 • Email: contacto@puntido.com • www.puntido.com • WiFi • Open from March to November (check outside these months). 40 beds. €6 bunk bed. €32 double room. €40 triple room. Restaurant with €10 menu. Food shop. Bike room. Pets accepted. Kitchen. Breakfast. Restaurant service. Reservations accepted.

→**Albergue Juan de Yepes** c/. Real, 1 • Tel. 638 938 546 • reservas@alberguejuandeyepes.com • www.alberguejuandeyepes.com • WiFi • Open from March to October. €8 bunk bed. €35 double room. Kitchen. Bike room with washing area. Area adapted for animals. Bar/restaurant. Reservations accepted.

## HONTO
🅷

→**Gîte Kayola** Route Napoléon • Right beside the Way, on the D428, an annex of the Orisson refuge but located 800 metres before it • Tel. 0033 559 49 13 03 / 0033 681 49 79 56 • refuge.orisson@wanadoo.fr • www.refuge-orisson.com • Open from April to 15 October. 15 beds. €15. Kitchen. Space for bikes. Reservations accepted.

## HORNILLOS DEL CAMINO
🏠🛏️🅳🅷🅰️

→**Albergue Municipal** Calle San Roman, 3 • Tel. 689 784 681 • hornillos.alberguemunicipal@gmail.com • http://hornillosalbergue.es • Open all year, reservations not accepted, with 32 beds in communal dormitories. Price €9 with breakfast. Complaints about the cold in winter.

→**Albergue El Alfar de Hornillos** c/. Cantarranas, 8 • Tel. 654 263 857 • elalferdehornillos@gmail.com • http://elalfardehornillos.es • Open from Easter to October, reservations accepted, with 20 beds in dormitories for 4, 6 and 10 people. Price €9. Breakfast €3 and communal dinner €9.

→**Albergue Hornillos Meeting Point** c/. Cantarranas, 3 • Tel. 608 113 599 • info@hornillosmeetingpoint.com • www.hornillosmeetingpoint.com • Open from March to October, reservations accepted, with 32 beds in rooms of 10 and 12 beds and two doubles. Price: €10 in communal rooms and €33-43 for doubles. Communal dinner €9 and breakfast

€3. Newly constructed building with a pretty garden.

## HOSPITAL (FINISTERRE)
🏠

→**Albergue O Casteliño** Hospital s/n • Tel. 615 997 169 • Open all year. 18 beds. €12 shared dormitory. Single rooms available: €20. Kitchen. Space for bikes. Reservations accepted.

## HOSPITAL (LUGO)
🏠

→**Albergue Hospital de Condesa** Hospital de Condesa • Tel. 660 396 810 • Open all year. 18 beds. €6 shared dormitory. Kitchen. Reservations not accepted.

## HOSPITAL DE LA CRUZ
🏠🏠

→**Albergue de peregrinos Hospital da Cruz** Hospital da Cruz • Open all year. 32 beds. €6 shared dormitory. Kitchen. Reservations not accepted.

## HOSPITAL DE ÓRBIGO
🏠🏠🏠🏠🏠🏠

→**Albergue parroquial Karl Leisner** c/. Álvarez Vega, 32 • Tel. 987 388 444 • info@alberguekarlleisner.com • Open all year, reservations accepted, with 90 beds in dormitories of between 4 and 12 beds. Price €5. Has a pretty courtyard with a well.

→**Albergue San Miguel** c/. Álvarez Vega, 35 • Tel. 987 388 285 and 618 183 420 • alberguesanmiguel@gmail. com • www.alberguesanmiguel.com • Open from March to October. Reservations accepted. 30 beds, with one room for 18 people and three rooms for 4 people. Price: €8 for communal room and €10 for the ones for 4 people. Organizes workshops and painting exhibitions and has a library, an area for reading with a wood stove and a large courtyard.

→**Albergue Verde** Av. Fueros de León, 76 • Tel. 607 671 670 and 689 927 926 • oasis@albergueverde. es • Open all year, reservations accepted, with 28 beds in shared rooms and one double. Price: €11 and €30 for the double with double bed and shared bathroom. Dinner and breakfast by voluntary donation. Yoga and meditation classes.

→**Albergue La Encina** Av. Suero de Quiñones, s/n • Tel. 987 361 087 • segunramos@hotmail.com • www. complejolaribera.com • Open all year, reservations accepted, with 22 beds in one communal room (€10) and doubles (€40). Has bar/restaurant where meals (€10) and breakfast (€3) are served.

I

## ILARRATZ
🏠

→**Albergue Ezpeleku** c/. San Martín, 3 • Tel. 948 304 721 • albergueezpeleku@gmail.com • albergueezpeleku.com • Open from Easter to 15 October. 6 beds. €15 • Restaurant. Massages. Space for bikes. Reservations accepted.

## ITERO DE LA VEGA
🏠🏠🏠🏠

→**Albergue Municipal** Pza. del Ayuntamiento, s/n • Tel. 605 034 347 and 979 151 826 • Open all year. 13 beds in a communal dormitory. Price €5. Reservations not accepted

→**Albergue La Mochila** c/. Santa Ana, 3 • Tel. 979 151 781 • lamochilaitero@gmail.com • Open all year, reservations accepted, with 28 beds in dormitories of between 2 and 8 beds. Price €6-10. Restaurant and bar with pilgrim's menu at €10 (vegetarian and gluten free option). Adapted for people with reduced mobility.

→**Albergue Puente Fitero** c/. Santa María, 3 • Tel. 979 151 822 • hostelpuentefitero@hotmail.com • Open all year, reservations accepted, with 22 beds in a shared dormitory (€8), single room (€30), double room (€40) and triple room (€48). Dinner provided at €10 and breakfast at €2.50. Has a large terrace, which during the day becomes the busiest bar in the village, and a food shop.

→**Albergue Hogar del Peregrino** c/. Santa María, 17 • Tel. 979 151 866 and 616 629 353 • alberguehogardelperegrino@hotmail.com • https://albergue-hogar-del-peregrino.negocio.site • Open all year, with 8 beds in one room and four double rooms. Reservations accepted. Price €12. Breakfast and dinner served. It is a private house fitted out as a hostel.

**L**

## LA FABA

→**Albergue El Refugio** c/. Camino de Santiago, 9 • Tel. 654 911 223 • caminarte.asociacion@gmail.com • www.facebook.com/caminarte.asociacion • Open from March to November. 8 beds. €5 shared dormitory. Space for bikes. Reservations not accepted.

→**Albergue de La Faba** c/. Iglesia s/n • Tel. 630 836 865 • lafaba.weebly.com • www.lafaba.weebly.com • Open from mid-March to October. 66 beds. €5 shared dormitory. Kitchen. Space for bikes. Reservations not accepted.

## LARRASOAÑA

→**AAlbergue Municipal de Larrasoaña** c/. San Nicolás, 16 • Tel. 626 718 417 • alberguelarrasoaina@gmail.com • Open from Easter to 30 October. If you arrive early and the hostel is closed, you need to enquire at the town hall. Pilgrims only. 52 beds. €8 per night. Breakfast €3.50. Kitchen. Bike room.

→**Albergue San Nicolás** c/. Sorandi, 5-7 • Tel. 619 559 225 and 659 815 961 • alberguesannicolas@gmail.com www.alberguesannicolas.com • WiFi • Open from March to October. 40 beds. €12 per night. Dinner €11. Kitchen. Bike room. Reservations accepted.

→**Albergue Bide Ederra** c/. San Nicolás, 27 • Tel. 625 673 057 and 948 304 156 • info@hostelbideederra.com • Open all year. 4 beds. €15 in bunk bed. €20 for double room. It is possible to rent the entire hostel. Linen and breakfast included in the prices. Reservations accepted.

## LAS HERRERÍAS

→**Albergue Las Herrerías** c/. Iglesia, 1 • Tel. 654 353 940 • alberguelove@gmail.com • www.facebook.com/Alberguelove • Open from April to November. 17 beds. €5-7 according to dormitory. Space for bikes. Reservations accepted.

→**Albergue-pensión Casa Lixa.** c/. Camino de Santiago, 35 • Tel. 987 134 915 • info@casalixa.com • www.casalixa.com • Open from March to October. 30 beds. €10 shared dormitory. Single and double rooms available, €35-45. Space for bikes. Reservations accepted.

## LA PORTELA

→**Albergue-hostal El Peregrino**
Ctra. antigua N-VI s/n • Tel. 987 543
197 • reservas@laportela.com • www.
laportela.com • Open from March
to mid-November. 26 beds. €10
shared dormitory. Single and double
rooms available: €28-40. Space for
bikes. Reservations accepted.

## LAVACOLLA

→**Albergue Lavacolla** c/. Lavacolla,
35 • Tel. 653 630 300 • reservas@
alberguelavacolla.com • www.
alberguelavacolla.com • Open all
year (winter, by reservation). 34
beds. €12 shared dormitory. Kitchen.
Space for bikes. Reservations
accepted.

## LA VIRGEN DEL CAMINO

→**Albergue municipal Don
Antonino y Doña Cinia** Av. Padre
Eustoquio, 16 • Tel. 615 217 335 and
987 302 800 • alberguevirgen@gmail.
com • Open from April to October,
reservations not accepted, with 40
beds in two communal rooms. Price
€7. Has garden and services for the
disabled.

## LÉDIGOS

→**Albergue El Palomar** c/. Ronda
de Abajo • Tel. 979 883 605 • info@
albergueelpalomar.com • www.
albergueelpalomar.com • Open from
March to November, reservations
accepted, with 47 beds in 18 bunks
(€6) and 29 beds (€7), as well
as doubles (€20). It has a large
courtyard with swimming pool and
bar/restaurant

→**Albergue La Morena** c/.
Carretera, 3 • Tel. 626 972 118 and 979
065 052 • info@alberguelamorena.
com • www.alberguelamorena.com •
Open all year, reservations accepted,
with 18 beds in shared dormitories
(€8), double rooms (from €35) and

triple rooms (from €55). Pilgrim's
menu from €10 and buffet breakfast
(only in high season) from €7.

## LEÓN

→**Albergue de peregrinos de
las Benedictinas Carbajalas** Pza.
Santa María del Camino, 7 • Tel.
680 649 289 • sorperegrina@gmail.
com • www.alberguesleon.com
• Accommodation of a religious
nature. Open all year. Pilgrims only.
132 beds. €5. Breakfast with payment
by voluntary donation. Pilgrim's
menu €9. Men and women sleep
in separate rooms. Reservations
accepted for groups of more than
4 people

→A**Albergue San Francisco de
Asís** Av. Alcalde Miguel Castaños, 4
• Tel. 987 215 060 • reservas.leon@
alberguescapuchinos.org • www.
alberguescapuchinos.org • WiFi •
This is a students' residence, part
of which takes in pilgrims. Open
all year. 166 beds. 54 beds in low
season. €10 bunk beds and €15
double room. Bike room. Restaurant.
Pilgrim's passport issued.

→**Albergue Miguel de Unamuno**
c/. San Pelayo, 15 • Between the
cathedral and the basilica of San
Isidoro • Tel. 987 233 010 and 601 377
423 • albergue@residenciaunamuno.
com • www.residenciaunamuno.
com • WiFi • Open from July to
September. 86 beds. €13-18 per
night. Bike room. Reservations
accepted.

→**Albergue Check in León** Av.
Alcalde Miguel Castaño, 88 • Tel.
987 498 793 and 686 956 896 •
checkinleon@gmail.com • www.
checkinleon.es • WiFi • Open all
year. 40 beds. €10 per night. Kitchen.
Bike room. Reservations accepted.

→ **Albergue La Muralla Leonesa** c/. Tarifa, 5 • Tel. 987 177 873 • info@alberguemurallaleonesa.com • www.alberguemurallaleonesa.com • WiFi • Open every day from March to October, the rest of the year from Thursday to Sunday. €12 for pilgrims. Kitchen. Bike room. Reservations accepted

→ **Albergue Santo Tomás de Canterbury** c/. La Lastra, 53 • Tel. 987 393 626 • info@alberguesantotomas.com • www.alberguesantotomas.com • WiFi • Open from March to November. 48 beds. €8-10 shared dormitory. Bike lending service for going around the city. Pilgrim's passport issued. Kitchen. Bar/restaurant. Bike room. Reservations accepted.

→ **Albergue Globetrotter Urban Hostel** c/. La Paloma, 8 • Tel. 987 103 267 • reservas@globetrotterhostel.es • WiFi • Open all year. 46 beds. €15-20. Bike room. Reservations accepted.

→ **Albergue León Hostel** c/. Ancha, 8 • Tel. 987 079 907 • info@leonhostel.es • WiFi • Open all year. 20 beds. €12-18 bunk beds. €28-32 double room. Kitchen. Terrace. Bike room. Reservations accepted.

→ **Albergue Hostel Urban Río Cea** c/. Legión VII, 6 • Tel. 636 946 294 and 639 179 386 • info@hostelurbanriocea.com • Open all year. €18 bunk bed. €30 rooms. Reservations accepted.

→ **Albergue Hostel Covent Garden** c/. Ancha, 25 • Tel. 987 004 428 and 601 082 002 • reservas@hostelcoventgarden.com • WiFi • Open all year. 10 beds. €17 per night. Kitchen. Bike room. Reservations accepted.

**Other options.** Furthermore, the city is well served by other types of accommodation. In the old quarter there is a variety of attractive offers: Pensión Blanca B&B (c/. Villafranca, 2. Tel. 987 251 991), Pensión La Torre (c/. La Torre, 3. Tel. 987 225 594), Pensión Sandoval (c/. Hospicio, 19. Tel. 987 212 041).

## LIGONDE
Ⓗ

→ **Albergue municipal escuela de Ligonde** • Tel. 679 816 061 • Open all year. 20 beds. €8 shared dormitory. Kitchen. Space for bikes. Reservations not accepted.

→ **Albergue La Fuente del Peregrino** Ligonde, 4 • Tel. 687 550 527 • lafuentedelperegrino@agape.org • www.lafuentedelperegrino.com • Open from May to October. 9 beds. Relies on voluntary donations. Reservations not accepted.

## LIÑARES
Ⓜ Ⓗ

→ **Albergue Linar do Rei** Liñares s/n • Tel. 616 464 831 • linardorei@gmail.com • Open from March to November. 20 beds. €10 shared dormitory. Single and double rooms available: €35-45. Kitchen. Space for bikes. Reservations accepted.

## LOGOSO
Ⓗ

→ **Albergue-pensión O Logoso** s/n • Tel. 659 505 399 • alberguelogoso@gmail.com • Open all year. 40 beds. €12 shared dormitory. Single and double rooms available: €35-40. Kitchen. Space for bikes. Reservations accepted.

## LOGROÑO
Ⓞ

→ **Albergue Albas** Pza. Martinez Flamarique, 4 bajos • Tel. 941 700 832 • albas@alberguealba.es • www.alberguealbas.es • WiFi • Open all year. Pilgrim's Passport issued. 22 beds. €12 per night. Bike room. Reservations accepted.

→**Albergue Check in Rioja** c/. Los Baños, 2 • Tel. 941 272 329 • info@checkinrioja.com • www. checkinrioja.com • WiFi • Open from March to October. Pilgrim's passport issued. 26 beds. €15 shared dormitory. €40 double room. Breakfast €3.50. Kitchen. Has a small library specialising in the Way.

→**Albergue parroquial Santiago El Real** c/. Barriocepo, 8 • Tel. 941 209 501 • info@santiagoelreal.org • Open all year. From October to May it is replaced by other premises - no. 58 in the same street. 30 beds. Pilgrims only. Relies on voluntary donations. Communal dinner and breakfast. Reservations not accepted.

→**Albergue Logroño** c/. Capitán Gallarza, 10 • Tel. 941 254 226 and 608 234 723 • info@casaconencanto. net • www.alberguelogrono.es • WiFi • Open all year (except from 25 December to 1 January). Pilgrims only. 30 beds. €10 shared dormitory. €20 single room. €30-40 double room. €45-55 triple room. Kitchen. Bike room.

→**Albergue Santiago Apóstol** c/. Ruavieja, 42 • Tel. 941 256 976 and 670 993 560 • Open all year (check beforehand in low season). 78 beds. €10-15 bunk beds. €40 double room. €64 triple room. Reservations accepted.

**Other options.** In the old quarter of Logroño there are half a dozen B&Bs, with very different facilities: La Redonda (c/. Portales, 21. Tel. 941 272 409), Hostal Niza (c/. Gallarza, 13. Tel. 941 206 044), Fonda La Bilbaína (c/. Gallarza, 10. Tel. 941 254 226), Hostal Sebastián (c/. San Juan, 21. Tel. 941 242 800) and Hostal La Numantina (c/. Sagasta, 4. Tel. 941 251 411), among others. The city also has Camping La Playa (Tel. 941 252 253. http://www.campinglaplaya. com), Open all year.

## LORCA

→**Albergue de Lorca** c/. Mayor, 40 • Tel. 948 541 190 • txerra26@mixmail. com • WiFi • Open from Easter to October. 14 beds (three rooms for four people and one double). €7 in bunk bed and €10 per person in the double. Kitchen and dining room. Bar/restaurant. Dinner available for €10. Bike room. Reservations accepted.

→**La Bodega del Camino** c/. Placeta, 8 • Tel. 948 541 162 and 948 541 327 • bodegacamino@gmail.com • http://www.labodegadelcamino. com • WiFi • Open from Easter to October (rest of the year, for groups by reservation). 30 beds in dormitories. €10 per night, €9 with pilgrim's passport). €30-45 for double room. Kitchen and dining room. Bar/restaurant. Breakfast (€3) and pilgrim's menu (€10). Bike room. Reservations accepted.

## LOS ARCOS

→**Albergue Isaac Santiago** c/. San Lázaro, 6 • Tel. 948 441 091 and 948 640 172 • WiFi • Municipal, on leaving the town. Open from Easter to October. 70 beds. €6 per night. Kitchen and dining room. Bike room. Massages €10-20.

→**Albergue Casa de la Abuela** Pza. De la Fruta, 8 • Tel. 630 610 721 and 948 640 250 • contacto@ casadelaabuela.com • www. casadelaabuela.com • Open from Easter to October (rest of the year it is possible for groups to rent it). 32 beds, 24 in bunks in communal dormitories and 8 in beds in double rooms. €10 for bunk and €35-45 for double room. No kitchen. Dining room. Breakfast at €3.50. Porch. Bikes in a separate garage. Reservations accepted.

→**Albergue Casa Alberdi** c/. El hortal, 3. Leaving the town • Tel. 650 965 250 • alberdikontxi@gmail. com • www.alberguecasaalberdi.

com/index.html • WiFi • 30 beds. Kitchen and dining room. Breakfast €4. Porch. Terrace. Parking for bikes. Reservations accepted, except in summer.

→**Albergue La Fuente - Casa de Austria** c/. Travesía del Estanco, 5 • Tel. 948 640 797 and 636 018 348 • lafuentedecasadeaustria@gmail.com • www.lafuentecasadeaustria.com • WiFi and computer • Open all year (except Christmas holidays and the month of January). Pilgrims only. 55 beds. €9-11 in dormitory and €35 for double room. Kitchen and dining room. Breakfast €3.50. Foot bath. Massages. Bike room. Reservations accepted.

**M**

### MANJARÍN
A
→**Refugio de Manjarín** Next to the main road • Open all year, reservations not accepted, with 30 beds in shared dormitories. Runs on voluntary donations. It is a special case since the refuge welcomes pilgrims at any time of year, despite the harsh winter conditions in the Montes de León and not having running water, showers or toilets.

### MANSILLA DE LAS MULAS
→**Albergue Municipal** c/. Los Mesones, 14 • Tel. 661 977 305 and 987 311 250 • alberguemansilla@gmail.com • www.ayto-mansilla.org • Open all year, reservations not accepted, with 75 beds in communal dormitories. Price €5.

→**Albergue El Jardín del Camino** c/. Camino de Santiago, 1 • Tel. 987 310 232 and 600 471 597 • olgabrez@yahoo.es • www.albergueeljardindelcamino.com • Open all year (except a few days in November and December, which it is advisable to confirm), with 40 beds in communal rooms. Price between €5 and €10 according to season. Has

a bar/restaurant with tables in a nice garden, where a pilgrim's menu for €10 and combined dishes are served. Reservations accepted.

→**Albergue Gaia** Av. Constitución, 28 • Tel. 987 310 308 and 699 911 311 • alberguedegaia@hotmail.com • https://alberguedegaia.wordpress.com • Open all year, except February, with 18 beds in two shared dormitories. Price €8. Breakfast by voluntary donation. Reservations accepted.

### MAÑERU
→**El Cantero** c/. Esperanza, 2 • Tel. 948 342 142 • info@alberguedecantero.com • www.alberguedecantero.com/inicio • WiFi • Open from Easter to October. 26 beds in shared dormitories. €10 per night. Kitchen and dining room. Has a bar/restaurant (lunch and dinner menus for €10). Garden. Bike room. Reservations accepted.

### MELIDE
→**Albergue de la Xunta** Rúa San Antonio s/n • Tel. 660 396 822 • Open all year. Pilgrims only. 156 beds. €6 per night. Kitchen without equipment. Dining room. Bike room. Reservations not accepted.

→**O Apalpador** Rúa San Antón, 23 • Tel. 679 837 969 and 981 506 266 • www.albergueoapalpador.com • WiFi • Open all year. 30 beds. €10 per night (in 2013 they opened another hostel, Novo Apalpador, with 24 beds, in c/. Cantón de San Roque, 24). Bike room. Reservations accepted.

→**O Cruceiro** Rda. de La Coruña, 2 • Tel. 616 764 896 • info@albergueocruceiro.com • www.albergueocruceiro.es • WiFi and computer • Open from Easter to October. 72 beds (rooms for 4 and 6 people). €10 per night. Bike room. Kitchen and dining room.

→**Albergue Pereiro** c/. Progreso, 43 • Tel. 981 506 314 • info@ albergepereiro.com • www. albergepereiro.com/• WiFi • Open from Easter to November. €10 per night. Kitchen and dining room. Terrace. Bike room. →**Albergue Melide** Av. Lugo, 92 • Tel. 981 507 491 and 627 901 552 • alberguemelide@ hotmail.com • www.albergemelide. com • WiFi and computer • Open from Easter to October. 42 beds. Kitchen and dining room. Bar. €10 per night. Breakfast €3. Menu €8. Terrace. Barbeque. Bike room. Reservations accepted.

→**Albergue Vilela** Rúa San Antonio, 2 • Tel. 616 011 375 • alberguevilela@ gmail.com • www.facebook.com/ profile.php?id=100008366078155 • Open all year (from November to mid-March, by reservation). 28 beds. €10 for bunk bed.

→**Albergue San Anton.** c/. San Antonio, 6 • Tel. 981 596 427 and 698 153 672 • alberguesananton@gmail. com • www.alberguesananton.com • WiFi and (chargeable) computer • Open from March to November (confirm during the rest of the year). 36 beds. €10 and €12 (high season). Bike room. Kitchen and dining room. Cafeteria. Breakfast €3-4. Terrace. Garden. Reservations accepted.

→**Albergue Afonso II El Casto** Av. Toques e Friol, 52 • 981 506 454 and 608 60 48 50 • info@ alberguealfonsoelcasto.com • www. alberguealfonsoelcasto.com • Open from Easter to October. Pilgrims only. 34 beds, 30 in bunks and 4 in a room with beds. €10 per night. No kitchen. Dining room. Terrace. Bike room €10. Reservations accepted.

→**Albergue Arraigos** Rúa Cantón de San Roque, 9 • Tel. 600 880 769 • albergue.arraigos@gmail.com • www.alberguearraigos.com • WiFi and computer with printer • Open all year. 20 bunk beds in a single dormitory. €10 per night. Kitchen and dining room. Reservations accepted.

→**Albergue Montoto** Rúa Codeseira, 31 • Tel. 646 941 887 • alberguemontoto@gmail.com • https://alberguemontoto. negocio.site/ • WiFi • Open from Easter to October. 48 beds in four dormitories. €12 for bunk bed. Jacuzzi. Kitchen and dining room. Garden. Terrace. Pool table. Bike room. Reservations accepted.

## MOLINASECA

→**Albergue municipal San Roque** Travesía Manuel Fraga, s/n • Tel. 722 616 347 and 692 886 721 • anam75513@gmail.com • Open from March to November, reservations not accepted, with 42 beds in shared dormitories. Price €6. Meals €8 and breakfast €3. On leaving the village, right beside the main road, in the former chapel of San Roque, refurbished as a hostel.

→**Albergue Compostela** c/. La Iglesia, 39 • Tel. 622 317 525 and 987 453 057 • alberguecompostela@ hotmail.com • Open all year, with 31 beds in shared dormitories. Price €9 in bunk and €11 in bed. Communal dinner €9 and breakfast €3. Reservations accepted.

→**Albergue Santa Marina** Travesía Manuel Fraga, 6 • Tel. 615 302 390 and 987 453 077 • alfredomolinaseca@hotmail.com • Open from March to October, with 56 beds in shared dormitories. Price €7, communal dinner €9. On leaving the village, just before the municipal hostel. Reservations accepted.

## MORATINOS

→**Albergue Hospital San Bruno** c/. Ontanón, 9 • Tel. 979 061 465 and 672 629 658 • brunobernoni@gmail. com • Closed in February and March, with 30 beds in communal and double rooms. Price €9 in communal room and €38 for double. Located in a typical Castilian house with courtyard and garden and has a bar/

restaurant with Italian specialities and a pilgrim's menu (€9.50). Reservations accepted.

→**Hostal-Albergue Moratinos** c/. Real, 12 • Tel. 979 061 466 • info@hostalmoratinos.es • www. hostalmoratinos.es • Open all year, reservations accepted, with 6 beds in a room with bunk bed (€10) and single (€40), double (€45), triple (€51) and quadruple (€60) rooms. Has a bar/restaurant.

## MURIAS DE RECHIVALDO

→**Albergue municipal** Carretera Santa Colomba • Tel. 638 433 716 • www.alberguemurias.wixsite.com • Open from March to October, with 18 beds in a shared dormitory. Price €5. Runs in the village's former school buildings with a large courtyard where you can camp in the summer. Reservations not accepted.

→**Albergue y Casa Rural Las Águedas** Camino de Santiago, 52 • Tel. 987 691 234 and 636 067 840 • lasaguedas@yahoo.es • https://lasaguedas.com • Open all year (from November to February, for groups only), with 30 beds in two rooms with bunks. Annexed to the hostel is a country house that is open all year with 5 double rooms. Price €12, doubles from €50 with breakfast. Dinner €12 and breakfast €4. A typical house of the León Maragatería region whose original architecture has been retained. Reservations accepted.

## MURUZÁBAL / MURUZABAL

→**El Jardín de Muruzábal** Camino Monteviejo, 21 • Tel. 696 688 399 • alberguejardindemuruzabal.com • Open from April to October (check during the rest of the year). The whole house is rented. 23 beds in a large dormitory with 14 bunks (€10), two double rooms with bath (€50), one double room (€40) and a triple

(€55) with shared bath. €4 breakfast and €12 dinner. Bike room with workshop. Kitchen and dining room. Bar and restaurant. Swimming pool. Tennis court. Swings. Reservations accepted.

→**Albergue Mendizabal** c/. Mayor, 7 • Tel. 678 010 119 and 948 344 631 • alberguemendizabal@gmail.com • https://albergue-mendizabal-en-muruzabal.negocio.site/ • WiFi • Open all year. 10 beds, 4 in bunks and 6 in beds. €18 with breakfast included. €8 lunch or dinner. Kitchen (without utensils) and dining room. Terrace/garden. Bike room. Reservations accepted.

**N**

## NÁJERA

→**Albergue de Peregrinos municipal de Nájera** Pza. de Santiago, s/n • Tel. 941 360 041 • Open all year. Pilgrims only. 92 beds in a communal dormitory with bunks. The sports centre is normally used when it is full. Computers with Internet. Relies on voluntary donations. Kitchen and dining room. Courtyard. Reservations not accepted.

→**Albergue Puerta de Nájera** c/. Ribera del Najerilla, 1 • Tel. 941 362 317 and 683 616 894 • reservas@alberguedenajera.com • www. alberguedenajera.com • WiFi • In the town centre. Open from March to October. 34 beds in rooms for 2, 4, 6 and 8 people. €10 in rooms of 4, 6 and 8 people, €15 in special rooms of 2 and 4 people and €40 for the double room. No kitchen, only microwaves. Dining room. Outside garden. Bike room. Reservations accepted.

→**Albergue Nido de Cigüeña** c/. Calleja Cuarta San Miguel, 4 • Tel. 611 095 191 • booking@alberguenajera. es • http://alberguenajera.es • WiFi • Open from April to October. 20 beds in a dormitory, one quadruple and one double. €10 per night in dormitory, €15 in quadruple and €50 in double. Kitchen and dining room. Courtyard and garden. Bike room in garage opposite the hostel. Reservations accepted.

→**Albergue La Judería – Sancho III** c/. San Marcial, 6 • Tel. 941 361 138 • Open from Easter to October. 10 beds. €8 per night. No kitchen or dining room. Meals served in Restaurante La Judería from €10. Reservations accepted.

**Albergue Las Peñas** c/. Costanilla, 56, on the outskirts • Tel. 621 209 432 and 621 209 410 • alberguelaspenas@ gmail.com • www.facebook.com/ AlbergueLasPenyas/• WiFi • Open all year. 12 beds. €10 in dormitory. €30 in double. Breakfast €2.50. Bike room. Stable. Reservations accepted.

**NAVARRETE**
🅰🅿⬛♿🏠🅿🅷🅷⬜〜🅤🅤@
→**Albergue de Peregrinos municipal de Navarrete** c/. San Juan, s/n • **Tel. 941 440 7**22 and 941 260 234 • info@santiago.org • www. asantiago.org • WiFi • Open from Easter to October. Pilgrims only. 48 beds in four communal dormitories. €7 per night. Kitchen and dining room. Balcony and porch. Place for bikes in bar opposite. Reservations not accepted.

→**Albergue El Cántaro** c/. Herrerías, 16 • Tel. 941 441 180 • info@ albergueelcantaro.com • www. albergueelcantaro.com • WiFi and computer • Open all year. 31 beds in two dormitories, four doubles and one single. €10 in dormitory, €20 for single and €30-40 for double. Breakfast €3. Kitchen with microwaves and utensils only. Dining room. Bike room. Pilgrim's passport issued. Reservations accepted.

→**Albergue La Casa del Peregrino** c/. Las Huertas, 3 • Tel. 630 982 928 • alberguenavarrete@gmail. com • https://alberguenavarrete. wordpress.com • WiFi • Open from Easter to mid-October. Pilgrims only. 18 beds in dormitory and double rooms. €10 in dormitory and €30 for double. Breakfast €2.50. No kitchen, only microwaves. Dining room. Terrace. Bike room. Pilgrim's passport issued. Reservations accepted.

→**Albergue Buen Camino** c/. La Cruz, 2 • Tel. 941 440 318 and 681 252 222 • www.alberguebuencamino.es • Open all year. 10 beds in dormitory and two doubles. €9 for bunk and €35 for double. No kitchen, only microwaves. Breakfast €3. Bike room. Reservations accepted.

→**Albergue Pilgrim's** c/. Abadía, 1 • Tel. 941 440 707 and 628 372 998 • www.albergue-pilgrims-navarrete. com • Open from February to November (rest of the year, according to demand). 36 beds. €10 in room without bath, €12 in room with bath and €15 in double room with shower. No kitchen. Dining room. Bar. Pilgrim's menu and vegetarian menu for €12. Terrace. Reservations accepted.

→**A la Sombra del Laurel** Carretera de Burgos, 52 • Tel. 639 861 110 • info@alasombradellaurel.com • www.alasombradellaurel.com • WiFi • On the Way itself, leaving Navarrete. Open all year (only for groups from October to February). 27 beds. €15 in bunk, €40-50 for double, €60-65 for triple and €80 for quadruple. No kitchen. Dining room. Breakfast €3. Communal dinner €10-13. Terrace. Bike room. Pilgrim's passport issued. Reservations accepted.

→**El Camino de las Estrellas**
Carretera de Burgos, 9 • Tel.
941 441 603 and 618 051 392
• alberguedelasestrellas@
gmail.com • http://
albergueelcaminodelasestrellas.
com • WiFi • Open all year. 48 beds.
€10 in bunk bed and €40 for double
room. No kitchen. Dining room.
Terrace. Bike room and workshop.
Breakfast €3. Reservations accepted.

## NEGREIRA

→**Albergue de Negreira** Rúa
Patrocinio, s/n • Tel. 981 886 046
and 664 081 498 • concello@
concellodenegreira.es • www.
concellodenegreira.es • Open all
year. Part of the Xunta de Galicia
network. 22 beds. €6 per night.
Kitchen and dining room. Picnic area.
Bikes kept in laundry rooms.
→**San José** Rúa de Castelao, 20 • Tel.
881 976 934 • info@alberguesanjose.
es • www.alberguesanjose.es • WiFi
• Open from March to November
(rest of the year, by reservation). 50
beds. €12 per night. Kitchen and
dining room. Terrace. Bike room.
Reservations accepted.
→**Albergue Lua** Av. Santiago, 22 •
Tel. 698 128 883 • www.alberguelua.
com • Open all year. 40 beds. €10
per night. Kitchen and dining room.
Breakfast served. Terrace. Place for
bikes. Reservations accepted.
→**AAlbergue El Carmen** c/.
Carmen, 2, on the first floor of the
Mezquita restaurant/guest house
• Tel. 636 129 691 and 981 881 652 •
info@alberguenegreira.com • www.
alberguehostalmezquita.com • WiFi
• Open all year. 34 beds. €10 per
night. No kitchen. Bar/restaurant.
Terrace in cafeteria. Menu €10.
Reservations accepted.
→**Albergue Alecrin** Av. Santiago, 52,
on entering the town • Tel. 981 818
286 • alecrin@albergueennegreira.
com • www.albergueennegreira.
com • Open from April to October.
40 beds. €10 per night. Kitchen and

dining room. Inner courtyard, where
the bikes are kept.
→**Albergue Anjana** c/. Chancela,
39, in a development on the
outskirts of Negreira • Tel. 722
501 720 • albergue.anjana@gmail.
com • www.anjanaalbergue.wix.
com/anjanaalbergue • Open from
March to October. 20 beds. €12. No
kitchen. Dining room. Terrace. Bike
room.
→**Albergue turístico** de Logrosa,
somewhat off the Way (in Chancela
you need to take the turn-off to
Logrosa, after the church, and the
hostel is the first house on the right)
• Tel. 981 885 820 and 646 142 554
• alberguedelogrosa@gmail.com •
www.alberguedelogrosa.es • Open
all year. 20 beds in rooms for 2, 3
and 4 people. From €17 per night.
No kitchen. Dining room. Library.
Garden. Bike room.

## O

## O CEBREIRO

→**Albergue de O Cebreiro** Pedrafita
do Cebreiro, s/n • Tel. 660 396 809
• www.xacobeo.es • At the end
of the town, the first in Galicia
of the Xunta network. Open all
year. Pilgrims only. 106 beds in
two dormitories. Gets very full in
high season. €6 per night. Kitchen
without utensils. Reservations not
accepted.
→**Albergue Turístico Casa
Campelo** O Cebreiro, s/n • Tel.
679 678 458 and 982 179 317 •
casacampelo@outlook.com
• www.facebook.com/CASA-
Campelo-117976538845093/• WiFi •
Open all year. 10 beds in dormitory
and four double rooms. €12 in
dormitory and €45 for double. Bike
room. Reservations accepted.

## ÓBANOS

⊗ ▢ ▢ H ▣ U @

→**Albergue Usda** c∕. San Lorenzo, 6 • Tel. 676 560 927 • Open from Easter to mid-October. Pilgrims only. 36 beds. €8 per night. Breakfast €3. Kitchen and dining room. Courtyard. Bike room. Reservations not accepted.

→**Albergue Atseden** c∕. Camino de Santiago, 2 • Tel. 646 924 912 • atseden1234@gmail.com • www. atsedenhostel.com • WiFi and computer • Open from 15 March to 15 October. 12 beds in one dormitory. €12 with breakfast for pilgrims, €15 for others. Kitchen and dining room. Garden. Bike room. Reservations accepted.

## OLVEIROA

▢ H

→**Albergue de Santiago de Olveiroa,** s∕n • Tel. 658 045 242 and 981 744 001 • www.dumbria. com • Open all year. Part of the Xunta network. Pilgrims only. 46 beds spread across various buildings, including a granary. €6 per night. Kitchen with no utensils. Bike room. Reservations not accepted.

→**Albergue Hórreo** Olveiroa, s∕n. DAlbergue Hórreo Olveiroa, s∕n. Restaurant and B&B Casa Loncho • Tel. 981 741 673 and 617 026 005 • casaloncho@gmail.com • www. casaloncho.com • WiFi • Open all year. 48 beds divided into five rooms. €12 per night. Kitchen and dining room. Has a shop and a bar that sells bread. Breakfast €3.50. Menu €10 in the restaurant. Bike room. Reservations accepted.

→**Albergue O Peregrino** Olveiroa, s∕n • Tel. 981 741 682 and 637 264 033 • Open all year. 12 beds. €10-12 per night. No kitchen. Bar/restaurant with menu. Reservations accepted.

→**Albergue Casa Pepa** In the neighbouring village of Santa Mariña, Maroñas-Mazaricos, next to the church • Tel. 981 852 881 and 686 234 342 • alberguecasapepa@yahoo. es • www.mazaricos.net • It is a bar on the ground floor. Open all year. 18 beds. €12 in bunk and €20 per person in double.

→**Albergue Santa Mariña** Santa Mariña, 14 • Tel. 981 852 897 and 653 626 864 • casaantelo@gmail.com • In the village of Santa Mariña. Open all year. Pilgrims only. 10 beds spread across two rooms. €10 per night. Kitchen and dining room. Cafeteria. Bike room. Reservations accepted.

→**Albergue municipal en Vilaserío** s∕n. Former school buildings • Tel. 648 792 029 • In Vilaserío. Open all year. 14 beds in one dormitory. Pilgrims only. No prices. Relies on voluntary donations. Reservations not accepted.

→**Also in Vilaserío:** Restaurante albergue O Rueiro. Vilaserío 28, Bugallido • Tel. 981 893 561 • contacto@ restaurantealbergueorueiro.com • WiFi • Open all year. 30 beds. €12 per night. No kitchen. Bar/restaurant. Menu €11. Bike room. Reservations accepted. Also Albergue Casa Vella (c∕. Vilaserío 23, 615 452 253, cvvilaserio@gmail.com, 14 beds. €12).

## ONCINA DE LA VALDONCINA

H

→**Albergue El Pajar** c∕. Arriba, 4 • Tel. 677 567 309 • elpajardeoncina@ gmail.com • Open all year, reservations accepted, with 9 beds in a shared dormitory. Price €10. Runs in a typical country house with more than 200 years of history.

## ORBANEJA

▢ Ⓗ Ⓐ

→**Albergue El Peregrino** Calle Principal, 1 • Tel. 947 430 980 and 622 931 076 • laura_crislaine@hotmail. com • Open all year, with 18 beds. Price €5. Bar/restaurant with menu on the ground floor. Reservations accepted.

P

## PADORNELO

▢ Ⓗ

→**Albergue El Puerto Alto do Poio** • Tel. 982 367 172 • Open all year (may close a few days in winter). 18 beds. €6 shared dormitory. Space for bikes. Reservations accepted.

## PALAS DE REI

◎

→**Albergue de peregrinos Os Chacotes** c/. As Lagartas s/n • Tel. 607 481 536 • Open all year. 112 beds. €6 shared dormitory. Kitchen. Reservations not accepted.

→**Albergue de peregrinos de Palas de Rei** Av. Compostela, 19 • Tel. 660 396 820 • Open all year. 60 beds. €6 shared dormitory. Kitchen. Space for bikes. Reservations not accepted.

→**Albergue Buen Camino** c/. Rua do Peregrino, 3 • Tel. 639 882 229 • alberguebuencamino@yahoo.es • www.alberguebuencamino.com • Open from Easter to October. 42 beds. €10 shared dormitory. Kitchen. Space for bikes. Reservations accepted.

→**Albergue Mesón de Benito** c/. Rua da Paz s/n • Tel. 636 834 065 • alberguemesondebenito@gmail.com • www.alberguemesondebenito.com • Open from Easter to October. 100 beds. €10 shared dormitory. Space for bikes. Reservations accepted.

→**Albergue Castro** Av. Ourense, 24 • Tel. 609 980 655 • info@ alberguecastro.com • www. alberguecastro.com • Open all year. 56 beds. €10 shared dormitory. Kitchen with microwaves only. Space for bikes. Reservations accepted.

→**Albergue San Marcos Travesía de la Iglesia s/n • Tel. 606 726 356 • info@alber**guesanmarcos. es • www.alberguesanmarcos.com • Open from March to November. 24 beds. €10 shared dormitory. Double and triple rooms available: €50-60. Kitchen. Space for bikes. Reservations accepted.

→**Albergue Outeiro** Pza. Galicia, 25 • Tel. 630 134 357 • info@ albergueouteiro.com • www. albergueouteiro.com • Open from March to October (rest of the year, by reservation). 50 beds. €10 shared dormitory. Kitchen. Space for bikes. Reservations accepted.

→**Albergue A Casiña di Marcello** Camiño da Aldeia de Abaixo s/n • Tel. 640 723 903 • alberguecasina@ gmail.com • www.alberguecasina. es • Open all year (winter, by reservation). 17 beds. €12-15 according to dormitory. Triple rooms available: €36. Space for bikes. Reservations accepted.

→**Albergue-pensión Zendoira** c/. Amado Losada, 10 • Tel. 629 727 605 • info@zendoira.com • www. zendoira.com • Open from March to October. 50 beds. €10 according to dormitory. Single, double and triple rooms available: €25-35-50. Kitchen. Space for bikes. Reservations accepted.

## PAMPLONA / IRUÑA
◉

→**Albergue Casa Paderborn** c/. Playa de Caparroso, 6 • Tel. 948 211 712 • jacobuspilger@paderborn.com • www.jakobusfreunde-paderborn. eu • WiFi • Open from March to November. Pilgrims only. 26 beds in dormitories of between 4 and 8 bunks. €7 per night. No kitchen. Dining room. Breakfast €3. Terrace. Bike room.

→**Albergue Plaza Catedral** c/. Navarrería, 35, bajo. In the old quarter, next to the cathedral • Tel. 948 591 336 and 620 913 968 • reservas@albergueplazacatedral. com • www.albergueplazacatedral. com • WiFi • Open all year. 46 beds. €15-18 in shared room with breakfast, from €44 for double, triple and quadruple. Kitchen and dining room. Bike room. Reservations accepted.

→**Jesús y María** c/. Compañía, 4 • Tel. 948 222 644 and 648 008 932 • jesusymaria@aspacenavarra.org • www.aspacenavarra.org/albergues-juveniles-y-peregrinos/albergue-jesus-y-maria • WiFi and computer • Open all year (except Christmas and the week of San Fermín, from 6 to 14 July). Pilgrims only. 114 beds. €10 per night. Breakfast €3.50. Kitchen and dining room. Courtyard. Bike room. Reservations accepted from October to April.

→**Hostel Hemingway** c/. Amaya, 26, 1º izq • Tel. 948 983 884 and 633 841 426 • info@hostelhemingway. com • www.hostelhemingway.com/ es • WiFi and computer • Open all year (except from 10 December to 1 January). 30 beds in five dormitories. €13-20 (according to season and day of the week) in shared dormitory with breakfast, €21-44 for double room and €32-35 for single room. Discount for pilgrims with pilgrim's passport. Kitchen and dining room. Bike room. Reservations accepted.

→**Albergue de Pamplona-Iruñako Aterpea** c/. del Carmen, 18 • Tel. 948 044 637 and 685 734 207 • alberguedepamplona@gmail.com • www.alberguedepamplona.info • WiFi • Open from 10 January to 15 December. Pilgrims only in high season. 24 beds. €15 per night with breakfast. Kitchen and dining room. Dinner €10. Breakfast €3. Courtyard. Bike room. Guests may use the Aquavox San Agustín spa and swimming pool. Reservations accepted.

→**Casa Ibarrola** c/. Carmen, 31, bajo • Tel. 948 223 332 and 692 208 463 • info@casaibarrola.com • www. casaibarrola.com • WiFi • Open all year except the week of San Fermín (from 6 to 14 July). 20 beds in one dormitory. €16 per night with breakfast included. Reservations accepted. Kitchen and dining room. Bike room. Reservations accepted.

**Other options:** Aloha Hostel (c/. Sangüesa, 2. 1º; 648 289 403; 26 beds; €15; www.alohahostel.es) and Xarma Hostel (Av/. Baja Navarra, 23; Tel 948 046 449; 18 beds. €15; www. xarmahostel.com).

## PARROCHA
▢ Ⓗ

→**Albergue de Mercadoiro, 2** • Tel. 982 454 359 • info@mercadoiro. com • www.mercadoiro.com • Open from March to mid-November. 22 beds. €12 shared dormitory. Double and triple rooms available: €50-60. Space for bikes. Reservations accepted.

## PEDROUZO
⊞ ⊠ ▢ ▢ ◔ ▢ ⊓ ⊓ Ⓗ ▱ ≋

→**AArca do Pino** c/. Arca, s/n • Tel. 660 396 826 • www.xacobeo.es • Part of the Xunta network. Open all year. Pilgrims only. 126 beds. €6 per night. Kitchen with no utensils. Bike room. Stable. Reservations not accepted.

→**Cruceiro de Pedrouzo** Av. de la Iglesia 7 • Tel. 981 511 371 and 629 518 204 • reservas@ alberguecruceirodepedrouzo.com • www.alberguecruceirodepedrouzo.com • WiFi • Open from March to November. 94 beds. €10 per night. Kitchen and dining room. Sauna (€2). Physiotherapy service. Bike room. Reservations accepted.

→**Porta de Santiago** Av. Lugo, 11 • Tel. 981 511 103 and 607 835 354 • portadesantiago@hotmail.com • www.portadesantiago.com • WiFi • Open from March to November. 54 beds. €10 per night. No kitchen but has microwaves. Dining room. Terrace. Bike room. Reservations accepted.

→**Albergue** Edreira Rúa da Fonte, 19 • Tel. 981 511 365 and 660 234 995 • info@albergue-edreira.com www.albergue-edreira.com • WiFi • Open from March to October. 52 beds. €10 in low season and €12 in high season. Bike room. Reservations accepted.

→**O Burgo** Av. de Lugo 47 • Tel. 981 511 406 and 630 404 138 • albergueoburgo@gmail.com www.albergueoburgo.com • WiFi • Open from April to October. 20 beds. €10 per night. Terrace. Foot massage. Bike room.

→**Albergue Otero** c/. Forcarei, 2 • Tel. 671 663 337 • info@albergueotero.com • WiFi • Open from April to November. 36 beds. €10 per night. No kitchen. Microwaves and fridge. Dining room. Bike room. Reservations accepted.

→**Albergue O Trisquel** Rúa do Picón, 1 • Tel. 616 644 740 • informatrisquel@gmail.com • Open from March to November. 78 beds. €10-12 per night. Kitchen and dining room. Bike room. Reservations accepted.

→**Albergue Rem** Av. de la Iglesia, 7 • Tel. 722 448 211 • reservas@ alberguerem.com • www.alberguerem.com • WiFi • Open from April to October. 40 beds. €10 in low season and €12 in high season. No kitchen. Bar/cafeteria. Bike room.

## PEREJE

→**Albergue de Pereje** Camino de Santiago s/n • Tel. 987 540 138 • Open all year. 30 beds. €5 shared dormitory. Kitchen. Space for bikes. Massages. Reservations not accepted.

## PIEROS

→**Albergue El Serbal y la Luna** c/. Pozo, 13 • Tel. 639 888 924 • alberguedepieros@gmail.com • Open from March to November. 20 beds. €5 shared dormitory. Space for bikes. Massages. Reservations accepted.

## POBLACIÓN DE CAMPOS

→**Albergue de peregrinos municipal** Paseo del Cementerio • Tel. 979 811 099 and 685 510 020 • info@amanecerencampos.net • Open all year, with 18 beds in a communal dormitory. Price €5. The owners also have a small rural hotel close to the hostel. Reservations accepted.

→**Albergue La Finca** Carretera 980, km 16 • Tel. 979 067 028 and 620 785 999 • info@alberguelafinca.es • www.alberguelafinca.es • Open all year, with 20 beds in shared dormitories. Price €10. Has a bar/restaurant with €10 menu and a large green space. Reservations accepted.

## PONFERRADA

→ **Albergue parroquial de Ponferrada** c/. La Loma, s/n • Tel. 987 413 381 • peregrinosflue@terra.es • www.sannicolasdeflue.com • WiFi • Open all year. Pilgrims only. 142 beds, increasing to 250 in summer. Relies on voluntary donations. Kitchen and dining room. Garden. Pilgrim's blessing on working days. Reservations not accepted.

→ **Albergue Alea** c/. Teleno, 33 • Tel. 987 404 133 and 660 416 251 • info@albergualea.com • www. albergualea.com • WiFi • Open from March to November. Pilgrims only. 18 beds. €10 per night. No kitchen. Dining room. Communal dinner €8. Breakfast €3. Garden. Bike room. Reservations accepted.

→ **Albergue Guiana** Av. Del Castillo, 112 • Tel. 987 409 327 • info@albergueguiana.com • www. albergueguiana.com • WiFi • Open from March to November. 90 beds in 14 dormitories and 6 private rooms. €12 per night. No kitchen. Dining room. Bike room. Breakfast €5. Sauna. Physiotherapy room. Reservations accepted.

## PORTOMARÍN

→ **Albergue de peregrinos de Portomarín** c/. Fraga Iribarne s/n • Tel. 660 396 816 • Open all year. 80 beds. €6 shared dormitory. Kitchen. Reservations not accepted.

→ **Albergue Ferramenteiro** c/. Chantada, 3 • Tel. 892 545 362 • info@albergueferramenteiro.com • www.albergueferramenteiro.com • Open from Easter to October. 130 beds. €10 shared dormitory. Kitchen. Space for bikes. Reservations accepted.

→ **Albergue-pensión El Caminante** c/. Sánchez Carro, 7 • Tel. 982 545 174 • info@pensionelcaminante. com • www.pensionelcaminante. com • Open from Easter to October. 12 beds. €10 shared dormitory.

Single, double and triple rooms available: €30-42-55. Space for bikes. Reservations accepted.

→ **Albergue-pensión PortoSantiago.** c/. Diputación, 8 • Tel. 618 826 515 • info@ albergueportosantiago.com • www. albergueportosantiago.com • Open all year (winter, by reservation). 16 beds. €10 shared dormitory. Single and double rooms available: €25-35. Kitchen. Space for bikes. Massages. Reservations accepted.

→ **Albergue-pensión Manuel** c/. Miño, 1 • Tel. 679 754 718 • pensionmanuel1@gmail.com • www. pensionmanuel.es • Open from April to November. 16 beds. €10 shared dormitory. Double and triple rooms available: €25-38. Kitchen. Space for bikes. Reservations accepted.

→ **Albergue-pensión Ultreia** c/. Diputación, 9 • Tel. 676 607 292 • Email info@ultreiaportomarin. com • www.ultreiaportomarin. com • Open all year. 14 beds. €10 shared dormitory. Single, double and triple rooms available: €35-40-50. Kitchen. Space for bikes. Massages. Reservations accepted.

→ **Albergue Novo Porto** c/. Benigno Quiroga, 12 • Tel. 610 436 736 • novoporto@gmail.com • www. alberguenovoporto.com • Open from April to November. 22 beds. €10 shared dormitory. Kitchen. Space for bikes. Reservations accepted.

→ **Albergue Folgueira** Av. Chantada, 18 • Tel. 659 445 651 • info@ alberguefolgueira.com • www. alberguefolgueira.com • Open all year. 32 beds. €10 shared dormitory. Kitchen. Space for bikes. Reservations accepted.

→ **Albergue Villamartín** c/. Peregrino, 11 • Tel. 982 545 054 • reservas@hotelvillajardin.com • www.alberguevillamartin.webnode. es • Open from April to October. 22 beds. €10 shared dormitory. Kitchen. Space for bikes. Reservations accepted.

→**Albergue Casa Cruz** c/. Benigno Quiroga, 16 • Tel. 652 204 548 • info@casacruzportomarin.com • www.casacruzportomarin.com • Open all year. 16 beds. €10 shared dormitory. Kitchen. Space for bikes. Reservations accepted.

→**Albergue Casa do Marabillas** Camiño do Monte, 3 • Tel. 744 450 425 • www.casadomarabillas. com • Open from March to October. 16 beds. €15 shared dormitory (breakfast included). Single and double rooms available: €30-35. Kitchen. Space for bikes. Reservations accepted.

→**Albergue-pensión Pons Minea** Av. Sarria, 11 • Tel. 610 737 995 • info@ ponsminea.es • www.ponsminea. es • Open from April to November. 24 beds. €10 shared dormitory. Single, double, triple and quadruple rooms available: €40-50-65-80. Reservations accepted.

→**Albergue-pensión Aqua Portomarín** c/. Barreiros, 2 • Tel. 608 921 372 • albergueaquaportomarin@ hotmail.com • Open from March to November. 10 beds. €10 shared dormitory. Single and double rooms available: €30-35. Kitchen. Space for bikes. Reservations accepted.

→**Albergue Pasiño a Pasiño** c/. Rua de Compostela, 25 • Tel. 665 667 243 • alberguepasoapaso@gmail.com • www.pasinapasin.es • Open all year (winter, by reservation). 30 beds. €10 shared dormitory. Kitchen. Space for bikes. Reservations accepted.

→**Albergue A Fontana de Luxo** c/. Fontedagra, 2 • Tel. 645 649 496 • info@afontanadeluxo.com • www. afontanadeluxo.com. Open all year (winter, by reservation). 10 beds. €15 shared dormitory. Single and double rooms available: €35-42. Kitchen. Space for bikes. Reservations accepted.

→**Albergue Casona da Ponte** Camiño da Capela, 10 • Tel. 686 112 877 • casonadaponte@gmail.com • Open from March to November.

47 beds. €10 shared dormitory. Kitchen. Space for bikes. Reservations accepted.

## PORTOS
Ⓗ
→**Albergue-pensión A Paso de Formiga Portos,** 4 • Tel. 618 984 605 • apasodeformiga@hotmail. com • www.apasodeformiga.com • Open from Easter to October. 12 beds. €10-12 according to dormitory. Double rooms available: €40. Space for bikes. Reservations accepted.

## PUENTE LA REINA
⊞✖▣🖉⬚🗑🛏🚪⬛@
→**Albergue de los Padres Reparadores** c/. Crucifijo, 1 • Tel. 948 340 050 and 689 447 222, mobile from Easter to November • econo.puente@esic.es • Open all year. Pilgrims only. 96 beds in 12 dormitories. €5 per night. Kitchen and dining room. Garden. Daily Mass at 7.30pm. Bike room. Reservations not accepted.

→**Albergue Jakue** c/. Irunbidea, 34 • Tel. 948 341 017 • www.jakue.com/el-albergue • Open from April to October. Pilgrims only. 85 beds (40 in bunks and 45 in beds. From €11-12 per night (double with sofa, bed and bath, €36-40). Kitchen and dining room. Bar/restaurant. Dinner €13 and breakfast €4. Reservations accepted.

→**Albergue Santiago Apóstol** 400 metres from the town, over the bridge • Tel. 948 340 220 and 660 701 246 • alberguesantiagoapostol@ hotmail.com • WiFi • Open from Easter to October. Pilgrims only. 100 beds. €10-12 in bunk, €14 per person in doubles, €15 per person in bungalows for 4-6 people. Camping for €6. No kitchen. Bar/restaurant. Menu for €10. Swimming pool. Bike room. Reservations accepted.

→**Albergue Puente** Paseo de
Los Fueros, 57 • Tel. 661 705 642 •
albergue@alberguepuente.com
• http://alberguepuente.com •
WiFi • Open from 15 March to 15
November. Pilgrims only. 38 beds.
€13 in shared rooms and €34 for the
double room. Kitchen and dining
room. Buffet breakfast included.
Pilgrim's menu €10. Bike room.
Reservations accepted.
→, **Albergue Estrella Guía** Paseo
de Los Fueros, 34, 2º • Tel. 622 262
431 • alberguestellaguia@gmail.com
• www.facebook.com/Albergue-
Estrella-Guia-723219327760570 •
Open from March to November.
6 beds. €15 (with breakfast).
No kitchen, only microwaves.
Communal dinner served (by
voluntary donation). Balcony. Bike
room. Reservations accepted.

## PUENTE DE VILLARENTE
🞌🞌🞌🞌🞌🞌 H A 🞌🞌
→**Albergue San Pelayo** c/. El
Romero, 9. Tel • 650 918 281,
615 459 919 and 987 312 677 •
alberguesanpelayo@hotmail.com •
Open all year (advisable to contact
in winter), with 66 beds in communal
rooms (€8-10), singles (€30), doubles
(€40) and triples (€57). Has bar/
restaurant and serves breakfast
(€3), dinner (€10) and menus. Pretty
garden with tables and balcony.
Reservations accepted.
→**Albergue-Hostal El Delfín Verde**
Carretera N-601, 15 • Tel. 987 312
065 • info@complejoeldelfinverde.
es • http://complejoeldelfinverde.
es • The hostel is annexed to the
guest house, opens from March
to October, and has 20 beds in
dormitories of 4, 6 and 10 people.
Communal dormitory €5, single
€25, double €40 and triple €55.
Swimming pool in summer and
bar/restaurant with menu at €10.
Reservations accepted.

## R

## RABANAL DEL CAMINO
🞌🞌🞌 H A
→A**Albergue Municipal** Pza.
Jerónimo Morán • Tel. 678
433 962 and 655 274 613 •
municipalrabanalbergue@gmail.
com • Open all year (confirm in
winter), with 36 beds in communal
dormitories. Price €5. It has a pretty
garden with the option to camp,
a picnic area and hammocks for
relaxation. It was renovated in 2018.
Reservations accepted.
→**Albergue Nuestra Señora del
Pilar** Pza. Jerónimo Morán • Tel.
616 089 942 and 987 631 621 •
rabanalelpilar@hotmail.com •
albergueelpilar.com • Open all
year, with 76 beds spread across
communal and double rooms. Price
€5 and €35 for doubles. Serves
combined dishes and breakfast for
€3. Reservations accepted.
→**Albergue Gaucelmo** Pza. del
Peregrino Julián Campo • Tel. 987
631 615 and 987 631 647 • Open from
Easter to October, with 44 beds in
dormitories of between 4 and 20
beds. Runs on voluntary donations.
The hostel belongs to the UK
association, the Confraternity of
Saint James, and the Asociación de
Amigos del Camino de Santiago del
Bierzo. It has a garden and offers
breakfast and meals. Reservations
accepted.
→A**Albergue La Senda** c/. Real, s/n
• Tel. 669 167 038 and 696 819 060
• alberguelasenda@hotmail.com •
http://hostel-caminodesantiago.
com • Open from Easter to October,
with 34 beds in shared dormitories.
Price €5. It has a camping area for
putting up a tent, a bar/restaurant
and massage service. Reservations
accepted.

## RABÉ DE LAS CALZADAS

→ **Albergue Liberanos Domine** Plaza Francisco Riberas, 10 • Tel. 695 116 901 • clementinadelatorre@gmail.com • www.liberanosdomine.com • Open all year, with 24 beds divided into four rooms of 8, 6 and 4 people. Prices: bed €9, dinner €8 and breakfast €3. Reservations accepted.

## REDECILLA DEL CAMINO

→ **Albergue municipal San Lázaro** c/. Mayor, 24, opposite the church • Tel. 947 585 221 and 686 563 548 • www.redecilladelcamino.es/alojamiento/albergue-de-peregrinos • WiFi and computer • Open all year. 50 beds in dormitories of between 2 and 12 bunks. €5. Kitchen and dining room. Restaurant: menus by voluntary donation from April to September and breakfast by voluntary donation all year. Courtyard. Bike room.

→ **Albergue Essentia** c/. Mayor, 34 • Tel. 606 046 298 • manuramirez6@hotmail.com • www.facebook.com/Albergue-Essentia-611390189025932 • It opened in 2016. Open all year. Pilgrims only. 10 beds in shared rooms. €10. Kitchen and dining room. Dinner €10 and breakfast €3. Bike room. Reservations accepted.

## RELIEGOS

→ **Albergue municipal Don Gaiferos** c/. Don Gaiferos, 1 • Tel. 686 527 505 and 987 317 801 • Open all year, with 45 beds in four communal dormitories. Price €5. Reservations not accepted.

→ **Albergue La Parada** c/. La Escuela, 7 • Tel. 987 317 880 • alberguelaparada@gmail.com • www.alberguelaparada.com • Open from April to November, with 40 beds in shared and double rooms. Price €7 and €30 for double room. Bar/restaurant with pilgrim's menu

(€10) or à la carte. Reservations accepted.

→ **Albergue de Ada** c/. Real, 42 • Tel. 691 153 010 • alberguedeada@gmail.com • www.alberguereliegos.es • Open from April to mid-October (rest of the year, by reservation), with 20 beds and a room for disabled people. Price from €8. Vegetarian dinner €9 and breakfast €4. Reservations accepted.

→ **Albergue Gil** Calle Cantas, 18 • Tel. 620 424 271 and 987 317 804 • albergueguil@outlook.es • Open from Easter to November, with 23 beds in communal rooms (€8) and double rooms (€30). Bar/restaurant service. Reservations accepted.

→ **Albergue Vive tu Camino** c/. Real, 56 • Tel. 987 317 837 and 610 293 986 • alberguevivetucamino@gmail.com • www.alberguevivetucamino.com • Open from March to October, with communal rooms and one double. Price €9 and €35 for the double. Provides communal dinner (€9) and breakfast (€3) and has an inner courtyard. Reservations accepted.

→ **Albergue La Cantina de Teddy** Camino Real, s/n • Tel. 622 206 128 and 987 190 627 • monteciber@hotmail.com • Previously it was the Piedras Blancas II. Open from April to October, with communal and double rooms. Price €9 and €30-40 for doubles. Bar/restaurant. Reservations accepted.

## RIBADISO DE BAIXO

→ **Albergue de peregrinos de Ribadiso de Baixo** Ribadiso s/n • Tel. 660 396 823 • Open all year. 70 beds. €6 shared dormitory. Kitchen. Space for bikes. Reservations not accepted.

→ **Albergue Los Caminantes** Ribadiso s/n • Tel. 647 020 600 • info@alberguloscaminantes.com • www.alberguloscaminantes.com • Open from Easter to October. 56 beds. €10 shared dormitory. Double rooms available at €35-40. Kitchen. Space for bikes. Camping area. Reservations accepted.

→**Albergue Milpés** Ribadiso, 7 • Tel. 616 652 276 • alberguemilpes@gmail. com • www.alberguemilpes.com • Open all year. 24 beds. €10 shared dormitory. Kitchen with microwaves only. Reservations accepted.

## RIEGO DE AMBRÓS
🅟 🄷 🄰

→**Albergue municipal de Riego de Ambrós** c/. Real, 100 (next to the hermitage of San Sebastián) • Tel. 640 376 118 and 669 413 491 • valdcarrizo@gmail.com • Open from March to October, with 27 beds in rooms of 2 and 4 bunks and 6 beds on mattresses on a platform. Price €6. Has bar/restaurant with dinner and breakfast for €16. Reservations accepted.

## RONCESVALLES / ORREAGA
→**Albergue de peregrinos de Roncesvalles** Real Colegiata de Roncesvalles • Tel. 948 760 000 and 948 760 029 • info@ albergueroncesvalles.com • www. albergueroncesvalles.com • WiFi • Open all year (from November to March it relocates to the Albergue de la Colegiata with 34 beds and in summer it becomes a camping area). 183 beds. Maximum stay of one night. €12. Kitchen and dining room. Bike room. Pilgrim's passport issued. Blessing of the pilgrim at 8pm and 6pm (weekends). Reservations accepted with five days' notice and by e-mail.

## RUA
🅟 🄷

→**Cámping Peregrino O Castiñeiro** A Rúa, 28 • Tel. 662 456 093 • info@ campingperegrino.es • www. campingperegrino.es • Open from April to October. 112 beds. €10-12 according to dormitory. Space for bikes. Reservations accepted.

## RUITELÁN
🄷

→**Albergue El Rincón de Pin** Ctra. N-VI, 41A • Tel. 616 066 442 • alberguepin@gmail.com • Open all year. 10 beds. €10 shared dormitory. Double and triple rooms available: €38-55. Reservations accepted.

## S

## SAHAGÚN
🔲 🔲 🔲 🔲 🔲 🄷 🄰 🄣🄐🄧 🔲 🔲 🔲 🄲 🔲

→**Albergue de Peregrinos Cluny** c/. Arco, 87, iglesia de la Trinidad • Tel. 987 781 015 and 662 147 431 • otsahagun@hotmail.com • Reservations not accepted, with 64 beds in communal dormitories. Price €5. The hostel closes in winter so, more or less until Easter, the town council fits out other premises with 16 beds, in calle Antonio Nicolás, 55. Tel. 987 780 001.

→**Albergue Santa Cruz** c/. Antonio Nicolás, 40 • Monasterio de Santa Cruz • Tel. 650 696 023 • alberguesantacruzsahagun@gmail. com • www.alberguesensahagun.es • Open from February to November, with 58 beds in dormitories of 4 and 6 beds and guest quarters with double and single rooms located in the former monastery of the Benedictine Mothers. Prices: €5 and €15-20 in double room. Provides shared dinner, a pilgrims' meeting at 5pm, Mass at 6pm and blessing of the pilgrim at 7pm. Reservations accepted.

→**Hostal-Albergue Viatoris** c/. Arco, 31 • Tel. 987 780 975 and 679 977 828 • aaocho@hotmail.com • www.domusviatoris.com • Open from March to November, with 50 beds in shared dormitories (€5-7) and an annexed guest house with single rooms (€18), doubles (€25) and triples (€36). Dinner €10, breakfast €4 and restaurant with à la carte menu. Reservations accepted.

→**Albergue El Labriego** Av. Doctores Bermejo y Calderón, 9 • Tel. 722 115 161 and 622 646 136 • reservas@alberguesellabriego. com • Open all year, with 19 beds in a shared dormitory. Price €8. Lunch €10, communal dinner €7.50 and breakfast €3.50. It is a former abbey, with inner courtyard and chapel, adapted as an inn and hostel. Reservations accepted.

## SAINT-JEAN-PIED-DE-PORT / DONIBANE GARAZI

🅟 ✖ 🖳 🛡 🏧 🍴 🛏 🅗 TAXI 🚍 🛢 @

→**Ospitalia Refuge municipal** Rue de la Citadelle, 55 • Tel. 0033 559 491 086 • www.amisvieillenavarre. fr/ospitalia-refuge-municipal-les-chemins-de-st-jacques • WiFi • Open all year. 32 beds in three dormitories. €10 per night with breakfast included (€30 for the only double room). Microwaves and fridge, no kitchen. Terrace. Reservations not accepted.

→**Refuge Accueil Paroissial Kaserna** Rue d'Espagne, 43 • Tel. 0033 559 376 517 • www.saintjeanpieddeport-paysbasque-tourisme.com/refuge-accueil-paroissial/151 • WiFi • Open from April to October. Pilgrims only. 14 beds in two dormitories. €20 half board, although can be paid for by working. Communal dinner and breakfast. Reservations only accepted the day before.

→**Gîte Ultreia** Rue de la Citadelle, 8 • Tel. 0033 680 884 622 • gite. ultreia@vertesmontagnes.fr • www. ultreia64.fr • WiFi • 17 beds • Open from April to October. €22 for bed and breakfast in room of 4 or 7 beds, €56-68 in the two double rooms. Kitchen and terrace. Bike room. Pilgrim's passport issued. Reservations accepted.

→**Gîte Beilari** Rue de la Citadelle, 40 • Tel. 0033 559 372 468 • info@beilari. info • www.beilari.info/es • Open from 15 March to October. 18 beds. €33 half board (accommodation, pilgrim's menu and breakfast). The kitchen cannot be used. Communal dinners. Bike room. Reservations accepted.

→**Le Chemin vers l'Etoile** Rue d'Espagne, 21 • Tel. 0033 559 372 071 and 0033 670 208 213 • www.pelerinage-saint-jacques-compostelle.com • WiFi • Open all year (between November and March it is essential to make a reservation 15 days in advance). 20 beds in dormitories for 8 to 12 people. €17-20 with breakfast included and €12 for dinner (take-away picnic, €5-7). Garden. Bike room. Guitar. Reservations accepted.

→**Gîte Izaxulo** Av. Renaud, 2 • Tel. 0033 524 341 900 • contact@gite-izaxulo.com • www.gite-izaxulo. com/legite.html • WiFi • Open from March to October. 18 beds in 3 dormitories and 2 private rooms. €24 per night, €27 with breakfast and €72 in the double. No kitchen. Bike room. Reservations accepted.

→**Gîte Buen Camino** Rue de la Citadelle, 30 • Tel. 00 33 663 261 202 and 0033 559 372 523 • gitebuencamino@gmail.com • www. gitebuencamino.com/• WiFi • Open all year. 15 beds. €16 in dormitory, €18 in quadruple, €46 in double. Dining room but no kitchen. Bar/restaurant. Breakfast €5. Dinner €13. Take-away picnic €7. Two terraces. Garden. Bike room. Reservations accepted.

→**Gîte Compostelle** Route d'Arneguy, 6 • Tel. 0033 559 370 236 • gitecompostella@sfr.fr • Open from March to October. 14 beds in 5 dormitories. €12. Kitchen and dining room. Reservation compulsory.

## SALCEDA

➜**Albergue-pensión turístico Salceda** Ctra. N-574 km 75 • Tel. 981 502 767 • pousadadesalceda@ gmail.com • www. albergueturisticosalceda.com • Open all year. 8 beds. €13 communal dormitory. Single, double, triple and quadruple rooms available: €40-47-65-75. Space for bikes. Reservations accepted.

➜**Albergue de Boni** Lugar de Salceda, 22 • Tel. 618 965 907 • elalberguedeboni@gmail.com • www.elalberguedeboni.blogspot. com.es • Open from Easter to mid-November. 20 beds. €12 shared dormitory. Kitchen with microwaves only. Space for bikes. Reservations accepted.

➜**Albergue-pensión Alborada** Lugar de Salceda s/n • Tel. 620 151 209 • pensionalberguealborada@ gmail.com • Open from May to November. 10 beds. €12 communal dormitory. Double rooms available: €50. Kitchen. Space for bikes. Massages. Reservations accepted.

## SAMOS

➜**Albergue del monasterio** c/. Monasterio de Samos, 1 • Tel. 982 54 60 46 • info@abadiadesamos. com • www.abadiadesamos.com • Open all year. 66 beds. Relies on voluntary donations. Space for bikes. Reservations not accepted.

➜**Albergue Val de Samos** Av. Compostela, 16 • Tel. 609 638 801 • info@valdesamos.com • www. valdesamos.com • Open from April to November. 48 beds. €10 shared dormitory. Kitchen. Space for bikes (chargeable). Reservations accepted.

➜**Albergue Albaroque.** c/. El Salvador, 1. Tel. 628 828 845 • Open all year. 10 beds. €10 shared dormitory. Space for bikes. Reservations accepted.

## SAN JUAN DE ORTEGA

➜**Albergue parroquial de San Juan de Ortega** c/. de la Iglesia, 1 • Tel. 947 560 438 • sanjuandeortega@gmail.com • www.alberguesanjuandeortega. es • Open from March to October, with 60 beds in shared dormitories. Price €10. Communal dinner €9. Mass and blessing of the pilgrim at 6pm. Garlic soup is served free of charge at the end of the blessing, an act of hospitality started by Father José María, who died in 2008. Reservations not accepted.

## SAN CRISTÓBAL DO REAL

➜**Albergue Casa Forte de Lusío** (past the village) • Tel. 659 721 324 • Open all year. 60 beds. €6 shared dormitory. Kitchen. Space for bikes. Reservations not accepted.

## SAN NICOLÁS DEL REAL CAMINO

➜**Alberguería Laganares** Plaza de la Iglesia • Tel. 979 188 142 and 629 181 536 • laganares@yahoo.es • www. alberguelaganares.com • Open from mid-March to October, with 20 beds distributed in rooms of 4 and 6 beds. Prices: €9, breakfast €2.50 and lunch/dinner €10. It is located in a typical house made of mud and packed earth with a wooden roof, restored so as to be in keeping with its traditional architecture. Reservations accepted.

## SANSOL

→**Albergue Sansol** c/. Barrio Nuevo, 4 • Tel. 948 648 473 and 609 203 206 • info@deshojandoelcamino.com • www.deshojandoelcamino.com • WiFi • Open from Easter to October. 26 beds in a communal dormitory. €10 per night. Lunch or dinner €10 (Moroccan menu option at the same price) and breakfast €4. Moroccan infusions. Garden and foot bath. Bike room. Reservations accepted.

→**Albergue Codés** Los Bodegones s/n, on the outskirts of the village • Tel. 689 804 028 • www. alberguerestaurantecodes.com • WiFi • Open from April to October. 20 beds. €12 in bunk bed. €15 in quadruple. Bar/restaurant. Terrace.

## SANTA CATALINA DE SOMOZA

→**Albergue Hospedería San Blas** c/. Real, 11 • Tel. 987 691 411 and 637 464 833 • Open all year (by reservation in low season), reservations accepted, with 24 beds in communal dormitories and double rooms. Prices: communal dormitory €5 (€7 with heating), single €30, double €35-40 and triple €45-50. Has a bar/restaurant that provides bed and breakfast.

→**Albergue-Casa Rural El Caminante** c/. Real, 2 • Tel. 987 691 098 and 638 102 837 • elcaminante. ctr@gmail.com • www.elcaminante. es • Open all year, reservations accepted, with 22 beds (€5 and €8 with heating). Besides the hostel, there is a country house with 12 rooms (€35-40 for doubles, €50-60 for triples and €60 for quadruples). It has a bar/restaurant and provides menus.

## SANTA IRENE

→**Albergue de peregrinos de Santa Irene** Santa Irene s/n • Open all year. 32 beds. €6 communal dormitory. Kitchen. Space for bikes. Reservations not accepted.

## SANTIAGO DE COMPOSTELA

→**Seminario Menor La Asunción** Av. Quiroga Palacios, s/n • Tel. 881 031 768 and 981 568 521 • santiago@ alberguesdelcamino • www. alberguesdelcamino.com • WiFi • Open from March to November. 177 beds. €12 in communal rooms and €17 in single rooms. Kitchen and dining room. Terrace. Bike room. Stays of more than one night are allowed. Reservations accepted.

→**Residencia de peregrinos San Lázaro** Rúa San Lázaro, s/n • Tel. 981 571 488 and 618 266 894 • Open all year. Pilgrims only. 80 beds. €10 for the first night and €7 for following nights (maximum three nights). From €25 to €35 in private rooms. No kitchen, only microwaves. Kitchen and dining room. Terrace. Bike room. Reservations accepted.

→**Santo Santiago** Rúa do Valiño, 3 • Tel. 657 402 403 • elsantosantiago@ gmail.com • www.elsantosantiago. com • WiFi and computer • Open all year. 38 beds. €12-20 per night. Bike room.

→**Albergue Fin del Camino** Rúa de Moscova, s/n • Tel. 981 587 324 • albergue@ fundacionperegrinacionasantiago. com • www.alberguefindelcamino. com/index.php/es/ • WiFi and computers • Open at Easter and from May to October. Pilgrims only. 110 beds in five dormitories. €9 per night. Kitchen and dining room. Garden. Bike room. Reservations not accepted.

→**Mundoalbergue** c/. San Clemente, 26 • Tel. 981 588 625 and 696 448 737 • info@mundoalbergue. es • www.mundoalbergue.es • WiFi and computer • Open all year. 34 beds. €17 in high season and €12 in low season. Breakfast €3. No closing time. Kitchen and dining room. Bike room. Reservations accepted.

→**O Fogar de Teodomiro**
Pza. Algalia de Arriba, 3 • Tel.
981 582 920 and 699 631 592 •
fogarteodomiro@aldahotels.com
• www.fogarteodomiro.com • WiFi
• Open all year. 20 beds. €15 per
night. Kitchen and dining room.
Reservations accepted.

→**Albergue La Estación** Rúa
de Xoana Nogueira, 14 • Tel. 981
594 624 and 639 228 617 • info@
alberguelaestacion.com • www.
alberguelaestacion.com • WiFi •
Open from Easter to September.
24 beds in dormitories. €15 from
June to August, €13 the rest of the
year. Massage service. Bike room.
Reservations accepted.

→**Albergue Acuario** c/. Estocolmo,
s/n • Tel. 981 57 54 38 • reservas@
acuariosantiago.com • www.
acuariosantiago.com • WiFi • Open
all year except January and February.
60 beds in rooms for 4, 6, 8 and
12 people. From €10 per night.
Microwaves and fridge. Bike room.

→**Roots & Boots** Rúa do Cruceiro
do Gaio, 7 • Tel. 699 631 594 •
info@rootsandboots.es • www.
rootsandboots.es • WiFi • Open all
year. 48 beds. From €15. Bike room.
Reservations accepted.

→**Albergue del Monte do Gozo** c/.
Rúa do Gozo, 18 • Tel. 660 396 827 •
Open all year. 500 beds. €6 shared
dormitory. Kitchen. Reservations not
accepted.

→**Albergue Meiga Backpackers** c/.
Rúa dos Barquiños, 67 • Tel. 981 570
846 • info_meiga@yahoo.es • www.
meiga-backpackers.es • Open all
year except Christmas. 26 beds. €13-
15 according to dormitory. Kitchen.
Space for bikes. Reservations not
accepted.

→**Albergue The Last Stamp** c/. Rúa
do Preguntoiro, 10 • Tel. 981 563 525
• reservas@thelaststamp.es • www.
thelaststamp.es • Open all year
except 15 December to 15 January. 62
beds. €15 shared dormitory. Kitchen.
Space for bikes. Reservations
accepted.

→**Albergue Porta Real** c/.
Concheiros, 10 • Tel. 633 610 114 •
reservas@albergueportareal.es •
www.albergueportareal.es • Open all
year. 24 beds. €10-20 according to
dormitory. Kitchen with microwaves
only. Space for bikes. Reservations
accepted.

→**Albergue Azabache c/. Rúa
Acibechería, 15 • Tel. 9**81 071 254 •
azabachehostel@yahoo.es • www.
azabache-santiago-com. Open all
year (by reservation in low season).
20 beds. €14-18 according to
dormitory. Kitchen. Reservations
accepted.

→**Albergue La Credencial** Fonte dos
Concheiros, 13 • Tel. 639 966 701 •
reservaslacredencial@gmail.com •
www.lacredencial.es • Open from
March to November. 36 beds. €10-14
according to dormitory. Kitchen.
Space for bikes. Reservations
accepted.

→**Albergue Monterrey** c/. Rúa
das Fontiñas, 65 • Tel. 655 484 299
• rstmonterrey@gmail.com • www.
alberguemonterrey.es • Open all
year. 36 beds. €10-14 according to
dormitory. Kitchen. Space for bikes.
Reservations accepted.

→**Albergue Blanco** c/. Rúa das
Galeras, 30 • Tel. 699 591 238 •
blancoalbergue@gmail.com • Open
all year. 20 beds. €12-20 according
to dormitory. Kitchen. Space for
bikes. Reservations accepted.

→**Albergue La Estrella de
Santiago** c/. Rúa dos Concheiros,
36-38 • Tel. 617 882 529 • info@
laestrelladesantiago.es • www.
laestrelladesantiago.es • Open from
February to December. 24 beds. €10-
16 according to dormitory. Kitchen

with microwaves only. Space for bikes. Reservations accepted.

→**Albergue Compostela** c/. San Pedro de Mezonzo, 28 • Tel. 628 306 556 • contacto@ alberguecompostela.es • www. alberguecompostela.es • Open all year. 66 beds. €15 shared dormitory. Kitchen. Space for bikes. Reservations accepted.

→**Albergue Basquiños 45** c/. Rúa dos Basquiños, 45 • Tel. 661 894 536 • albergue45@gmail.com • www. albergueb45.com • Open all year (by reservation in low season). 6 beds. €10-16 shared dormitory. Space for bikes. Reservations accepted.

→**Albergue Santiago km 0** c/. Rúa Carretas, 11 • Tel. 881 974 992 • info@ santiagokm0.es • www.albergueb45. com • www.santiagokm0.es • Open from the end of February to the end of December. 46 beds. €18-26 according to dormitory. Kitchen. Space for bikes. Reservations accepted.

→**Albergue El Viejo Quijote** c/. Rúa dos Concheiros, 48 • Tel. 631 649 910 • Open all year. 22 beds. €13 shared dormitory. Reservations accepted.

→**Albergue turístico La Salle** c/. Rúa de Tras Santa Clara • Tel. 682 158 011 • Open all year except 22 December to 31 January. 84 beds. €17 shared dormitory. Kitchen with microwaves only. Space for bikes. Reservations accepted.

**Other options.** Santiago is full of hotels, B&Bs and guest houses for all tastes and budgets. Some Wayfarers decide that they have earned a night in the Parador Nacional, in the Plaza del Obradoiro itself (Tel. 981 582 200). The city has a lot to offer in terms of accommodation. For more modest budgets: Pensión da Estrela. Pza. San Martiño, 5. Tel. 981 576 924; Hostal Alameda. Rúa San Clemente, 32. Tel. 981 588 100; Hostal Pazo de Agra. c/. Caldeirería, 37. Tel. 981 882 660; Hostal La Carballinesa. c/. Patio de Madres, 14. Tel. 981 586 261.

## SANTIBÁÑEZ DE VALDEIGLESIAS
**H**

→**Albergue parroquial** Carromonte, 3 • Tel. 987 377 698 • Open from March to November, with 20 beds in dormitories of 4 and 6 beds. Price €6 and €16 with half board. Serves breakfast, lunch and communal dinner. Holds pilgrim's Mass and blessing at 8pm. Reservations not accepted.

→**Albergue Camino Francés** c/. Real, 68 • Tel. 987 361 014 • albergcaminofrances@gmail.com • http://alberguecaminofrances. com • Open from March to October, with 14 beds spread across one communal room for 12 people and one double room with en-suite bathroom. Price €8.50 and €35 for the double. Lunch and dinner €9.50, breakfast from €1.20. Reservations accepted.

## SANTO DOMINGO DE LA CALZADA

→**Abadía Cisterciense** c/. Mayor, 31 • Tel. 941 340 700 • hospederia@ cister-lacalzada.com • www.cister-lacalzada.com/albergue • WiFi • Open from May to September. Pilgrims only. 33 beds. €8 per night. Kitchen and dining room. Dinner €10 and breakfast €4. Bike room. It is possible to take part in religious ceremonies. Reservations not accepted.

→**Cofradía del Santo** c/. Mayor, 38-42 • Tel. 941 343 390 • albergue@ alberguecofradiadelsanto.com • www.alberguecofradiadelsanto. com • WiFi and computer • Open all year. Pilgrims only. 143 beds in the new building and 74 in the old. Dormitories of between 10 and 26 beds (including one for snorers). €7 per night. Kitchen and dining room. Pilgrim's passport issued. Bike room. Reservations accepted.

## SARRIA

◎

→**Albergue de peregrinos de Sarria** c/. Rúa Mayor, 79 • sarria@alberguesdelcamino.com • www.alberguesdelcamino.com • Tel. 982 533 568 • Open all year. 40 beds. €6 shared dormitory. Kitchen. Reservations not accepted.

→**Albergue Monasterio de la Magdalena** Av. La Merced, 60 • www.xacobeo.es • Tel. c/. Rúa Mayor, 79 • Open from March to October. 100 beds. €6 shared dormitory. Kitchen. Space for bikes. Reservations accepted.

→**Albergue Don Álvaro** c/. Rúa Mayor, 10 • Tel. 686 468 803 • info@alberguedonalvaro.com • www.alberguedonalvaro.com • Open all year. 40 beds. €9 shared dormitory. Single and double rooms available: €35-45. Kitchen. Space for bikes. Reservations accepted.

→**Albergue O Durmiñento** c/. Rúa Mayor, 44 • Tel. 600 862 508 • durmiento_sarria@hotmail.com • www.alberguelosblasones.com • Open from March to November. 42 beds. €8-9 according to dormitory. Reservations accepted except in summer.

→**Albergue Los Blasones** c/. Rúa Mayor, 31 • Tel. 600 512 565 • info@alberguelosblasones.com • www.facebook.com/Albergue-O-Durmiñento • Open from April to November. 41 beds. €10 shared dormitory. Kitchen. Space for bikes. Reservations accepted.

→**Albergue dos Oito Marabedís** c/. Conde de Lemos, 23 • Tel. 629 461 770 • Open from May to October. 22 beds. €9-10 according to dormitory. Kitchen. Space for bikes. Reservations accepted.

→**Albergue Internacional** c/. Rúa Mayor, 57 · Tel. 982 535 109 • info@albergueinternacionalsarria.es • www.albergueinternacionalsarria.es • Open all year (in winter by reservation). 43 beds. €10 shared dormitory. Double rooms available: €45. Kitchen with microwaves only. Space for bikes. Reservations accepted.

→**Albergue San Lázaro** c/. San Lázaro, 6 • Tel. 659 185 482 • alberguesanlazaro@hotmail.com • www.alberguesanlazaro.com • Open from April to October. 28 beds. €10 shared dormitory. Single, double and quadruple rooms available: €28-35-48. Kitchen with microwaves only. Space for bikes. Reservations accepted.

→**Albergue Casa Peltre** c/. Escalinata Mayor, 10 • Tel. 606 226 067 • alberguecasapeltre@hotmail.com • www.casapeltre.es • Open from April to October. 22 beds. €10 shared dormitory. Kitchen. Space for bikes. Reservations accepted.

→**Albergue Mayor.** c/. Rúa Mayor, 64 • Tel. 671 659 998 • alberguemayor@gmail.com • www.alberguemayor.es • Open from March to October. 16 beds. €10 shared dormitory. Kitchen. Space for bikes. Reservations accepted.

→**Albergue-pensión A Pedra** c/. Vigo de Sarria, 19 • Tel. 652 517 199 • info@albergueapedra.com • www.albergueapedra.com • Open from March to November. 15 beds. €10 shared dormitory. Single and double rooms available: €35-42. Kitchen. Space for bikes. Reservations accepted.

→**Albergue Oasis.** Camino a Triacastela, 12 • Tel. 605 948 644 • reservas@albergueoasis.com • www.albergueoasis.com • Open from March to October (rest of the year, by reservation). 27 beds. €10 shared dormitory. Kitchen. Space for bikes. Reservations accepted.

→**Albergue Obradoiro** c/. Rua Mayor, 49 bajo • Tel. 647 209 267 • reservas@albergueobradoirosarria.es • www.albergueobradoirosarria.es • Open from Easter to October. 28 beds. €8-10 according to dormitory. Kitchen. Space for bikes. Reservations accepted.

→**Albergue Credencial** c/. Rua do Peregrino, 50 • Tel. 654 535 333 • alberguecredencial@gmail.com • www.alberguepuenteribeira.com • Open all year. 28 beds. €9-10 according to dormitory. Space for bikes. Reservations accepted.

→A**Albergue-pensión Puente Ribeira** c/. Rua do Peregrino, 23 • Tel. 698 175 619 • info@ alberguepuenteribeira.com • www. alberguecredencial.es • Open from March to October. 41 beds. €9 shared dormitory. Single and double rooms available: €20-30. Kitchen with microwaves only. Space for bikes. Reservations accepted.

→**Albergue Alma do Camiño.** c/. Rua Calvo Sotelo, 199 • Tel. 629 82 20 36 • sarria@almadocamino.com • www.almadelcamino.com • Open from March to October. 100 beds. €9 shared dormitory. Kitchen. Space for bikes. Reservations accepted.

→**Albergue Matías** c/. Rua Mayor, 4 • Tel. 683 243 335 • info@matiaslocanda.es • info@ matiaslocanda.es • Open all year. 30 beds. €9 shared dormitory. Reservations accepted.

→**Albergue La Casona de Sarria** c/. San Lázaro, 24 • Tel. 670 036 444 • info@lacasonadesarria.es • www.lacasonadesarria.es • Open all year (by reservation in winter). 24 beds. €10 shared dormitory. Single, double and triple rooms available: €25-35-75. Space for bikes. Reservations accepted.

## SAN XULIÁN DEL CAMIÑO

🅷

→**Albergue O Abrigadoiro** San Xulián do Camiño • Tel. 676 596 975 • medeagomez@yahoo.es • Open from Easter to October. 18 beds. €12-14 according to dormitory. Space for bikes. Reservations accepted.

**T**

## TARDAJOS

🆇🔲♨🌙◯🅗🅰🖳

→**Albergue municipal de Tardajos** c/. Asunción, s/n • Tel. 947 451 189 • Open from March to October, with 18 beds. Runs on voluntary donations. Reservations not accepted.

→**Albergue La Fábrica** Camino de la Fábrica, 27 • Tel. 620 111 939 • cristina@alberguelafabrica.com • www.alberguelafabrica.com • Open all year, with a shared dormitory (€12), twin room (€40) and double room (€48). Breakfast and dinner served. Operates in a large stone building that was home to a flour mill. Reservations accepted.

→**Albergue La Casa de Beli** Av. General Yagüe, 16 • Tel. 629 351 675 • lacasadebeli@gmail.com • https:// lacasadebeli.com • Open all year, with 34 beds distributed across five shared rooms (€10) and an annexed hotel with single rooms (from €35), doubles (from €45) and triples (from €70). Restaurant with dinner (€10) and breakfast (€3.50). Reservations accepted.

## TERRADILLOS DE LOS TEMPLARIOS

→**Jacques de Molay** c/. Iglesia • Tel. 979 883 679 and 657 165 011 • yaquesdemolay@hotmail.com • WiFi and computer (chargeable) • Pilgrims only. 49 beds. Open all year (closes from 22 December to 10 January). €8 in bunk and €10 in bed. No kitchen. Dining room. Bar/restaurant with dinner for €10. Breakfast €3. Terrace. Bike room. Shop, butcher's and bakery. Reservations accepted.

→**Albergue Los Templarios** Entering the town, alongside the N-120 • Tel. 667 252 279 and 979 065 968 • alberguelostemplarios@hotmail. com • www.alberguelostemplarios. com • Internet and WiFi • Pilgrims only. 52 beds. €8. Single rooms

(€28) and double rooms (€38). Shop. No kitchen. Dining room. Bar/restaurant. Serves dinner (€10) and breakfast (€3). Bike room. Reservations accepted.

## TORRES DEL RÍO

→**Albergue La Pata de Oca** c/. Mayor, 5 • Tel. 948 378 457, 692 221 710 and 608 250 121 • alberguelapatadeoca@gmail.com • WiFi • Open all year. Pilgrims only. 42 beds, 32 in shared dormitories (€10-14), four double rooms (€50) and one triple (€70). No kitchen. Dining room. Restaurant with menu (€10) and breakfast (€3). Terrace. Courtyard with foot bath. Bike room. Reservations accepted.

→**Albergue Casa Mariela** Pza. Padre Valeriano Ordóñez, 6 • Tel. 948 648 251 and 603 359 218 • fergusmar_thiago@hotmail.com (check availability) • www.facebook. com/fernando.albergue.5 • WiFi and computer (chargeable) • Open all year. 70 beds in dormitory for €10 per night and in double rooms at €45. No kitchen. Dining room. Bar and small shop. Menus at €12 and breakfast at €3.50. Accommodation and dinner €22. Terrace. Bike room. Reservations accepted.

## TOSANTOS

→**Albergue parroquial San Francisco de Asís** C. Santa Marina, 2 • Tel. 947 580 371 • Open from April to mid-November, runs on voluntary donations. 30 beds in shared dormitories. Provides communal dinner and breakfast, also by voluntary donation. Reservations not accepted.

→**Albergue Los Arancones** c/. de la Iglesia, s/n • Tel. 947 58 14 85 and 693 299 063 • carloseguiluz@ outlook.es • Open all year, reservations accepted. 16 beds in a shared dormitory. Price €10. Serves breakfast, lunch and dinner in the bar. Reservations accepted.

## TRABADELO

→**Albergue de Trabadelo** Camino de Santiago s/n • Tel. 987 566 447 • Open from March to November. 36 beds. €6 shared dormitory. Kitchen. Space for bikes. Reservations accepted.

→**Albergue parroquial** c/. Iglesia s/n • Tel. 630 628 130 • arrifersa@hotmail.com • www. albergueparroquialtrabadelo. com • Open all year (in winter by reservation). 20 beds. €5 shared dormitory. Double rooms available: €20. Kitchen. Space for bikes. Reservations accepted.

→**Albergue Crispeta** Ctra. antigua N-VI s/n • Tel. 987 566 529 • osarroxos@gmail.com • Open all year (in winter, by reservation). 32 beds. €6-8 according to dormitory. Kitchen. Space for bikes. Reservations accepted.

→**Albergue Camino y Leyenda** Camino de Santiago s/n • Tel. 987 566 446 • alberguecaminoyleyenda@ gmail.com • Open from April to October. 8 beds. €9-14 according to shared dormitory. Double rooms available: €32. Space for bikes. Reservations accepted.

→**Albergue Casa Susi** c/. Camino de Santiago, 123 • Tel. 683 278 778 • alberguecasasusi@gmail.com • www. facebook.com/alberguecasasusi • Open from April to October. 12 beds. €5 shared dormitory. Space for bikes. Reservations accepted.

## TRIACASTELA

→**Albergue de peregrinos de Triacastela** Rúa do Peregrino, s/n. In a meadow, before entering the town centre • Tel. 660 396 811 and 638 962 814 • www.xacobeo.es • Administered by the Xunta. Open all year. Pilgrims only. 56 beds in 14 dormitories. €6 per night. Kitchen without utensils. Dining room. There is a bar where you can dine just 50 metres away. Possibility to camp. Reservations not accepted.

→**Complexo Xacobeo** c/.
Leoncio Cadórnigo, 12 • Tel. 982
548 037 and 982 548 426 • info@
complexoxacobeo.com • www.
complexoxacobeo.com • WiFi and
computer • Open all year except
Christmas holidays. 48 beds. €10
in dormitory, €37 in single room,
€45 in double and €57 in triple.
Kitchen and dining room. Restaurant
with menu. Bike room. Reservations
accepted.

→**Refugio del Oribio** Av. de Castilla,
20 • Tel. 982 548 085 and 616 774 558
• albergueoribio@gmail.com • WiFi •
Open all year. 27 beds. €9 (€8 from
November to March). Kitchen and
dining room. Bar/restaurant. Terrace.
Bike room. Reservations accepted.

→**Albergue Aitzenea** Pza. Vista
Alegre, 1 • Tel. 982 548 076 and 670
452 476 • info@aitzenea.com • www.
aitzenea.com • WiFi • Open from
15 April to 15 October. 44 beds. €8.
Kitchen and dining room.

→**Berce do Caminho** c/. Camilo
José Cela, 11 • Tel. 982 548 127
• www.facebook.com/profile.
php?id=100008373844955 • WiFi and
computer • Open all year except
December and January. 27 beds. €8.
Kitchen and dining room. Terrace.
Bike room. Reservations accepted.

→**Albergue A horta de Abel** Rúa
do Peregrino, 5 • Tel. 608 080 556
• ahortadeabel@hotmail.com •
http://albergueahortadeabel.com
• WiFi and computer • Closed from
October to April (check the exact
dates). 20 beds. €10 for bunk, €35
for single and €40 for double room
with bath. Kitchen and dining room.
Garden. Bike room. Reservations
accepted.

→**Pensión Albergue Lemos** Av.
de Castilla, 24 • Tel. 677 117 238 •
pensionalberguelemos@outlook.
com • www.pensionalberguelemos.
com • WiFi • Open all year. €9 in
bunk bed. Kitchen and dining room.
Terrace. Bike room.

→**Albergue Atrio** Rua do Peregrino,
1-3 • Tel. 982 548 488 and 699 504
958 • xoan65@gmail.com • www.
facebook.com/albergueatrio.
triacastela • WiFi • Open from
February to November. 20 beds.
€10 in bunk bed. Kitchen and dining
room. Bar/restaurant. Terrace. Bike
room. Reservations accepted.

## TRINIDAD DE ARRE

→**Albergue de peregrinos de
la Trinidad de Arre** Puente del
Peregrino, 2 • Tel. 948 332 941 and
629 270 863 • www.facebook.com/
suseiarre • Open from March to
mid-December. Pilgrims only, with
priority for those travelling on foot.
34 beds. €8. Kitchen and dining
room. Terrace. Bike room. Daily Mass
at 8am. Reservations not accepted.

## U

### UHART-CIZE

→**Albergue Ferme Ithurburia** Route
Napoléon. Right beside the Way,
on the D428 • Tel. 0033 559 371 117 •
Jeanne.ourtiague@orange.fr • www.
gites-de-france-64.com/ferme-
ithurburia/• Open all year (except
from 15 November to 20 December).
14 beds. €60 double room. €80
triple room. €90 quadruple
room. Kitchen. Library. Animals
not accepted. Dinner service.
Reservations accepted.

→**Refuge Orisson T**el. 0033 559 491 303 • refuge.orisson@wanadoo.fr • www.refuge-orisson.com • Open from April to October. 18 beds. €36 half board (dinner, bed and breakfast). Kitchen and dining room. Terrace. Bike room. Email reservation recommended.

## UTERGA

→**Albergue Camino del Perdón** c./ Mayor, 61 • Tel. 948 344 598 and 690 841 980 • info@caminodelperdon. es • www.caminodelperdon.es • WiFi and computer • Open from March to September. 22 beds in a dormitory (€10) and three doubles with bath (€50). No kitchen. Bar and restaurant. €12 meals. Terrace. Supplemented by a guest house with five rooms located 300 metres away. Bike room. Reservations accepted.

→**Albergue Casa Baztán** c./ Mayor, 46 • Tel. 948 344 528 • albergue@casabaztan.com • www. casabaztanalbergue.com • Open all year. 26 beds in a dormitory (€10) and one double (€45). Kitchen and dining room. Restaurant. Dinner €10. Breakfast €4. Terrace. Bike room. Reservations accepted.

## V

## VALCARLOS / LUZAIDE

→**Albergue municipal de Luzaide/ Valcarlos** Pza. Santiago, on the ground floor of the school • Tel. 948 790 199 and 696 231 809 • turismo@ luzaide-valcarlos.net • http:// luzaide-valcarlos.net/es/inicio • WiFi • Open all year. 24 beds. €10 per night with breakfast (sheets €3 and towel €3). Dining room and kitchen. Bike room. Reservations accepted.

## VEGA DE VALCARCE

→**Albergue de Vega de Valcarce** c./ Pandelo, 3 • Tel. 606 792 791 • alberguemunicipal@vegadevalcarce. net • Open all year. 64 beds. €5 shared dormitory. Kitchen. Space for bikes. Reservations accepted.

→**Albergue do Brasil-El roble** Ctra. antigua N-VI s/n. Tel. 634 242 642 • Alberguebrasil.elroble@gmail.com • Open from March to November. 18 beds. Relies on voluntary donations. Kitchen. Space for bikes. Reservations accepted.

→**Albergue Santa María Magdalena** c./. Carqueixeide, 2 • Tel. 684 045 491 • caminomagdalena2018@gmail. com • www.facebook.com/ alberguesantamagdalena • Open all year (in winter, call in advance). 15 beds. €9 shared dormitory. Double and triple rooms available: €30-45. Space for bikes. Reservations accepted.

→**Albergue El Paso** Ctra. antigua N-VI, 6 • Tel. 628 104 309 • info@ albergueelpaso.es • www. albergueelpaso.es • Open all year. 28 beds. €10 shared dormitory. Kitchen. Space for bikes. Camping area. Reservations accepted.

## VENTAS DE NARÓN

→**Albergue Casa Molar** c./. Ventas, 4 • Tel. 696 794 507 • casamolar_ ventas@yahoo.es • Open from March to November (rest of the year, by reservation). 18 beds. €10 shared dormitory. Double rooms available: €30. Space for bikes. Reservations accepted.

→**Albergue O Cruceiro** c./. Ventas, 6 • Tel. 658 064 917 • delinavazquez@ hotmail.es • www.albergueocruceiro. blogspot.com.es • Open from March to December. 22 beds. €10 shared dormitory. Double rooms available: €30. Space for bikes. Reservations accepted.

## VENTOSA

➔**Albergue San Saturnino** c/.
Mayor, 33 • Tel. 941 441 899 and 657
823 740 • ventosa@jacobeos.net •
www.jacobeos.net • WiFi • Open all
year. Pilgrims only. 42 beds in shared
dormitories. €10. Kitchen and dining
room. Terrace. Groceries sold. Bike
room. Disabled access. Reservations
accepted.

## VIANA

➔**Albergería Andrés Muñoz**
c/. Ruinas de San Pedro, s/n •
Tel. 948 645 530 and 609 141 798
• albergueviana@hotmail.com
• www.viana.es/turismo/donde-
dormir/albergues/• Municipal.
Internet for guests. Pilgrims only.
Open all year. 46 beds distributed
across rooms for 6, 8 and 12 people
in bunk beds. €8. Washing machine.
Drinks machine. Dining room and
kitchen. Bike room.
➔**Albergue Izar. c/. El Cristo, 6 •
Tel. 660 071 349** and 948 090 002
• info@albergueizar.com www.
albergueizar.com • WiFi • Open from
March to October (check the rest of
the year). 42 beds in rooms of 8 to 18
bunk beds (€10) and doubles at €30.
Breakfast €3. Kitchen. Bike room.
Reservations accepted.
➔**Albergue Parroquial** Pza. de
los Fueros, next to the church •
Tel. 948 645 037 and 646 666 738 •
parroquiaviana@gmail.com • Open
from June to September. 17 beds in
four shared dormitories. No prices,
voluntary donations. Provides dinner
and breakfast. Pilgrims' Mass at 8pm.
Bike room.

## VILLAFRANCA DE MONTES DE OCA

➔**Albergue del Hotel San Antón
Abad** c/. del Hospital, 4 • Tel. 947
582 150 • hotelsanantonabad@
gmail • www.hotelsanantonabad.
com • WiFi • Open from 15 March
to 15 November. Shared dormitory
(€10) and double rooms (€30-45).
Menu €13. The hostel is the property
of the Hotel San Antón Abad and
is located in a former 14th century
pilgrims' hospital. You need to go
to the hotel reception to register in
the hostel.

## VILLALCÁZAR DE SIRGA

➔**Albergue municipal de Villalcázar
de Sirga** Pza. del Peregrino,
behind the town hall • Tel. 979
888 041 (town hall) • secretario@
villalcazardesirga.es • Open from
April to October, with 20 beds
in communal dormitories. Runs
on voluntary donations and is
administered by the Order of Malta.
Reservations not accepted.
➔**Albergue Don Camino** c/. Real, 23
• Tel. 979 888 163 and 620 399 040 •
aureafederico@hotmail.com • www.
casas-aurea.es. Open from March
to October, with 26 beds in three
shared dormitories. Price €8. Besides
the hostel, the owners run the bar/
restaurant and three independent
country houses. They also provide
a taxi service. Reservations not
accepted.

## VILLAMBISTIA

➔**Albergue Municipal de San
Roque** Pza. Mayor, 13 • Tel. 680 394
585 • carmentrimont@hotmail.com
• www.villambistia.es • Open all year,
with 12 beds in shared dormitories.
Price for bed €6 and €16 with half
board. Reservations not accepted.

## VILLARES DE ÓRBIGO

→**Albergue Villares de Órbigo**
c/. Arnal, 21 • Tel. 987 132
935 and 722 833 373 • info@
alberguevillaresdeorbigo.com •
http://alberguevillaresdeorbigo.
es • Open all year, except from 15
December to 31 January, with 24
beds spread across four rooms. Price
for communal dormitory €8, double
€25, double with bath €35 and
quadruple with bath €45. Communal
dinner and breakfast by voluntary
donation. It is a refurbished old
country house and the owner speaks
various languages. Reservations
accepted.

→**Albergue el Encanto** Camino
de Santiago, 23 • Tel. 682 860
210 and 987 388 126 • info@
albergueeencanto.es • https://
albergueeencanto.es • Open from
Easter to October, with 24 beds
spread across five double rooms
with bath (€50 including breakfast),
one with 4 beds and bath (€90
including breakfast) and one with 10
beds (€14 including breakfast). It is
a house that is more than 100 years
old, refurbished as a hostel in 2018.
Reservations accepted.

## VILLARMENTERO DE CAMPOS

→**Albergue Amanecer** c/. José
Antonio, 2 • Tel. 629 178 543 •
albergueamanecer@gmail.com
• Open from March to October,
reservations accepted, with 20 beds
in two shared dormitories. Prices:
bunk bed €6, communal dinner
€8. It also has log cabins (€18),
hammocks and tipis (€3). There is
a bar in the hostel and the hostel
owner leaves breakfast ready so
that pilgrims can have it at any time
before they start walking.

## VILLAVANTE

→**Albergue Santa Lucía** c/.
Doctor Vélez, 17 • Tel. 987 389 105
and 692 107 693 • informacion@
alberguesantalucia.es • www.
alberguesantalucia.es • Open from
April to October, with 30 beds
in communal and double rooms.
Price €10, double €28 and double
with bath €40. Bar/restaurant
with communal dinner for €9 and
breakfast for €4. Massage room
with professional staff. Reservations
accepted.

## VILORIA DE RIOJA

→**Refugio Acacio y Orietta** c/.
Nueva, 6 • Tel. 679 941 123 and 947
585 220 • acaciodapaz@gmail.com
• http://acacioyorietta.com WiFi
• Pilgrims only. Open from April to
October. 10 beds. €6. Voluntary
donation for dinner and breakfast.
Kitchen. Bike room. Reservations
accepted.

→**Albergue Parada Viloria** c/.
Bajera, 27 • Tel. 610 625 065 and 639
451 660 • alberguepadaviloria@
gmail.com www.facebook.com/
MariajeToni • WiFi • Open from
March to October. 16 beds in rooms
for 10, 4 and 2 people. €5. Dinner
and breakfast by voluntary donation.
Bike room. Reservations accepted.

## VILLAFRANCA DEL BIERZO

→**Albergue municipal** Just before
entering the town centre • Tel. 987
542 356 and 987 540 028 • www.
villafrancadelbierzo.org/albergue/•
WiFi • Open from Easter to
November. Pilgrims only. 62 beds. €6
per night. Kitchen. Bike room.

➜**Albergue Ave Fénix** c/. Santiago, 10 • Tel. 987 542 655 • albergueavefenixgmail.com • www. albergueavefenix.com • WiFi • Just after passing the Puerta del Perdón. Open all year. Pilgrims only. 80 beds. €6 per night (breakfast €3 and communal dinner €7). Bike room. Massages.

➜**Albergue de la Piedra** c/. Espíritu Santo 14 • Tel. 987 540 260 • amigos@alberguedelapiedra.com • www.alberguedelapiedra.com • WiFi • On the outskirts, 10 minutes on foot. Open from April to November. 32 beds. €10 in shared room, €30 in double and €36 in triple. Breakfast €2. In summer, beds are made available for pilgrims in the Colegio Divina Pastora. Bike room.

➜**Albergue Leo** c/. Ribadeo, 10 • Tel. 987 542 658 and 658 049 244 • Email: info@albergueleo.com • www. albergueleo.com • WiFi • Open from March to November. Pilgrims only. 24 beds in dormitories of 2, 4 and 6 people. €10. Breakfast €2.50. Has winery/bar. Kitchen dining room. Terrace. Bike room. Reservations accepted.

➜**Hospedería San Nicolás del Real** Travesía de San Nicolás, 4 • Tel. 696 978 653 and 620 329 386 • info@sannicolaselreal.com • www. sannicolaselreal.com WiFi • Open all year (in winter, by reservation). 75 beds. €5-8 in dormitory, from €30 in single room, from €50 in double and from €60 in triple. Serves meals at €11, pilgrim's menu. Kitchen. Bike room. Reservations accepted.

➜**Albergue El Castillo** c/. del Castillo, 8 • Tel. 987 540 344 • albergueelcastillo@gmail.com • reservas. www.albergueelcastillo. es • WiFi • 24 beds in three shared dormitories and one private room. €10-12 and €30 for the double. Breakfast €3. Kitchen and dining room. Terrace. Reservations accepted.

➜**Albergue La Yedra** c/. La Yedra, 9 • Tel. 636 586 872 • alberguelayedra@gmail.com • WiFi. 18 beds in a shared dormitory. €10.

## VILLAMAYOR DE MONJARDÍN

➜**Albergue Villamayor de Monjardín** c/. Mayor, 1 • Tel. 948 537 139 and 677 660 586 • www. alberguevillamayordemonjardin. com • WiFi • Open from March to October. 20 beds in three rooms. €15 in communal dormitories and €20 per person in the double room, both with breakfast included. Kitchen and dining room. Bike room. Reservations accepted.

➜**Albergue Hogar Monjardín.** c/. de la Plaza, 4 • Tel. 948 537 136 • www.facebook.com/ oasistrailsalbergue • Open from April to October. 25 beds in four dormitories. €8 per night. €23 half board. €25 double room. €10 dinner. €5 breakfast. Dining room. No kitchen. Bike room.

## VILLAMAYOR DEL RÍO

➜**Albergue San Luis de Francia** Carretera de Quintanilla, s/n • Tel. 947 580 566 and 659 967 967 • www.facebook.com/ alberguesanluisdefrancia/• WiFi and Internet • Old refurbished farmhouse, located on the right-hand side on entering the village, 300 metres from the Way. Open from mid-March to October. 26 beds. €5 per night. Pilgrim's menu €8. Breakfast €3. Dining room. No kitchen. Bike room. Terrace. Reservations accepted.

## VILLAR DE MAZARIFE

→**Albergue San Antonio de Padua** c/. León, 33 • Tel. 987 390 192 and 687 300 666 • alberguesanantoniodepadua@ hotmail.com • www. alberguesanantoniodepadua.com • WiFi • Open all year. 60 beds. €8 in bunk and €50 in double rooms. Offers lunch (€9), dinner and breakfast (€3). Dining room and kitchen. Bike room.

→**Albergue de Jesús** c/. Corujo, 11 • Tel. 987 390 697 and 686 053 390 • refugiojesus@hotmail.com • WiFi and computer • Open all year. 50 beds in bunks. €7. Dinner €9. Breakfast €3. Garden with a small swimming pool. Bar that serves breakfast and menus. Kitchen. Bike room. Reservations accepted.

→**Mesón Albergue Tío Pepe** c/. El Teso de la Iglesia, 2 • Tel. 987 390 517 and 696 005 264 • informacion@ alberguetiopepe.es • www. alberguetiopepe.es • WiFi • 26 beds in rooms of 2, 3 and 4 beds. €9 per person, €40 in double without bath and €50 in double with bath. €20 half board. Restaurant. Breakfast €3. Pilgrim's menu €9. It usually closes from December to February. Dining room. No kitchen. Inner courtyard. Bike room.

## VILLATUERTA

→**Albergue La Casa Mágica.** c/. Rebote, 5 • Tel. 948 536 095 • hola@lacasamagica.eu • www. alberguevillatuerta.com • WiFi and computer • In a stately home over 400 years old. Open from March to October. 39 beds (five shared rooms and one double). €14 in dormitory, €40 for single and €50 for double. No kitchen. Dining room. Restaurant. Serves breakfast (€5) and a communal vegetarian dinner (€13). Massages. Meditation room. Reservations accepted.

## VILLAVA / ATARRABIA

→**Albergue municipal de Villava** c/. Pedro de Atarrabia, 15-17, raer • Tel. 948 517 731 and 649 713 943 • info@alberguedevillava.com • www. alberguedevillava.com • WiFi • Spa, sauna, Turkish bath, thermal bath and jacuzzi. Guests may use the swimming pools for €3.50. Open all year. 54 beds. €13.50 per night, €17.50 with breakfast, €24.50 with half board and €32 with full board. Kitchen. Dining room. Terrace. Bar and restaurant attached, with pilgrim's menu at €8. Bike room. Accessible for people with reduced mobility. Reservations accepted.

## Z

### ZABALDIKA

→**Albergue parroquial** c/. San Esteban de Arriba, 8 • Tel. 948 330 918 • zabaldika@rscj. es • www.facebook.com/ ZabaldikaCaminoSantiago • Open from 15 April to 15 October. 18 beds. Relies on voluntary donations. Free kitchen. Space for bikes. Camping area. Reservations not accepted.

### ZARIQUIEGUI / ZARIKIEGI

→**Albergue de Zariquiegui** c/ San Andrés, 16 • Tel. 670 360 888 • albergue@elalberguedezariquiegui. com • Opened in 2009, renovated in 2016 and extended in 2017. Open from March to October. 22 beds. €10. Bar/restaurant. Communal dinner €11. Reservations accepted.

→**Albergue San Andrés.** c/. Camino de Santiago, 4 • Tel. 948 353 876 • WiFi • info@alberguezariquiegui. com • www.elalberguedezariquiegui. com • Open all year. 18 beds. €10. Serves breakfast, lunch and evening meals. Laundry service. Reservations accepted.

## ZUBIRI

→**Albergue Municipal de Zubiri**
Ctra. de Francia, s/n, in the former
school buildings • Tel. 948 304 378,
628 324 186 • concejozubiri@yahoo.
es • WiFi • Open from mid-March to
October. 44 beds. €8. The showers
and toilets are outside the hostel.
When it is full, beds are made
available in the pelota court. Dining
room with kitchen and vending
machines.

→**Albergue Zaldiko** Puente de
la Rabia, 1 • Tel. 609 736 420 •
reservas@alberguezaldiko.com •
www.alberguezaldiko.com • WiFi •
Open from March to October (by
reservation the rest of the year).
24 beds. €10. The owners manage
the Baserri bar, where they serve a
pilgrim's menu.

→**Albergue El Palo de Avellano** Av.
Roncesvalles, 16 • Tel. 666 499 175 •
http://elpalodeavellano.com/es/
inicio • Internet for guests • Open
from March to mid-November (the
rest of the year you need to check
availability). 59 beds. With breakfast
included, €16 in bunk and €18 in
bed, €46 single, €58 double and
€84 quadruple. Dinner €13. Bike
room. Reservations accepted.

→**Albergue Segunda Stage** Av.
Roncesvalles, 22 • Tel. 948 304
170 and 697 186 560 • info@
albergueseguendaStage.com •
http://albergueseguendaStage.
com • WiFi • 12 beds. €15 with
breakfast. Dining room with kitchen.
Reservations accepted.

→**Albergue Río Arga c**/. Puente
de la Rabia, 7 • Tel. 948 30 42 43
• hrioarga@gmail.com • www.
alberguerioarga.blogspot.com • 12
beds. €15 in bunk and €40 in double
room. Dining room with kitchen.
Reservations accepted.

→**Albergue Suseia** c/. Murelu, 12 •
Tel. 948 304 353 • info@suseiazubiri.
com • www.suseiazubiri.com • Open
from March to October. Out of
season for groups only and by prior
consultation. €15 with breakfast.
€28 half board (from May to
September). Menus at €13.

## ZURIAIN

→**Albergue La Parada de Zuriain**
Landa, 8 • Tel. 699 556 741 and
616 038 685 • laparadadezuriain@
yahoo.es • WiFi • Open from March
to October. 16 beds. €10 in bunk,
€13 with breakfast and €30-50
for double room. Bar/restaurant.
Serves breakfast, lunch and dinner.
Reservations not accepted.

# Index of Place Names

# Notes

# Notes

# Notes

Brimming with creative inspiration, how-to projects and useful information to enrich your everyday life, Quarto Knows is a favourite destination for those pursuing their interests and passions. Visit our site and dig deeper with our books into your area of interest: Quarto Creates, Quarto Cooks, Quarto Homes, Quarto Lives, Quarto Drives, Quarto Explores, Quarto Gifts, or Quarto Kids.

First published in 2020 by Aurum,
an imprint of The Quarto Group.
The Old Brewery, 6 Blundell Street
London, N7 9BH,
United Kingdom
T (0)20 7700 6700
www.QuartoKnows.com

Original edition first published in Spanish by Ecos Producciones Periodisticas, SCP. 2019.

A catalogue record for this book is available from the British Library.

ISBN 978-0-7112-5613-2

10 9 8 7 6 5 4 3 2 1

Design by Ginny Zeal

Printed in China